Grace and Disgrace

"From early in my life, I heard tales of the infamous 'Dixie Mafia' gangster, Billy Sunday Birt. As with most people who become famous—or infamous, in this case—there are often exaggerations and untruths. Phil Hudgins' account of the life led by Birt's wife, Ruby Nell, his son, Shane, and of Birt himself is a telling of a bizarre life in which right and wrong get turned upside-down. It's a world controlled by a man who lived by his own strange codes of conduct and whose love, while genuine, was hard to understand, much less live with. Regardless, the tale is fascinating and attempts to explain that even a cold-blooded killer has many sides to his life."

— **Robert Williams**, former president, now consultant, National Newspaper Association

"*Grace and Disgrace* is a famous/infamous Georgia story that has been waiting for a capable storyteller for too long. Now Phil Hudgins has stepped up to that plate and has given us the horror and the history of this true story through the voice of a sympathetic narrator. No one would accept Billy Sunday Birt as a hero. Instead, Hudgins gives us the story of his wife and the mother of his five children. Ruby Nell Birt is truly heroic. Only twelve when they married (he was nearly seventeen), Ruby Nell stayed with Birt. By the time he was known as a man who would kill for money and had done so uncountable times, she had five children and feared for her own life. After Birt was in prison, Ruby Nell spent her life working to feed and clothe her children and to teach them that they had done nothing wrong through their father. The times she received help and encouragement from the people of Barrow County are moving and heart-lifting. You will not be sorry to meet Ruby Nell Birt."

—**Sally Russell,** author of *Roots and Evergreen* and *Shatter Me with Dawn*

"A 12-year-old 'angel' marries a handsome 16-year-old, who becomes a 'devil,' murdering more than 50 people. Billy Sunday Birt spent most of his life on Georgia's Death Row, and his angelic ex-wife Ruby never stopped praying for him and their five children. If evangelist Billy Sunday knew that a ruthless killer was named after him, the revered man of the cloth would roll over in his grave. Read journalist Phil Hudgins' *Grace and Disgrace: Living with Faith and the Leader of the Dixie Mafia*, written in the voice of the now 80-year-old 'angel.' Your heart will be chilled one moment and warmed the next."

—**Dink NeSmith,** Co-owner, Community Newspapers Inc.

"This book offers a welcome and enriching new dimension on the astonishing life and expanding legend of one of the most cold-blooded killers in modern-day Georgia history."

—**James C. Cobb**, author of *Georgia Odyssey* and history professor emeritus of University of Georgia

Grace and Disgrace

Living with Faith and the Leader of the Dixie Mafia

Grace and Disgrace

Living with Faith and the Leader of the Dixie Mafia

Ruby Nell Birt

As told to Phil Hudgins

Copyright © 2022 Shane Birt

All rights reserved. No part of this book shall be reproduced or transmitted in any form or by any means, electronic, mechanical, magnetic, photographic including photocopying, recording, or by any information storage and retrieval system, without prior written permission of the publisher. No patent liability is assumed with respect to the use of the information contained herein. Although every precaution has been taken in the preparation of this book, the publisher and author assume no responsibility for errors or omissions. Neither is any liability assumed for damages resulting from the use of the information contained herein. Billy Shenandoah "Shane" Birt is solely responsible for the content of this publication.

Second Edition

ISBN: 978-1-6653-0644-7 - Paperback

ISBN: 978-1-6653-0645-4 - eBook

These ISBNs are the property of BookLogix for the express purpose of sales and distribution of this title. BookLogix is not responsible for the writing, editing, or design/appearance of this book. The content of this book is the property of the copyright holder only. BookLogix does not hold any ownership of the content of this book and is not liable in any way for the materials contained within. The views and opinions expressed in this book are the property of the Author/Copyright holder, and do not necessarily reflect those of BookLogix.

INTRODUCTION

If you've ever heard of a loosely organized group of criminals who became known as the Dixie Mafia of the late 1960s and early '70s, you may have heard the name Billy Sunday Birt. He was my father. A lot of things have been said and written about my dad, but much of it is not true. You're invited to read this book, one that sticks to the truth as closely as documents and memory will allow.

One thing is certain: My father was really two people in one, a man who would not swat a bug if it landed on him, but also a man who would kill a fellow human being without blinking an eye. He would occasionally give money and groceries to the needy, but he would steal and rob with no qualms whatsoever. He was the man to call if you wanted a building destroyed for insurance. He was the man to call if you wanted revenge. He was the man to call because he was good at what he did. He was a hit man's hit man. People in law enforcement knew him as the deadliest man in Georgia.

The real hero of this story is my mother, Ruby Nell Birt. Unless you've lived in Barrow County, Georgia, you've probably never heard of my mother. But she was—and is—the strongest, kindest, most godly person I know. She was trapped in a one-sided marriage. She was kept in the dark for years about what her husband did after he left home most every night. And yet, she refused to leave him and move away from the county she loved.

Early on, Billy Birt provided for his family, but when he went to prison in 1974, my mother was left with thirty-five dollars in her pocketbook and five children to feed and clothe. She worked five jobs at one time to get her family off food stamps. She prayed constantly for us Birt children when we got into trouble. In fact, if it hadn't been for my mother and her fervent prayers, I might not be here today. I was a severe drug addict headed for destruction.

"I lived for my children," Mom says often. And she lived to worship God.

So, the purpose of this book, number one, is to thank my mother for all she's done for me and my four siblings. She has always been there for us. But there are other reasons I approached journalist Phil Hudgins about helping us write this story. I want to set the record straight. I want to tell the story of the Birt family as it was, not as we wanted it to be. People need to know why my mother is the real hero of the Barrow County Birts. She endured untold torment from the man who said he loved her, and she kept the faith.

Another objective is to offer hope to women who are in bad marriages. My mother's hope was found in her strong faith. "If you will do your best, the Lord will do the rest," she says. She really believes that. So do I.

I'd also like to apologize to the families of my father's victims. Reliving all those horrible times will not be easy for them or for us. In fact, we never even considered writing a book until untrue descriptions of my father were disseminated. We certainly do not want to glorify him or what he did.

Finally, we want to thank several people who helped our family survive over the years. I'm referring to people like Lynn Walls, the late Dr. Ed Etheridge, the late Dr. C.B. Skelton, former Winder mayor John Mobley, and others. Of course, we can't leave out the late Sheriff Earl D. Lee of Douglas County, Georgia, who was to have been one of my father's "hits," but who befriended his would-be killer in prison, told him about forgiveness through Jesus Christ, and even played Santa Claus to us children for several years.

Now you know why this book was written. And you know what it's about. It's a story about unbelievable evil and manipulation; it's about perseverance and determination; it's about hard work; it's about commitment, faith, love, and redemption. More than anything, perhaps, it's about forgiveness.

Please understand that this book is my and my mother's version of what happened over the years my father lived on this Earth. There are other versions, which may be right or wrong. But the stories my father told me came from a clear mind, a mind unaffected by drugs. They are not my opinions. The huge hands others knew as those of a killer eventually were the hands I knew as a man who joined them in prayer.

Today, at fifty years old, I must say that everything good in my life has come from my savior Jesus Christ, from my wife and family, from second chances, and from my earthly hero, Ruby Nell Birt, my mother.

—Billy Shenandoah "Shane" Birt

Young Billy Birt.

CHAPTER ONE

He called me Pretty Woman. I was just a child, just shy of twelve years old when we met, but to Billy Sunday Birt I was a woman. Pretty Woman. I met him when my Aunt Florence Mathis and I were walking down the street in front of People's Bank in downtown Winder, Georgia, a small town about fifty miles east of Atlanta. He knew my aunt—my mother's sister—and spoke to her. "This is Billy Birt," she said to me. He asked my name, and I told him.

I had heard of Billy Birt—we both had attended County Line School, although Billy dropped out early to go to work. My parents knew him, but I'd never been around the guy, even in school. All I knew was that he was several years older than I was and that my cousins thought he was one of the best-looking boys in Winder. He was good-looking, I'll have to say, and I guess I was impressed that he thought I was attractive, too. I could tell by the way he looked at me. He was about five feet, ten inches tall with dark hair and penetrating eyes. I was a skinny girl, five feet three, with long, dark hair. He was outgoing; I was quiet and timid.

The day after we met, he came to my house. We lived on Highway 53 in Winder at the time, and Billy lived with his family on Chicken Lyle Road, about three miles away. He visited on the pretense of talking to my daddy about something. Both of them worked at a sawmill—Daddy actually ran one—so I thought maybe he was telling the truth. But it wasn't long before I knew that he really came to see me.

On another visit, he asked me out, and we went to a walk-in movie theater downtown. My younger sister Betty went with us. In fact, Betty was always there, I guess to chaperone. Billy and I were never alone on a date. It was me, Billy, and Betty. But being chaperoned didn't bother me. After all, I was just a kid.

I was born on May 16, 1942, in a house located across from my present home near the Barrow-Gwinnett county line. That house is gone now, but I have fond memories of my time there.

My childhood dream was to get married and live happily in a Christian home. But not right then, not when I was still a child. My parents, Nellie and Myron Columbus Lee—everybody called my daddy Mack—needed me, depended on me. They both worked, Daddy, of course, at the sawmill and Mama at Carwood Manufacturing, where she sewed clothes for men and boys. It was left up to me to cook and clean the house. At just nine or ten years old, I was preparing beans and potatoes and biscuits and other dishes just like Mama did when she was at home to cook, mostly on weekends. I tried to keep the house as clean as she wanted. Mama was a cleanliness freak, so everything had to be spotless.

Despite my household chores, we kids still had time to play. We played typical children's games: "Ring Around the Rosie," "Hide and Seek," "Kick the Can." During the summer, we caught lightning bugs at night and in the daytime flew June bugs on a string. Eventually, there would be six of us: Betty, Freddie, Frances, Quinton, Runette, and me. I was the oldest, so I was in charge when Mama and Daddy were at work. I think I was a pretty good supervisor.

At one time, we lived where Fort Yargo State Park was developed later on. Behind our house was a great big rock, one about the size of a six-person supper table, and we children would climb all over that rock playing cowboys and Indians. The game was appropriate, I guess, because the original log fort there was built in 1792 by settlers for protection against Creek and Cherokee Indians. I'm not sure what my great-granddaddy on my mother's side would have thought about the fort. He was a full-blooded Cherokee. I met him only one time. He walked into our house one night dressed in his Cherokee regalia—headdress and all—and stood there in the dim light of a kerosene lamp in our living room. It was a little spooky. He never spoke. He soon left, and I never saw him again.

In 1810, historians say, auctioneer George Humphrey sold Fort Yargo and 121 acres of land to John Hill for 167 dollars. The home Hill built was destroyed by fire in 1954, but the Hill family cemetery is still located on the Fort Yargo tract.

We Lees were a close, happy family, especially on weekdays. Daddy was an alcoholic who drank heavily every weekend. He knew it wasn't a good idea to mix alcohol with sawmill work, so he never drank on work days. But he made up for lost time on weekends. Starting Friday evenings, he would guzzle white lightning—he liked the strong stuff—and transform himself from an easygoing, responsible man into a knees-wobbly drunk for the next forty hours or so. The family never suffered from his drinking, though; he was a good provider. But Mama hated every bit of his drinking, and she fussed at him all weekend long. On the big rock where we children played, Mama and Daddy sometimes fussed and fought.

I remember many nights going to bed crying and praying, "Lord, get Mama to hush. If she'll just be quiet, Daddy will sober up like he always does and be good as new by dinnertime Sunday." Mama always cooked a big meal on Sundays, and Daddy was sober enough to enjoy it. But for nearly two full days, Mama felt compelled to yell at Daddy continuously.

Sometimes she had a right to be furious. When Daddy ran out of money for booze, he found a way to get it. One day, Mama struck up a conversation with a woman from the Glenwood section of Barrow County, and Mama said, "I sure like your dress because I have one at home just like it."

"Lord have mercy," the woman said, "I bought this from Mr. Mack."

Mama went home and looked inside her cedar chifferobe, which she always kept locked just in case her husband was tempted. The pretty dress was not there. Daddy wasn't going to let a measly lock keep him from getting what he wanted. He had taken the back off the chifferobe, stolen Mama's dress and sold it. And it wasn't the first time. Turned out, the woman with the pretty, stolen dress had bought other nice garments from Mama's chifferobe.

My mother pitched a fit.

As I said, Mama was a fanatic about cleanliness. All her clothes had to be washed, starched, and ironed before they were put away. And she couldn't even imagine another woman wearing her pretty, clean dresses.

But Daddy could.

Daddy always stood up for me, though, weekend toot or weekday sober. I was his baby, he told everybody. So, when he found out that Billy was driving me and Betty around in a car with bad brakes, he insisted that the brakes be fixed. But Billy kept putting it off and putting it off. Finally, one day, Daddy spotted the car parked on the shoulder of Highway 211 and decided to take matters into his own hands. I guess Billy had run out of gas and abandoned the car. Well, Daddy went and got some gas, but not to start the car. He doused the vehicle and set it on fire. Brakes problem solved. We didn't find out until much later that Daddy was the arsonist.

Mama and Daddy were not churchgoers before Billy and I started dating, but they let us children attend the Church of the Nazarene close to our home. The preacher there would come by in a van on Sundays and pick us up. And if it was raining and I was wearing my nice, white, high-top shoes all polished for church, the preacher would take me in his arms and carry me to the van. He was such a nice man—a tall, elderly man—and I wish I could remember his name.

It was at that church that I became a Christian. I asked Jesus Christ into my heart, and I have tried to keep the faith ever since.

CHAPTER ONE

I'll never forget my conversion experience. Something went out of me the day I said yes to Christ. I felt suddenly alive, and I believe my life changed right then. I was baptized in a lake off Hal Jackson Road in Barrow County. Later, I would be baptized again when I joined the Church of God in Winder. I'll tell you more about that later.

I didn't read the Bible much when I was an adolescent—I was a typical kid in that way, I guess—but my faith grew as I got older, and prayer and reading of the Word sustained me during my darkest days. Mama and Daddy eventually started attending church, and they also became Christians. They were baptized in a river.

As a family, we always enjoyed attending the Easter morning worship service on top of Stone Mountain near Atlanta. There was something mesmerizing about being up high like that and watching the sun rise over the horizon, knowing that it was on the third day after His crucifixion that Jesus arose from a borrowed tomb and offered believers eternal life after death. The next Easter after we started dating, Billy attended the service with us.

We had been dating about a year when Billy proposed as we sat on that humongous mountain of granite. He turned to me and said, "Pretty Woman, let's get married before we break up again. I don't want to break up again." We had broken up several times, but he would always come back after he'd done something deceitful, like seeing other girls. I would take him back, even though it wasn't in his nature to apologize. He never apologized for anything, at least not sincerely.

I agreed to marry him, but first he had to convince my parents to sign a paper giving us permission to marry. I was underage. At first, Mama and Daddy didn't take him seriously when he said he wanted me to be his bride. But then they found out he was dead serious. One day, I'm told, Billy was helping Daddy dig a well. Daddy was down in the well, and Billy was pulling up buckets of mud Daddy had filled.

"Mack," Billy called down, "I'm going to marry Ruby."

"I can't let you marry her, Billy," Daddy said. "That's my baby."

"Look up," Billy yelled. Daddy looked up, and Billy was holding a bucket of mud over the opening of the well. He obviously was threatening to drop it onto my defenseless father as he stood below. As I said, Billy was dead serious about marrying me.

Later on, when the subject came up again, Billy told my parents he would marry me and take me to Texas to live. He had a sister who lived there. Mama offered me her car, one with a rumble seat, if I wouldn't marry Billy. I turned her down. Finally, Billy said, serious as he could be, "If you ever want to see your daughter again, you'll sign this paper and let us get married."

My parents had no choice. They signed.

I was in the fifth grade, but I was about to quit school, which I always enjoyed, especially when we studied history. I was going to marry Billy Sunday Birt, ready or not.

I was about a month shy of thirteen years old.

Eunice and Pete Phillips with dog.

CHAPTER TWO

O N THE AFTERNOON OF APRIL 14, 1954, a Wednesday, my mother and daddy rode with Billy Birt and me to Monroe, Georgia, about fifteen miles from Winder, and stopped at the home of a justice of the peace. It was a simple wedding, as you might expect, held in the man's living room. My parents had given me permission to marry Billy, a name I soon shortened to Bill. He was almost seventeen, born August 11, 1937. Actually, he was born on August 12, but Bill had a speech impediment—he was tongue-tied, I called it—and he couldn't say "twelve" or "twelfth" clearly. But he could say "August eleventh" pretty well.

At the time of our marriage, as I said, I was almost thirteen, born May 16, 1942. I weighed ninety-eight pounds.

But, as far as the justice of the peace was concerned, I was sixteen. That's what I had to say, anyway. In Georgia, a girl was supposed to be at least sixteen before she could legally marry, even with her parents' or guardians' permission. She could marry at a younger age if she happened to be pregnant. I certainly wasn't pregnant. So I guess you could say our marriage began with a little fib.

I look at my granddaughters and great-granddaughters today and can't imagine them being married at twelve or thirteen years old. Actually, I can't imagine *any* girl being a wife at that tender, impressionable age. But I officially became Bill Birt's Pretty Woman that afternoon, and I was determined to be a good wife.

We drove home. Home for Bill and me was my parents' place off Highway 53 near Winder, a big house my daddy built. That evening, Bill and I went to my bedroom to spend our wedding night. There would be no fancy honeymoon.

I don't remember what any of us said the next morning, if we said anything at all besides "Good morning," and perhaps something about the weather. But I know I was embarrassed to face my parents after their adolescent daughter, Daddy's baby, not even a teenager yet, had gone to bed with a man, actually a boy, I guess, but at least an older boy. I was terribly embarrassed. So were my parents. Bill might have been, too. I don't know.

My mother fixed breakfast, and we sat down together and ate quietly. This was to be my first full day as Mrs. Billy Sunday Birt. All of a sudden, it was like we were playing house, and I was the child bride.

It didn't take me long to figure out what Bill thought of me and how he would treat me. He really loved me, I believe, but I was more than his wife. When I say that I officially became Bill Birt's Pretty Woman, I mean just that. I was his prized possession. He owned me, and it was up to him to please me. If I saw something in a store and commented favorably on it—"That's pretty, isn't it?"—I would own that something the very next day. Bill would go back and buy it for me.

It was also his duty, he felt, to correct and scold me. One time, I turned my back on him while he was talking to me. "Don't you ever do that again," he growled. "You look at me and listen when I'm talking."

I knew I had been properly admonished. He picked up raising me, a child, where my parents left off, but in a much different way.

My duty was to serve him, to talk about him and what he was doing and how he felt and who he knew and what he wanted to do the next day. It was all about him. He wanted me to wash his back and feet when he took a bath. I did that. He wanted me to cook what he liked and get all dressed and pretty, hair combed, before he came home for supper. I did that. He wanted me to keep his shoes polished and shined. I did that. He wanted me to

CHAPTER TWO

wash, starch, and iron his shirts and pants. I did that. When we didn't have a washing machine, I scrubbed his clothes in a tub of well water. Bill changed clothes every day. He always had a fresh haircut. He wanted to look good.

Bill Birt was my master and I worshiped him.

My husband was insanely jealous. If we went out—which was almost never—I had to look down if we were in the company of others. I didn't dare make eye contact with a strange man, or even with one I knew. I couldn't even speak to Bill's brothers. If we went to a movie theater and a man spoke to me, Bill would want to know what he said and why he was speaking to me. He wouldn't let me attend church. We didn't have a phone. He didn't want me talking to anybody but him.

I never got to know Claude and Eunice Birt, Bill's parents, very well, but I know that Eunice was extremely jealous just like my husband. Bill never talked about his folks or about growing up in a family so poor they sometimes went out and picked wild berries for their breakfast. Eunice birthed ten children, eight by Claude, who died in September of 1946, and two by her second husband. Claude and Eunice had four boys—Bill, Bobby, Ray, and Jimmy—and four girls—Louise, Frances, Ruby, and JoNell. Several years after Claude died, Eunice married Pete Phillips, who was a really good man. Children by Eunice and Pete were Betty Jean and Charles. Charles died when he was about nine months old, and Louise died at eighteen when her clothes caught on fire in a freak fireplace accident.

All the boys except Jimmy were scrappers, always ready for a fight if the opportunity arose, but Bill was different. He was more than a scrapper.

After Claude died, Bill's mama was left with a house full of kids, a crop in the field, and no money. Before Pete Phillips came along, the sheriff came to the Birt house one day to take all the children to a home somewhere. Eunice fetched a shotgun and ran him off. Nobody was going to take her kids. Sometime after that, the children's grandfather, Pink Hegwood, took in the whole family and raised them like his own.

After we'd been living with them for several months, my parents moved a few miles away, to near the little town of Bethlehem, Georgia. They turned over to us the house off Highway 53. Daddy had a job opportunity in Bethlehem, which in the fifties wasn't much of a town at all. It was rugged country, mostly, a perfect place to make and sell moonshine and grow cotton. That was Daddy's job opportunity, making illegal liquor. He hid quarts and pints of his product in the terraces of the cotton field, and when a customer came calling, he would fetch a jar, brush the dirt off, and make a sale. Daddy was never caught making or selling.

I was a skinny little thing at thirteen and fourteen, and when I went to a department store in town to buy new clothes, the clerk would say, "Honey, you need to go over to the little girls' section. We can't fit you here."

I would break down crying. Here I was a married woman, and I was being directed to the little girls' department. I was humiliated. But I found a solution: I taught myself to sew. I would scissor apart a dress and draw off a pattern around the different sections. I used that pattern to make my future dresses. I would vary the types of material and the style of the sleeves, making some puffy, some straight, so that all my dresses didn't look the same. I got my material at Belks and McConnell's department stores downtown.

Bill bought an electric sewing machine at Western Auto—the first one was missing a motor and he had to swap it for a good one—and I was in business. I became a pretty good seamstress, if I do say so myself. Bill liked what I turned out and got me to make shirts and pants for him. But for nobody else. If folks in his family or my family wanted something sewn, they couldn't come to me. Bill wouldn't allow it.

I was fast becoming a competent housewife. I already knew how to cook and soon learned what foods Bill liked best. If I had

CHAPTER TWO

cooked turnip greens, he was happy. He also liked smoked link sausages and bologna. I would buy a hunk of bologna from a country store on Highway 211 and cut it into slices to cook for our supper meat or for sandwiches. Bill also loved fried rabbit and gravy, so he put out traps in a field across the road from our house to capture future meals.

Bill worked at a sawmill within walking distance of the house and usually came home for lunch—or dinner, as we called it. I had gone back to school for a month to complete the fifth grade. Then I became a dropout.

Part of Bill's job at the sawmill was hauling lumber to some of the mountain counties in North Georgia, and sometimes he wanted me to ride with him. He would blow his truck horn, and I would run out and hop in the truck. Off we'd go. Those were good days, just riding in the beautiful mountains, me and Bill.

Most of the time, though, I was a stay-at-home housewife. That's the title Bill thought I deserved. I was a housewife. His personal housewife and servant. He wanted me at home where I belonged. But, believe it or not, one time he allowed me to check out a job sewing men's and boys' clothes at Carwood Manufacturing. I applied and was told I would need a work permit from the county board of education. Apparently, I was too young to decide on my own about working. It was just humiliation on top of humiliation. I swallowed my pride, got my permit, and worked at Carwood about a year. But I didn't dare take a different route from home to work or work to home. Bill was suspicious of any route changes.

I must confess: I was driving at that young age. I didn't get a driver's license until I was about thirty, but I drove for many years without one.

If you're wondering what my parents thought of Bill after we were married, I can tell you quickly: They never said anything against him. Bill was a charmer. Yes, he had a speech impediment, but when he turned on his charm, he could've made Simon Legree feel good about himself, even though sometimes he was Simon Legree himself. His one consistent compliment to me was about my cooking. "That was a good meal, Pretty Woman," he would say, standing by my chair, after almost every meal we shared together. One compliment from Bill could make me feel good for hours.

But if you're thinking Bill Birt quit his philandering after we were married, you're wrong. He never stopped seeing other women. In our early married years, he was home nearly every night during the week. But on the weekend, he was gone. I suspected he was with other women, but I didn't know for sure. And then, later on, he started making little remarks about his running around. It was always in a joking manner, like, "Pretty Woman, these women don't mean nothing to me. They're just whores. You're the only one I love." And he would laugh. I guess that was his way of apologizing. Many nights, I hugged up to his back in bed and cried myself to sleep. He probably didn't know why I was crying. And I'm not sure he cared.

On weekends sometimes, he would take me to his parents' home or my parents' home and come back for me after two days of partying and debauchery. I spent those weekends, and other days, too, praying to God. I found my strength in the Bible and in prayer. "In the day that I cried Thou answeredst me, and strengthenedst me with strength in my soul," Psalm 138:3 says. This is just one of many passages in the King James Bible that comforted me during my darkest times. I spent many hours in our yard praying. Just praying. I had spent too many nights crying and praying when my parents fussed, and I promised myself that I would not fuss with my husband when I got married.

The main reason for writing this book is to show my children and everybody else that it is impossible to live the life I've lived, and to come through it blessed, without the Lord. It's just impossible. That's what I want everybody to see. There's no other way out. The Lord got me out of bad situations many times. He saved my life. He saved my children's lives.

CHAPTER TWO

We eventually moved from my parents' old home place and into another house off Maddox Road. Bill and I lived in five different houses in Barrow County; we lived twice in the house on Maddox. One of the worst days of my life happened in our second home. I had been taken for the weekend to the home of my parents, who were living in nearby Gainesville, Georgia, at the time. At the end of the weekend, Bill came and got me and took me home.

I walked into our home and couldn't believe what I was seeing. And smelling. Bill and his girlfriend—whoever it was that weekend—had been together in my home and in my bed, and, because it was wintertime, they needed to build a fire in our wood-burning stove. Bill apparently couldn't find any wood, or didn't look for any, so he burned rubber tires in the stove. Black, smelly smoke and soot were everywhere. The place was a mess. Even the bed in our bedroom had collapsed.

I sat down on the floor and cried.

Bill laughed.

Billy Sunday Birt, by the way, was named after Billy Sunday, the famous American evangelist and prohibitionist who preached Christ's love and forgiveness to thousands of people.

Ruby and Bill with young Stoney

CHAPTER THREE

MY HUSBAND DIDN'T BECOME INVOLVED in the so-called Dixie Mafia until the late 1960s—in fact, the Dixie Mafia didn't exist until the late 1960s. Bill started running moonshine with Harold Smith Chancey, son of Ruth Chancey, leader of what lawmen called the Chancey Gang. Ruth was following in the ill-fated footsteps of her husband, Hoke, who was killed in a tractor accident in the early 1960s. Ruth Chancey and her lieutenants—her brother Clarence W. Royster and son Harold—built an illegal empire that engaged in car stealing, liquor making, burglary, robbery, arson, and even murder. Ruth Chancey's farm in Barrow County was considered the gang's headquarters for many years. Vehicles used in the operation were hidden in farm buildings and behind her house.

Bill was about to find himself hip deep in evil. Not that he'd ever been a good man as a husband. In 1954, as soon as we were married, he was running around with other women practically every week. And he treated me like a misbehaving puppy if I got in his way.

At one time in our young marriage—when we were living with my parents near the hospital in Winder—Bill had a girlfriend within walking distance of our home. One day, as was his custom, he wanted to go see this woman. I asked him to stay home. Like a child would do—I was still a child, after all—I followed along behind him begging him not to go. He grabbed me by the arm, led me to my parents' house and locked me inside. He told me I'd better not call for help. Then he walked over to his girlfriend's house. A couple of hours later, he came and let me out. He laughed. But he never apologized. As I said, it was not in Bill Birt's nature to sincerely apologize.

When our first child was about to be born, Bill was not around. He was in jail, sentenced for joyriding in a stolen car, if I remember correctly. But he was released the day before Billy Sunday Birt Jr. made his brief appearance on February 23, 1955. Delivered by Dr. Richard Forrest Graves, Billy Jr. lived for about thirty minutes. Before the birth, Dr. Graves looked straight at me and said, "Young lady, how old are you?"

I said, "Fourteen."

He said, "I ought to spank you good."

Yes, I was too young to become a mother, but I desperately wanted Billy Jr. to live. It wasn't to be. Monroe Wise, a local funeral director, brought my baby's little casket to my bedside to show me my handsome little guy. Bill saw him, too.

And that was the first time I saw Bill Birt cry.

It would be almost five years before our next child would come along. Those were lonely years for me. I quit working at the garment factory after about a year, so I busied myself with cleaning and sewing and cooking. Bill didn't want me out of the house unless I was going to work. After I quit work, he didn't want me to see other people, nor for them to see me. His jealousy seemed to grow as the years passed. He even swept our driveway every day, and if he saw footprints or tire tracks when he came home, he wanted to know who visited our house and why.

Then, thankfully, on October 20, 1959, came Billy Stonewall Birt—named after Confederate General Stonewall Jackson. Bill was in prison at the time, along with my parents, apparently for stealing a well pump. That's what I remember, anyway.

Suddenly, I had gone from playing with dolls a few years earlier to having my very own baby. Stoney, as we called him, was a healthy, handsome, blond boy and the first grandchild on my side of the family. The family I dreamed about was about to begin. Or so I thought.

CHAPTER THREE

Stoney was a delightful, outgoing child who loved to play outside when he got old enough. He didn't have a brother or sister to play with at first, so he invented his own invisible playmate. His name was David. You could hear him outside talking to David. We even set a place at the supper table for our imaginary friend. One day, Stoney ran inside screaming: "David is gone. He went down in the ground in the garden." Stoney and David were planting beans in the garden, and invisible David apparently disappeared.

Stoney wasn't the only one in the family who liked to work in the garden. I loved to see things grow, to see what God could produce. But Bill didn't want me to do anything in the vegetable garden, especially when he was not at home. It was all right if I watched while he worked, but he didn't want me out there by myself. I would have been in view of people driving by on Highway 29 in Statham, where we were living at the time. One day, Bill said, "Pretty Woman, if I ever catch you alone in that vegetable garden, I'm going to plow it up."

Well, I couldn't help myself. I went outside one pretty day and was digging in the garden when Bill came home. He didn't say a word. He just laughed. Then he went and got his tractor and plowed it all up. Plowed up everything. I couldn't do anything to stop him. "Pretty Woman, I told you," he said, and he walked away.

I was always watchful and careful with children, but one time we accidentally left Stoney all by himself at Holsenbeck Elementary School, where we had gone to play basketball one Sunday afternoon. Driving home, I saw a rabbit run 'cross the road and said, "Look, Stoney, there's a rabbit." But Stoney wasn't in the car. I was frantic. I turned the car around and headed back to the school. I found a man I didn't know holding my baby in his arms. Trying to find out who this boy was and where he lived, he had asked Stoney, "What's your mama's name?"

"Mama," he said.

"Who's your daddy?"
"Daddy."
"Where do you live?"
"Home."

Fortunately, Stoney was fine, even if he couldn't provide a lot of information about who he belonged to. But I was a bundle of nerves for a while.

Stoney was Daddy's little man, and they adored each other. Stoney hung out with Bill more than any of the other children. That was good and bad. It was good because Stoney had a father figure in his life—even though later in our marriage Bill was not the father he should have been, taking Stoney on moonshine runs with him. It was bad because Stoney was deprived of playing sports like other children. He wasn't able to attend church. He was always with his dad. He did become involved in Scouts for a short time, but that was just about it. I always felt bad for Stoney. He deserved better.

Believe it or not, Bill was a gentleman in some ways. He wasn't much of a drinker—although he hauled plenty of booze—and he wasn't one to cuss. He certainly didn't use bad words around women and children, and he would scold others who cussed in their presence. He loved most old people, all children, animals, and insects. Seeing a child, or anyone else, mistreating a lightning bug or any other insect put him into a rage. He also loved horses and dogs and once owned a quarter horse named Miller B. Twist, called Miller for short. Miller died from injuries sustained after he got loose and was hit accidentally by a local law officer driving by.

One day, the family's three-legged dog, Sam, was chasing Miller, and Bill went outside to put a stop to it. "Bill was shooting up in the air," our daughter Ann, our second born, recalled, "and Sam jumped up, and Daddy accidentally shot him. We were digging a hole to bury Sam, and then he took a breath. Away to the vet we went. Sam lived."

CHAPTER THREE

When the county fair came to town, Bill was known to walk around the fairgrounds giving money to children he didn't even know. He would take groceries to elderly people and shut-ins. Don't ask me to explain Bill's personality completely. I can't.

I do believe this, however: Bill was two people. When he was happy, his eyes were as blue as the sky. When he was angry, his eyes were green as grass. And, if his chin started quivering, you'd better move out of his way. He never hit me, though. I'd seen him ball up his fists at me. But then he walked away. He never laid a hand on me.

I had a lot of grit, and I could get in the face of just about anybody if I'd been wronged. But seldom with Bill. I did confront him one time when Stoney was a baby. And it was in front of one of Bill's many girlfriends, somebody he had been seeing at lunchtime at a relative's home. Holding Stoney in my arms, I told him, "OK, here's your choice. It's me or her."

"Pretty Woman," he said, "nobody backs me into a corner and tells me what to do."

Bill and I would add four more children—Ann, Montana, Norma Jean, and Shane—over the next dozen years, and I tried my best to shield them from all the notoriety that eventually would surround their father. I lived in terror over how their bearing the name "Birt" would affect their lives.

My children kept me going. They were part of me. Stoney was the first part. I had somebody who loved me and somebody I loved.

I couldn't have made it without my children, and I couldn't have made it without God. I prayed every day. One of my prayers was, "Lord, let me live long enough to raise my children. Lord, be with them and protect them."

God has done that.

"What time I am afraid," Psalm 53 says, "I will trust in Thee. In God I will praise His word, in God I have put my trust; I will not fear what flesh can do unto me."

I read that passage and found comfort. Sometimes I wasn't afraid. What could someone in the flesh do to me? But then, if I'm honest, I'll have to admit that sometimes I was very afraid of Billy Sunday Birt. I had many reasons to be fearful in our first few years of marriage.

And the fear, I soon discovered, would get worse.

From left, Montana, Ann, Shane, Norma Jean and Stoney pose for a photo probably from the 1990s.

CHAPTER FOUR

"To us, family means putting your arms around each other and being there." Barbara Bush, wife of George H.W. Bush, the forty-first president of the United States, made that statement on August 19, 1992, during a speech to the Republican National Convention.

I couldn't agree more. My family is what I have lived for; in fact, I believe my family is the *reason* God has kept me alive, despite many health problems, for more than seventy-nine years. My happiness—no, a better word is *joy*—has come from God and my five children. The children haven't been perfect; nor have I. All of us are not as close now as we were back during the hard times. But we survived because we put our arms around each other back then, because we were there for each other. We weren't always proud of the Birt name, but we were proud of each other.

My immediate family—*our* family, Bill's and my family—grew quickly after the birth of Stoney in 1959. We added another child every three years or so.

Rubyann—named after a country song Marty Robbins wrote—born January 26, 1963, was the first of those. Bill was working in construction at the time; fortunately, he wasn't in prison. All of my children were in construction work at one time or another, and my three sons would've made a great team: Stoney was best at bidding projects; Montana at operating machinery, and Shane at running the jobs. But they never worked as a team.

Rubyann—we usually call her Ann—was about four or five years old when Bill got involved with the so-called Dixie Mafia.

It may have been the Dixie Mafia getting involved with Bill. Whatever the case, I had to protect Ann and Stoney—and later the other children—from all the news on television about Bill's illegal dealings. I would cut the TV off as soon as I heard the name "Billy Sunday Birt" announced as part of a news story.

But Ann loved her daddy. She was Daddy's girl. She didn't know what he did to make a living when she was little. She thought he was a businessman. In fact, that's what she wrote on papers at school: "Father's occupation: Businessman."

We never let Ann or the others attend court when one of Bill's cases was being heard. Bill didn't want them there, and neither did I. My job was to protect them from the bad news about their daddy. I wanted the kids to have a good father figure in their lives, but, with Bill, it wasn't always easy. Shane said Bill was "as good a father as he knew how to be, but to compare him to Mr. Rogers, well, he was nowhere close."

Ann was an independent soul. I would dress her in a red velvet dress and pantaloons, but she would have no part of such prissiness. She hated girly things. She was strong and ready to fight anyone who said something bad about her daddy or her siblings. She didn't want them to get hurt.

Actually, it was Ann who got hurt at times. Physically hurt. She was sitting in a windowsill one day, and Stoney pushed her out. She landed on the ground outside, not hurt that badly, mainly mad at Stoney, who, by the way, said she simply fell out of the window. That was debatable.

Another time, she fell into and broke the glass door of our shower, cutting her bottom severely. She could have bled to death, but luckily we got her to the hospital in time.

I wanted Stoney to help discipline Ann, but she would say, "He's not my daddy, and I'm not going to let him correct me." And she didn't. I guess I was a bit naive back in those days—during the 1960s and early 1970s—and it was hard for me to go up against my own children. They were headstrong, every one of them. Ann asked me one time when she was older, "How did you do it, Mama?" I said, "Well, baby, I just prayed a lot and had the Lord with me."

Ann was eleven years old when her daddy was locked up for the last time, and she missed him very much. As I said, she loved her daddy, but she couldn't get along with me. She was rebellious, to say the least. She could talk about anything with Bill, but she and I never saw eye to eye on any subject. When she was about fourteen, she left our home and moved in with Aunt Jody, officially JoNell, Bill's sister.

"After I got grown and had a daughter-in-law," Ann said, "I don't know how many nights I called Mama crying and apologizing: 'Mama, I'm so sorry. How did you ever raise us? I don't know how you did it. It just blows my mind.' I got on the wild side—we all did at one time or another."

Ann has said many times that I was the strongest woman she'd ever met. But I'll be the first to tell you I didn't do it by myself. I had the Lord, and I had good friends who supported me.

Ann, now a mother and grandmother, is retired from construction work. She was great operating a scraper, or pan, in construction work. She was one of the best around. She and her Aunt Jody helped build most of Highway 316, the four-lane that goes from near Athens to Interstate 85 north of Atlanta. Ann now lives with her family in Wisconsin, where she owns a house and two small businesses.

My third child, Billy Montana Birt, was born on September 28, 1965. He was different from the others. He actually listened to me, and when I scolded him, he tried to straighten up. He was well-behaved most of the time. Sometimes when I did scold him, he had a way of getting me tickled about something. That took the sting out of the scolding—for both of us.

Montana was a very sick boy when he was seven years old. A couple of times when I went to the ball field after a game to pick him up, I would find him sitting down vomiting. The coach told me he was sick with a headache. I would take him home and put him to bed. The headaches kept occurring, so I took him to Dr. Ed Etheridge, our regular doctor. He sent us to a surgeon in Atlanta. Montana was hurting and terrified.

The surgeon's assistants ran tests and x-rayed Montana's head. They found a spot on his brain. But the surgeon didn't want to operate at that time because of Montana's young age. There was a great risk that he wouldn't pull through. So we had to wait and see.

Not long after that, evangelist Ernest Angley was holding a faith-healing revival in Atlanta, and Montana and I attended. During the service, Angley was pointing to people in the congregation who apparently had ailments of some kind. He pointed straight at Montana and said, "There's a young person here who has a brain tumor. The Lord told me."

Someone with the ministry came and got Montana and me and led us to the stage. Angley put his hands on my forehead and Montana's forehead. Next thing I knew, I was being helped up off the floor. My legs were like rubber. It was a wonderful feeling, let me tell you. Montana and I don't remember if he had fallen out, too.

Now, I know what some of you are thinking. You're saying to yourself, "Yeah, I've seen those people fall out when the preacher touched them, and I don't believe anything happened. I don't believe anybody was healed." I had had those same thoughts in the past. Some of it undoubtedly was fake. But what I can tell you for a fact is that I collapsed on that stage that night, and I had never fallen out in the Spirit before. And when I took Montana back to Atlanta, his brain was x-rayed again—and the tumor was not there. Doctors compared the two x-rays. The second x-ray was clean. There was no tumor.

On the way home from Atlanta, Montana kept saying, "It's gone. The feeling is gone."

CHAPTER FOUR

God does work miracles. He showed me I needed to have faith.

Montana turned out to be the preacher in the family. One night when he was about ten years old, he walked up quietly while I was sewing and said, "Mom, I talked to the Lord."

"Well," I said, "what do you think we should do?"

"I think we should go to church," he said.

I put my sewing aside, and we drove over to the Church of Lord Jesus Christ, where we worshiped every Sunday. Bill was in prison and couldn't stop us from attending church. The preacher was up on a ladder working on something, and he said, "Hey, what are y'all doing?" I said, "Montana wants to talk to you." The preacher climbed down and said, "Montana, what's up?"

"The Lord called me to preach," my boy said. The preacher talked to him about his decision. He encouraged him. Now, you need to know that Montana was no angel—that night or a few years later. One day, when he was about fifteen, somebody gave him some beer to drink, and he drank it. Then in class, he fell out of his desk and onto the floor, in front of all of his classmates. But Montana told the truth to the preacher that night: He really was called to preach, even if the road to his ministry was filled with potholes.

After Montana was grown, married and the father of two, Shane, my youngest child, and I got a call from Lisa, Montana's wife. Montana needed help. He was sitting on a sofa when Shane and I arrived with Brother Tommy Baker, our preacher. Montana looked like he was in a trance.

"Mom," he said, "the devil has come after my soul."

I got down on my knees in front of him and held onto him, crying. "He can't take you," I managed to say. "He can't do it."

Shane, then a teenager, said, "Mama, hold onto that Bible because when that demon comes out of Montana, it can go into you or anybody."

"Satan, you can't have him. You can't do it," I said.

Brother Baker then took over. "Montana," he said, "I'm going to pray to bind him so you can get some rest tonight." So the preacher put the Bible on Montana's hands and put his hands on my son. "I bind you, Satan," he said. "I bind you. He's a child of God, and you can't touch him, you can't have him. In the name of Jesus, I bind your power now."

I was holding onto Montana's legs. And, suddenly, the most ungodly roar came out of Montana's mouth. It was literally like fire coming from him. That was the demon leaving.

Montana slept well that night. Everything was fine.

Montana has encountered other ups and downs in his life and in his ministry, but today he's doing well. He and his wife and children live in Wisconsin, where Montana owns a construction company and leads a successful prison ministry.

Norma Jean Birt, my fourth child, named after a country singer, was born on February 24, 1968. She was my little drama queen. You'll find out later how this impressionable little girl, only a kindergartner at the time, was changed when she saw her daddy arrested outside our home and taken off to prison. That was real drama in her life, and it took her a long time to recover.

Norma Jean was a free spirit at a young age. When she was a baby, she would climb up onto a picnic table in our backyard, lie down on her back, cross her legs, and take her bottle. She was her own person even as a baby. She would do her own thing from that time on.

Bibbie—that's what most people called Norma Jean—was always sure about what she wanted and how she wanted to act. Sometime after she received her driver's license, she decided she wanted a white Chevrolet Blazer. She taught aerobics, and a girl in her class had a white Blazer, and she had to have one, too. I went to the bank, borrowed money, and bought her a white Blazer with a removable top.

CHAPTER FOUR

Well, somebody gave Norma Jean a bunch of old hats, and one of them was mostly feathers sticking up. One day, she asked her Uncle Freddie, my brother, to remove the top of her car; she wanted to go cruising.

"It's going to rain," he warned her. But she didn't care. "Take that top off, anyway." He did and she did go cruising—in the rain. She headed out for the Kentucky Fried Chicken restaurant wearing that feathered hat blowing in the wind, rain pouring down. I had two or three phone calls that day from people who had seen this feather-laden teenager getting soaked in her white Blazer.

Norma Jean had other problems with cars. One day, she rode with me to take Montana to wrestling practice. Her job was to pick up her brother's restored Ford Falcon at the mechanic's shop and drive it home. She was following me and a little girl I was babysitting that day.

As we were rounding a curve near the Winder middle school, the child looked back and said to me, "Bibbie go turn over." I ignored her. She said it again, louder, "Bibbie turn over." She sure did. Norma Jean was going too fast around the curve and flipped Montana's Falcon onto the side of the road.

I don't think Norma Jean was accident-prone, but you might get that impression as I tell you one more story about her mishaps. Montana, bless his heart, loved animals, and he had a guinea pig that he kept at our house. Well, Bill found a female guinea pig to give Montana's male a little company, not to mention extra activity. Montana was getting the boy out of his cage to meet his new wife, and Norma Jean sat down on the female guinea pig and killed her. She certainly didn't mean to, of course, but it took a while to console Montana.

Actually, Norma Jean is a talented lady who can do a little of everything. She was a waitress at the Master's Table. In fact, she was responsible for getting me work there many years ago. I still work there for Lynn Walls's catering business.

Norma Jean once served as human resources director for Barrow County and was the first woman elected county commissioner. She gave up her commissioner's post to give birth to twin boys. She also worked as a guard at Arrendale State Prison in Alto, Georgia, where Bill was incarcerated at one time. It's now a prison for women.

"Fortunately," she said, "I didn't associate the prison with Daddy. . . . Others in the family think I'm the weak one. 'Don't tell Norma Jean,' they'll say. 'It'll upset her.' Well, the thing that upset me was when somebody messed with my mama. I called her every night after I got married."

One time, Norma Jean asked me, "Mama, are we poor?"

"Do you think we're poor?" I said.

"No, ma'am," she said. And that settled that. Bill usually made money from his illegal dealings, but he mostly kept it for his own pleasures. He did provide for the children, though.

Norma Jean always sent me a card for Mother's Day *and* Father's Day, "because Mama was both mother and father to us," she said.

Billy Shenandoah Birt, my youngest, was born on August 17, 1971. We call him Shane. His name could have been a lot worse. We first named him Shenandoah Wyoming. But I knew that Bill would want "Billy" as part of his name, the way it is for Stoney's and Montana's names, so Shenandoah Wyoming became Billy Shenandoah.

Bill was around only one time when I went into labor. That was for Montana. The other times, we had to hunt him down—or he was in prison. For Shane, he showed up the next day.

"We were having a picnic under a bunch of shade trees while Mama was in the hospital having Shane," Ann remembered. "There was me and Montana, Norma Jean, Daddy, and somebody

CHAPTER FOUR

else I can't remember. Daddy had loaf bread, bologna, smoke links, and weenies, and we parked right there under the shade and had a picnic."

Shane was a good-looking baby, but he suffered from hiccups from the time he was born until he was three years old. Didn't matter to Bill. He was proud of his last-born, hiccups and all. He was proud of all of our children—all of them had blond hair when they were young—but he put Shane on display for anyone around. He even showed him off to a crew of men working on a road near our home. But he didn't have long to be with him. When Shane was about nine months old, Bill began a term in the federal prison near Atlanta for possession of a gun by a felon. And then, several months after his release, he went to prison for the last time, first for bank robbery, later for murder. Shane never really knew his dad outside of a prison.

That was a tough time. After Bill left—I always say "left," rather than sent to prison—I put Shane to bed night after night and then lay down and cried. I didn't want to cry in front of the other children. I had to be strong for them.

Shane was a curious child, always investigating things he should have left alone. When he was four or five years old, he found a couple of .30–30 rifle cartridges in our yard at the projects. This was during deer season. Shane knew that when he banged on a cap from a cap pistol, it would go bang. So he fetched a hammer and beat on one of the bullets. It didn't explode. Unfortunately, he was successful with the second one.

I heard an explosion and rushed outside to find Shane holding his dirt-covered face and, nearby, a hole in the ground. I grabbed a wet towel, threw it over his face and took him to the emergency room. He checked out okay.

I said to him, "Shane, what made you want to do that?"

"My just wanted it to go boom," he said. And it did.

Shane was always into something. As he grew older, I found myself refereeing some disagreement between him and one of the other children. Sometimes he would wear Montana's clothes—the boys were about the same size at the time—despite his brother's warnings not to. One day, I received a call at the restaurant. It was Shane. "Mom," he whined, "do you know what Montana done to me? Him and Norma Jean held me down and took my pants off of me. Are you going to let them treat me that way?"

I wasn't going to scold Montana because he had told Shane that morning not to wear his pressed pants. I just laughed at Shane's whining.

On December 17, 1987, I received word about Shane that was no laughing matter. Lynn Walls came in while I was working and said, out of breath, "You need to go with me. Shane has been in an accident." It happened at "Thrill Hill," the kids called it. A young driver had raced up this hill near the high school with his headlights off, and his truck went airborne and landed on Shane's truck on the other side. The driver and one passenger in the other boy's truck were killed.

I found Shane in the hospital, very much alive but severely injured. The accident broke practically every bone in his body. Both of his legs were broken in a couple of places. His recovery took weeks.

(On January 18, 2019, Shane met the man who saved his life. "Was it you or your brother who was injured in a bad wreck on Thrill Hill several years ago?" Tim Wallace asked Shane when he approached him on a construction site. "It was me," my son said. "Well, I saved your life," he said. Yes, Tim Wallace, a fireman with the Winder Fire Department, was one of the first responders to that accident. Shane's truck was on fire, and this wonderful man pulled Shane to safety. Wallace asked Shane where he hurt, and the answer was, "Everywhere." Shane will be forever grateful to Tim Wallace.)

When Shane got hooked on methamphetamine, I took it hard. All my other children had abused drugs—one of them prescription drugs—at one time or another. But I took it personally when

CHAPTER FOUR

Shane became involved. He not only *used* meth, he *made* and *sold* it. And he knew better. He had seen what drugs did to his siblings.

Shane couldn't understand why I didn't take him in and protect him when he was on drugs. I decided I had to show tough love—although Shane says now there was never any tough love in me; it was just love. Lynn Walls is the one who took Shane in and looked after him for some time.

Besides Lynn, Shane had two other supporters, his Uncle Bob—Shane sometimes called him Homer, his first name—and Harold Chancey. He and his uncle lived together for about three years in a house in Bethlehem, Georgia, where Shane owned property at the time. And, it's sad to say, Shane was homeless for a couple of years. He slept wherever he could find a bed.

I wasn't the only one who showed tough love to our youngest child. Most everybody, Shane said, turned their backs on him. But I guess my love was tougher than anybody's. One day, I talked to my other children about teaching Shane a lesson he wouldn't forget. We wanted him to get arrested.

"They thought," Shane said, "that if they could have me put in jail and try to show me the 'bad police,' that would straighten me up. What they didn't realize was that I was already mad at the whole world."

We talked to the sheriff, Joel Robinson, a good friend, about finding something to charge Shane with so he could spend some time in the pokey. The sheriff obliged. One night, in the fall of 2003, two sheriff's deputies parked their patrol cars near where Shane would turn off driving to his home in Bethlehem, and when he drove by, they pulled him over.

Turned out, neighboring Gwinnett County had issued a bench warrant on Shane for driving with an expired tag. They took him to the Barrow County Jail and, after spending some time in the holding tank, he was face-to-face with a huge, rough-looking deputy who demanded that he get undressed. "We're going to de-lice you," the deputy said.

"I'm not going to get undressed for nobody, especially on an expired ticket," Shane told the lawman.

"If you don't get undressed, we'll undress you," the deputy said.

"Well, you better get started."

So the deputy called for help, and he and several other deputies stripped Shane down to his birthday suit. They took him to the booking room, strapped him to a chair and sprayed him down with an insecticide formulated to kill lice, something Shane didn't have. "And then they took a water hose and washed me off," Shane recalled.

"They tried to teach me a lesson for absolutely nothing," he said. "I was sitting in a chair in the booking room, butt naked, cold, and wet, people coming in and out. They would ask me, 'Mr. Birt, are you willing to play fair now?' At first, I just cussed them out, which made the situation worse." Finally, Shane said he would do whatever they wanted him to do.

Gwinnett County officers wouldn't come and pick Shane up, "not for a seventy-dollar expired tag ticket," Shane said. So Deputy Gerald Thomas, who had retired as Winder's police chief, delivered him to Gwinnett County Jail, where he spent one night before a cousin came and posted bond for him.

Shane was on meth at the time, mad at everybody, as he said, and being de-liced, humiliated, and spending time in the slammer didn't change him one bit, he said, except maybe making him angrier. But we figured it was worth a try.

Shane said he had two friends who stood by him when he was on drugs: Lynn Walls and Harold Chancey. "As long as Harold Chancey was alive—he died September 11, 2003—no one would dare lay a hand on me," Shane said. "It was pure hell for me when Harold died."

Shane was living on the very bottom when he was on meth, but he thought for a while he was living the American dream. Then somebody got to him, and that somebody, believe it or not, was his father. Strung out on drugs, our son had quit working and

CHAPTER FOUR

couldn't find another job, mainly because of the way he looked. He wore pants with a 28-inch waist. He was emaciated, nothing but breath and britches. One day, he walked into the prison at Reidsville to see his daddy, but Bill didn't recognize him at first.

When the door slams in prison, all the inmates turn and look to see who's coming in. On this particular day, it was Shane. "Dad didn't recognize me until I was six feet away from him," Shane said. "He looked up and saw me, and tears ran down his face. Dad was worried about me. He looked at me and said, 'Now, who's going to give it (drugs) to *your* boy? You and your so-called friends?'"

Shane told him that if somebody gave drugs to his son, he would burn them down where they stood. Bill told Shane to give him the name of one dealer, "and I'll show you what I can do." Tears flooded his father's eyes.

Shane said this one encounter with his dad "was the straw that broke the camel's back." He was already tired of the life he was living. After that day, he began to straighten up and get off drugs. He and his wife, Jill, whom he married in 1992, had divorced in 2004 when they were expecting their fourth child. Shane had been on meth since 1998. After nearly eight years apart—with Shane sitting on one side of our church on Sunday mornings, Jill on the other side—Jill was convinced Shane was a changed man, and they remarried. They have been a happy couple ever since.

Today, Shane is very much involved with a church and with Gideons International, which places Bibles in hotels, prisons, and other institutions all over the world. He speaks regularly for the Gideons, often in prisons. In 2019, he became eligible to speak in any prison in Georgia.

But, because his daddy was in prison nearly all of Shane's life, my youngest child never developed a close relationship with Bill. He had to turn to other men, mostly relatives, for his father figure. Bill wasn't there for him. Did Bill love his children? Yes, I know he loved them. But his love sometimes was a moving target. When Shane was living in a house owned by Ruth Chancey Daws, Bill told him to move out. "He grabbed my knee," Shane said, "and he said, 'Son, if you're there after this point, I love you, but you're gone. I'm going to blow you from one end of the county to the other.' And the man was not bluffing." Bill could have made one phone call and gotten the job done.

How do you understand love like that? I never figured it out. I never understood how Bill could love me and say that "all those other women didn't mean nothing to me; they're just whores."

Billy Sunday Birt was a complex man. As I said before, he really was two men—one who could be kind and loving, even to animals, and another man who would blow up his own son if he disobeyed him.

I wish he had known someone in his younger life who could have told him about the love and forgiveness of our Lord and savior Jesus Christ. Surely, he would've taken a different route.

Dick Hoard in kitchen.

CHAPTER FIVE

If Bill birt had gotten his way, Floyd "Fuzzy" Hoard might have lived a long, happy, productive life. But he didn't get his way, and Hoard died a horrific death in his prime, at forty years old.

First impressions might indicate that Bill Birt had suddenly grown a new heart for people, that he believed killing another human being was plain wrong. But he was only looking out for himself. When a public official like Hoard is assassinated, federal, state, and local authorities from all over converge on the region. They look into every nook and cranny, investigating not just the murder, but other crimes, too. And Bill Birt did not want that to happen.

So, his urging others not to murder the man cracking down on bootlegging in the area obviously fell on deaf ears. And Hoard's family members had to live with the horror of August 7, 1967, the rest of their lives.

His son, G. Richard "Dick" Hoard, fourteen years old at the time, was there to witness the unthinkable aftermath on that morning, and fifty-two years later, in August of 2019, he sat at his kitchen table in Watkinsville, Georgia, and talked about it all. Over time, he has come to grips with the memories. He's personable, friendly, and content with his life. But it wasn't always that way.

"I knew stuff was going on with my father," he began. His dad was solicitor general of the Piedmont Judicial Circuit and a resident of rural Jackson County, Georgia. Today, he would be called the district attorney.

He and his dad were headed toward nearby Gainesville, where the Hoards had purchased a cabin on Lake Lanier. It was March and they planned to do some early spring cleanup of the place. At dusk, they rode by Cliff Park's house, and Dickey spotted all of the sedans and pickup trucks parked outside the man's garage. "Well," he said, "it looks like Cliff Park is doing his bootleg business tonight."

"Now, son," his father said, "how do you know Mister Park is bootlegging?"

"I just know."

"How do you just know?"

"Everybody knows. Everybody knows he's the biggest bootlegger in the state."

"But how do you know that?"

Dickey didn't want to say too much, lest he incriminate himself and his friends. "I've just heard some people talking about how they bought beer from him."

"High school students?"

"Yes, sir."

"Boys your age?"

"No, sir, older boys, seniors mostly, saying how they could get beer any time they wanted it." Dickey was going into the tenth grade in the fall.

His father dropped the questioning, and they drove on to the cabin, where they spent the night. The next day, back home, the weather was cold enough to stay inside, but Dickey got bored and wandered outside to look for his daddy. He found him in the yard talking to a young man dressed in blue jeans and tennis shoes. He was introduced as Ronnie Angel, who, Dickey would soon find out, was an agent with the Georgia Bureau of Investigation (GBI). They stopped talking immediately as Dickey walked up.

"What was Mister Angel doing here?" he asked his father after the agent left.

"He and I just had a little business to discuss," his daddy answered. "That's all."

CHAPTER FIVE

"What business?"

"I'm not sure it's anything you need to know about right now," he said. "When it is time to let you know, then I'll let you know. All right?"

A week or so later, his daddy knocked on Dickey's bedroom door. "Mister Angel needs your help," his father said when Dickey answered the door. Mister Angel, this time dressed in proper office attire, stood outside the room. "He needs to borrow some of your clothes. Why don't you let him look through your closet and your chest-of-drawers and see if he can find a few things he might can wear?"

Why does this man need some of my clothes? Dickey wondered. The first time he saw Mister Angel, he was dressed in blue jeans and tennis shoes. *Maybe he cannot afford anything better.*

"I don't mind you borrowing my stuff at all, but Daddy's stuff is—well, it's nicer," Dickey said.

Mister Angel smiled. "I just wanted to get some clothes that a younger man might wear," he said. He picked out a couple of pairs of pants and found an old sweatshirt, a blue one with a torn sleeve, and asked if he could borrow it. Then he discovered a pair of brown and white saddle oxfords and asked, "What about these?"

"Those'll be fine," Dickey said. "But if you don't mind, I would like to have 'em back when you're through with 'em."

Mister Angel said he would make sure everything was returned, and, if not, he'd buy him new clothes.

Well, if he can buy new clothes for me, Dickey thought, *surely he can afford to buy his own clothes.*

That evening, right after the GBI agent went shopping in his room, Dickey interrupted his father's eating Raisin Bran and asked why Mister Angel wanted to borrow some of his clothes.

"Mister Angel is going to buy some tax-free whiskey and beer at different places," his father said.

"Is he going to make a raid?"

"Yes, if he makes enough purchases, he'll make a raid."

A few weeks later, law enforcement officers raided Cliff Park's establishment. In all, officers raided twelve places across Jackson County and removed nearly twenty-two thousand dollars' worth of inventory—31 cases of whiskey and 2,054 cases of beer. Fourteen people were arrested, including Park, on a total of fifty-three charges. Sticking to protocol, Hoard had alerted the sheriff, L.G. "Snuffy" Perry, that the raid would go down.

"Bootleggers expected to get fined occasionally," Dick Hoard said. "They figured, 'Well, we ought to go pay our fine. We're not paying taxes. No big deal. It's part of the game.' But the fact that Dad had taken the inventory was a real loss to them. Dad began padlock proceedings to shut them down."

Ronnie Angel put it this way: They'd been doing business for fifty years, and this whippersnapper, Floyd Hoard, comes in breaking up everything they'd ever done.

Something must be done to stop Floyd Hoard.

On the morning of August 7, 1967, someone, no doubt his mother, Imogene, came into his bedroom and turned off the lamp Dickey had left on all night. Again. He halfway woke up, but was drifting again toward sleep when a tremendous boom outside shook the whole house. *Was it thunder? Or someone shooting to scare the goats out of the yard? No, we sold the goats two months ago.*

Dickey stood up and stumbled through the door leading to the back porch. He walked into the yard. The time was about 7:30.

"Dickey," his mother screamed. "Hurry. Come quick." She was standing in the corner of the front yard. Suddenly, she bolted toward him. "I think your daddy has just been killed," she yelled, grabbing at her hair. "Get some water. Quick! We've got to put out this fire."

Dickey walked across the yard to where his daddy had parked his 1967 Ford Galaxy 500. The car was unrecognizable. It had been demolished. Flames were shooting up from the engine.

CHAPTER FIVE

Dickey, the only boy in the family with three daughters, helped his mother gather buckets of water to douse the flames. The oldest daughter, Peggy Jean, knelt where the car door would have been, reached toward the back seat where her daddy lay, and patted his cheek. "Daddy, listen. Daddy. You're going to be all right now. We're getting some help. Horace is coming. Everything is going to be all right."

Her daddy suddenly breathed—or groaned—and Peggy Jean parted his charred lips to give mouth-to-mouth resuscitation. All of his teeth were missing. His throat was blocked. Air was not getting through.

Peggy Jean went to check on her mother and asked Dickey to see if he could get their daddy breathing. Dickey tended to his father, lowering his face toward him, fighting nausea at the taste of burned flesh, and exhaled into the nose—mouth-to-nose resuscitation—attempting to breathe life into his father a different way, as his sister instructed.

"He was dead, but I was there trying to breathe this in," he said later.

Soon, Horace Jackson, owner of the local funeral home, was there with an ambulance. And Uncle Albert Westmoreland, Jefferson's chief of police, drove up in his white patrol car. He cursed and pounded his fist into the palm of his hand, tears streaming down his face, and asked over and over, "Who would have done this? Who would have done this?"

An adult led Dickey away from the car and into the house. Inside, Dickey thought, *You mean somebody* did *this?* He had assumed it had been a terrible malfunction of the car. *But somebody wanted this to happen, wanted us to experience this.*

Dickey entered his parents' bedroom and grabbed his father's gun. He had an idea that whoever had been there hadn't meant for it to go this far and would come back and apologize. "And I was going to blow their brains out," he said.

His uncle saw that he had the gun and took it away from him. "I'm going to kill the son of a bitches," Dickey said. Normally, he would not say something like that in front of adults, but nobody reprimanded him on this day.

As the yard filled up with people, thirty minutes after the explosion, Dickey was sent to burn garbage in a barrel in the backyard. *The child doesn't need to see all of this,* the adults obviously thought. But he'd already seen it and tasted it and smelled it. As the garbage caught fire, Dickey sensed the odor of bacon grease from the brown paper sack. He looked toward the heavens and said, "Oh, God. Oh, God." That's as far as he got. The sky was blue. The birds were singing. Dickey was fourteen. His daddy was dead. "No, there's no God," he said to himself. "With God, this kind of thing wouldn't happen."

Hopelessness is not a word strong enough to explain how he felt. How his mother felt. How his sisters felt. Everyone was numb. What are we going to do now? There was nowhere to turn.

As an adult, Dick Hoard has told this story many times: at club meetings, at the University of Georgia law school, in his book *Alone Among the Living,* written when he was forty and published by University of Georgia Press. Years ago, when he was in college, he wrote down notes from that morning, but didn't write the book and get it published until 1994. *Alone Among the Living* has had a long shelf life. In 2017, it was reprinted and named in the Georgia Reads selections for that fall. His book, however, did not reveal the career he chose as a man approaching thirty years old.

In the weeks after his father's death, Dickey was practically smothered by isolation. He wanted to be understood, wanted to be consoled, wanted someone to take his grief away. But nobody could do that. In today's world, he said, a tragic death affecting a young person would bring "every counselor from the Southeast down to work with not just me and my family, but with our neighbors." Not so in 1967.

People who knew of the tragedy—that was everybody in the county—would say things like, "Don't bring this up. Don't talk about this to that young man." It appeared hardly anyone wanted to acknowledge that it happened. Dickey was angry. He wanted to yell at people: *Do you not realize what has happened?*

When someone did say something, it never seemed to be the right thing: "Well, you've got some big shoes to fill." "You're the man of the house now." "Your daddy is in a better place." Even the preacher, bless his heart, a good friend and a close friend of his dad's, had said before the funeral, "We're not going to open the casket. You just remember your dad as you last saw him."

Dickey looked at him and said, "I was at the car." But the preacher's heart was right. Dickey saw it in his face: the sadness, the despair, perhaps the hopelessness that he felt. His expressions helped more than his words.

Tragedies have happened to other people and brought suffering families together, but family members comforted each other. That did not happen in the Hoard family. The whole thing was polarizing. "We didn't talk about it," Dickey remembered. "It was sort of reminiscent of the sign on the locker room at school: 'When the going gets tough, the tough get going.'" Somehow, Dickey had to show that he was tough.

Dickey rebelled over the next weeks, months. He talked back disrespectfully to his mother, and sometimes to others, including teachers. He hated going to church, the Methodist church in town that he and his family had always attended. He'd had enough of boring sermons and pretty talk about God. If God were real, then the ten sticks of dynamite someone attached to his dad's car ignition would have blown up in the bomber's face. And he would have died, not his father. Nightmares and daydreams were all the same.

Dickey was good at basketball—he scored twenty-five points in a high school game once, and everybody congratulated him—and he ran cross-country. He also played baseball. But he had quit football because he was no good. He knew his dad was disappointed in him; he wanted him to play football. He felt guilty for not playing. It was a man's sport, and he wanted to be a man.

He even considered suicide. He was sixteen by then, and he had a gun to his head one day in his bedroom. But then he heard his grandmother down the hall, and he put the gun away. The Hoard family had moved in with Mammie, his mother's mother, never to return to their house in the country because of the unrelenting, bad memories that permeated the place. He tried running away from home once, but his mother caught him walking down the road.

"You're in such pain," he said, "and nobody understands. You want others to feel that pain, too. The only way for them to feel it would be for something to happen to them what happened to you. You have awful thoughts."

Finally, the self-imposed guilt and the taunting from some of his classmates got to him. He went out for football again. Twenty-eight people dressed out that year, and Dickey was seventh string. But he was going to be out there trying to appease his dad. Maybe trying to play, as bad as he was, would quiet Daddy in his head. His father had always been a good athlete, in high school and even in college.

Dickey was a terrible football player, even in a B-Team game. He was scared. He didn't want to hit people. The night after he tried to run away from home, his team was playing Morgan County. He decided not to talk to anybody all day long. Teachers asked him questions, and he just stared at them. He did not speak to players on the trip to Morgan County. He got in the game one time, on the kickoff team. He wanted somebody to kill him on that play, but he was ten yards away from anybody when the whistle blew. His team lost, and he was angry about that, too.

CHAPTER FIVE

The next Monday evening, something happened during football practice. He went crazy. He went on a body rampage. He was hitting everybody. He was going after the ball wherever it was, all out, hoping somebody would put him out of his misery. His coach, Jim Lofton, would say, "Can't somebody stop Dickey Hoard?" "No," the players said, "nobody can stop him." The Bible says it is more blessed to give than to receive, and he was enjoying giving it to these guys.

Believe it or not, he became a pretty good football player. The next week, he was in the lineup, and he became a letterman. He had gone from seventh string to being a starter. Football saved him for a while.

Then God intervened.

Dickey got suckered into attending a church retreat one night. And something happened. There was this old, handmade, rugged cross hanging up there at the retreat. It was primitive. He always found his church to be too pretty: stained glass, polished brass, fine carpet. But the death of Jesus, like the death of his father, was not pretty.

He didn't remember what was being said. He just kept looking at that primitive cross and thinking, "That really happened. That was a helluva way to die." In his image, as though he were filming a movie, there were flames. And the cameraman panned down from the head and the shoulders, and you looked around, and in the cordoned-off area is a GBI agent picking up pieces of evidence with tweezers. In his image, he combined those two horrific deaths. He had seen it happen: somebody died for what he believed in.

A song he learned as a kid kept going through his mind, one he had made fun of in the fourth grade by singing it with an Italian accent. He had sung a lot of insipid songs as a little church boy, inspiring him to want to hurry up and get out of fourth grade. But this song wasn't one of them: "Everybody ought to love Jesus, Jesus, Jesus. He died on a cross to save us from sin. Everybody ought to love Jesus."

Yes, he thought, *everybody should.* And that very night, he quit fighting with God.

For a long time, Dickey—now "Dick" because the name of his youth aged out—fought entering the ministry. "I did not want to be a pastor," he said. "I saw them as boring people having to go to a meeting of the flowers committee. I didn't want to do that. People on your case all the time about picky stuff, stuff that wasn't important."

He fought that calling for about five years. He had worked one year at a church, and afterward was fully convinced he didn't want to be a pastor. But after working as a high school football coach and teacher of literature for several years, he decided, at age twenty-eight, that ministry was what he was supposed to do. In 1981, he began studies at the Asbury Theological Seminary in Kentucky.

His seminary studies over, he served as pastor of four churches in Indiana, then a church in South Georgia for eight years, and an independent Methodist church in Watkinsville, Georgia, for nine years. In 2001, he helped launch another Wesleyan church, where he stayed until he retired in 2018. He and his wife, Candise, live in Watkinsville, where Dick writes novels, and occasionally speaks in churches and elsewhere. He also serves as color commentator at football games for a Christian school in nearby Athens, Georgia. The Hoards have three children and five grandchildren.

In January of 1968, five men were found guilty of conspiring to assassinate Floyd Hoard. Andrew Clifford "Cliff" Park, proved the mastermind of the murder, received the death penalty, although he was never executed. He died in 1978 at the Colony Prison Farm for aged and infirm inmates in Milledgeville, Georgia. Also convicted were Douglas Pinion, associated with Park and the go-between with Lloyd Seay, another defendant, in

CHAPTER FIVE

soliciting the murder; J.H. Blackwell, who placed the dynamite in the solicitor's car; and George Worley, who showed Seay and Blackwell where the Hoards lived.

Bill Birt was totally innocent this time. The word is, he even refused to furnish dynamite for the job. The explosives, court documents showed, were purchased in South Carolina. After Floyd Hoard was killed, Bill Birt called a meeting of criminal leaders he knew. They gathered at an Athens night club to coordinate their response to the heat they were feeling from law enforcement in the wake of the assassination. Members of the group agreed not to assassinate any more public officials in the area unless the others were informed beforehand. Soon after the Hoard assassination, the term "Dixie Mafia" was first used for the gang.

"Although the Floyd Hoard murder is sometimes linked to the 'Dixie Mafia,' that's a misnomer," wrote Mike Buffington in his book, *A Conspiracy of Silence: The Murder of Solicitor General Floyd Hoard*.

"The term 'Dixie Mafia' came into use only after Hoard's murder. It was used to describe associations of criminal gangs across the South that reached their peak in the 1970s. . . . The 'Dixie Mafia' was never organized as the name suggested and was a rather loose affiliation of criminal groups. The name evolved and is now linked mostly to criminal rackets that operated out of Biloxi, Mississippi, into the 1990s."

In his book, *Alone Among the Living*, Dick Hoard wrote of visiting in an Athens hospital Cliff Park, the mastermind of the plot to kill his daddy. "It's just something I've got to do," he told his sister, Peggy Jean, who was a nurse at the hospital, when she tried to discourage his visit. At twenty years old and a journalism major in college, he had been working on his notes for the book, and he wanted to interview Park.

"I heard he was in the hospital in Athens," he said, "and twenty minutes later, I was on my way to see him." He walked into Park's hospital room—there were no policemen or guards—and told Park he was related to Floyd Hoard. The "old man," as people in Jackson County called him, said he wasn't interested in being interviewed.

Dick Hoard, once a bitter, confused, seemingly hopeless young man, ended his book this way:

"He had clicked the lower teeth from his mouth and left them over his lip. I reached out my hand. He took it and I said, 'Goodbye.' He did not acknowledge my departure as I walked to the door, but when I turned and said, 'Mister Park,' he flinched, his eyes widening when he saw my raised elbow and extended arm, and it occurred to me that maybe he had expected to find aimed between his eyes not my index finger, but a pistol. He had been every bit as afraid of me as I of him. And for good reason. I could have walked in that room and blown his head off. He stared at my hand, curious now. I smiled and straightened my shoulders. 'Mister Park,' I said after I raised my finger and pointed toward the ceiling. 'Somebody up there still loves you.'

"He said nothing but turned again toward the wall, clicking his teeth, staring at nothing. I closed the door behind me and walked down the hall, a free man."

Couple before arrest.

CHAPTER SIX

At about ten o'clock on the morning of April 3, 1974, a Wednesday—April 3rd was his mother's birthday—Bill walked out of our home bound for a local store to buy milk for me to make sweet biscuits for him. Sweet biscuits are different from regular biscuits, and Bill loved them.

He was without a shirt, without shoes, without a gun. I think he was wearing black pants.

Norma Jean had been riding her bicycle on the dirt road in front of our house when she saw her daddy about to drive my station wagon across the road to the store, which was about 150 yards away. She put her bike down and asked to go with him. "No, honey, you can't go," he said.

"He picked me up and threw me up in the air," Norma Jean remembered decades later. "And he said, 'Daddy loves you a whole bunch,' and I said, 'I love you, too.'"

"I'll be right back," he told her.

After Bill reached the road, Virginia Avenue in Winder, the station wagon was surrounded by law enforcement officers, cars in front, cars in back of him. Cops were everywhere.

"In my five-year-old mind," Norma Jean said, "thousands of soldiers surrounded him. In reality, it was thirty to fifty officers, I guess. I went driving my bike up there, and I stopped way back. And it was the strangest thing: Daddy just looked at me. And something told me, *Go get your mama and don't say a word.*"

Norma Jean ran into the house, and Aunt Betty Jean, Bill's younger sister, was standing with me.

"Mama," Norma Jean said, "they got my daddy like this," and she leaned on the back of a chair, demonstrating how Bill was spread-eagled against a cop car. "And they have guns to his head."

Betty Jean and I walked outside. I went back inside to get Shane, who was about two and a half years old, as Betty Jean, who was pregnant at the time, continued to walk toward the arrest scene.

Norma Jean recalled that one of the law officers said something to Betty Jean, her Aunt Bet, and Bill obviously didn't like it. "I remember them knocking my daddy and him falling," Norma Jean said.

Norma Jean was five years old, a kindergartner. And that horrible scene—her daddy surrounded by men with guns, and then being hit and knocked to the ground—that was too much for this little girl.

"It was very traumatic for me," Norma Jean said. "I went into a funk and didn't speak for a long time. I don't believe in coincidences. I think God knows everything that's going to happen. God didn't put me through that. He carried me through it later in life."

I'm thankful Bill didn't have his gun with him. He told Shane during a prison visit many years later, "If I'd had my gun, I would have finished it right there." In other words, he would have gone down in a blaze of glory. The man who had lived by the gun would have died by the gun. Bill was almost thirty-seven years old, and he was going to prison for good.

Bobby Gene Gaddis, who was married to a first cousin of mine, was arrested that same day.

A third suspect, Billy Wayne Davis of Austell, Georgia, had been arrested a couple of weeks earlier. Bill and Gaddis faced an eight-count federal indictment in connection with a bank robbery and were tried in May 1974 in the U.S. District Court in Athens. Davis pleaded guilty, testified for the government in the trial, and was granted "safekeeping."

These three had been charged with robbing the National Bank of Walton County in Loganville, Georgia, on March 6, 1974.

CHAPTER SIX

I didn't know until years later how much money they got in that holdup.

Bill and Gaddis told investigators they were in Winder at the time of the robbery. But of course they were not. They, along with Davis, had driven to Loganville on the night of February 25, soon after Davis showed up at Winder Truck Stop on Highway 29 to collect money he claimed Bill owed him for a car. Bill owned the truck stop, and Gaddis managed it at night.

Bill told Davis he didn't have the money, but he did have an idea: We can rob the bank in Loganville. So, later that night, they went to Loganville looking for escape routes to take after their robbery. But they almost got in trouble before they even committed the crime. Three Walton County deputies spotted their car on a dirt road near the town and pulled them over. They searched the car. They didn't find anything illegal. That's because Bill had seen the deputies turn their car around to come after them, and he threw his pistol out a car window. Bill already had four felony convictions on his record and would have been returned to prison if the deputies had discovered his gun.

Three days later, on February 28, the trio went to Athens, about 25 miles from Winder, and stole a car from a motel parking lot. Bill stole a second car, a station wagon, also to be used in the holdup. And on March 6, they hit the bank, the National Bank of Walton County. Davis and Bill wore ski masks and overalls. Gaddis wore a long wig. Officers said a shotgun blast narrowly missed Bill after the robbery. A policeman, William R. Cody, forty-two years old, wasn't as fortunate. In a gunfight with Bill, he suffered wounds to his mouth and shoulder, but, thank goodness, he survived.

Cody and another policeman were on the scene in a matter of seconds, and Bill wondered how the Loganville police got to the bank so quickly. Must be a snitch somewhere, he figured, and he suspected one of his mistresses. He had spotted a federal agent's car parked in front of her house, and he knew something was going on.

About three weeks later, Bill, Davis, and Gaddis were planning to rob the Crawford Commercial Bank in tiny Crawford, Georgia, 37 miles southeast of Winder. Bill always drove through a town before robbing a bank to see where the cops were stationed. Both police cars were parked in front of the Crawford police station. That was good.

But then he spotted what looked like farmers wearing overalls and straw hats sitting in pickup trucks all over town. Each one had a gun rack in his truck. That was bad.

"That really got me suspicious," Bill told Stoney in a letter, "for a farmer might wear overalls thirty percent of the time, if he's old. But if he's young, most of the time he wears blue jeans." I told Bobby and Billy, 'This just don't look right. What in the hell is all these farmers doing in town on a Friday morning?' Both of them said nothing [was] wrong. But I told them I wasn't going to get the bank. That we would get it another day."

Everybody knew that Bill had a sixth sense, something that told him things weren't right. And something wasn't right in Crawford, Georgia, that Friday morning.

The three men argued for a while. Davis and Gaddis said Bill was just paranoid. "But that day I really wanted to hit the bank for we had been planning it for a week," Bill wrote, "and I almost didn't listen to my sixth sense."

Bill agreed to walk into the bank and check it out. If everything looked okay, they would carry through with their plan.

"The second I walked into that bank I knew I had been set up," he wrote. "There was five men and one woman. And none of them was in the bank last Friday when I came to Crawford to check the bank out. And I could always spot an FBI a mile away, and the six people I saw in the bank was FBI. The second I got inside that door and saw who was behind the windows I wanted to run. But I couldn't. I walked up [to] the window with a woman standing behind it and got change for a hundred. While she was giving me change, she was looking me straight in the eyes. She was FBI, too. To tell you the truth, when I turned my back to

CHAPTER SIX

walked out of that bank, I was looking to be shot all to pieces. I sure did feel good when I got outside of that bank."

Bill joined Davis and Gaddis in the stolen Ford station wagon parked outside, and they hightailed it out of town. Davis and Gaddis insisted Bill was paranoid, and they should have robbed the bank. They arrived at the place where they'd parked their second car—they always used three cars in a bank robbery, two stolen and one of their own—and they were still arguing.

"We'd been sitting there for over an hour arguing about it," Bill said in his letter. "I had the radio on, and it came over the news that Crawford bank had just been robbed and there was a big shootout and a couple was dead." Both Davis and Gaddis "went to hollering, we better get out of here; if the law finds us with two stole cars and these masks, we will never get out of prison. We were lucky that the law, while looking for the other bank robbers, didn't drive down the old field road where we parked."

They buried their masks in a wooded area and drove the stolen car back to a church where Bill had parked his personal car. They made it without running into the law.

It turned out that two men from Athens picked the wrong day to rob the Crawford bank. Actually, according to a newspaper report, only one of the two robbers, William D. Wilson, was killed. The other one, identified as Marvin Leonard Mahle, was wounded.

Again, Bill smelled a rat. Somebody had tipped the feds about their robbery plans.

From February of 1974 to the end of March, Bill and his partners robbed three banks: the Dacula Bank, eleven miles west of Winder; the Loganville bank, sixteen miles southeast of Winder; and the Manville Bank, in west Atlanta. Charlie Reed helped with the Dacula robbery; Gaddis was the driver. A policeman shot at them leaving town, and later the men found four bullet holes in their car. The take was only about ten thousand dollars, including five hundred rolls of pennies Reed hauled to the car in a sack. "This was a poor bank," Bill said.

No shootout occurred at the Manville Bank, Bill said, mainly because the men set fire to a church a half-mile away to divert attention. They waited until all the fire trucks and police cars in the district got to the church and then hit the bank. No shooting, but the job did not go completely smoothly. Bill and Reed went inside, robbed the bank, and ran outside to the stolen station wagon. They jumped in the back seat and covered themselves with blankets and sheets to avoid being spotted, Shane said. But then Gaddis, who was driving, got confused, Bill said, and tried to drive out the entrance of the drive-through lane. He blew his horn at an elderly woman driving toward him, but she refused to move. She blew back. He blew again. She blew back. Finally, he backed up, drove over a curb to get around her car, and sped through the parking lot to get to the highway. "Daddy said he kicked Gaddis in the back of his head for being stupid," Shane said.

The men had been lucky; they hadn't been caught or shot in three bank robberies, and they missed being wiped out at the Crawford bank. But their luck was coming to an end.

Following the Loganville robbery, Bill wrote in his letter to Stoney, "I didn't tell the boys where to hide the money, but I did tell them not to spend none of the hundred-dollar bills for ninety days because they stayed on a hot list for ninety days. Davis always hid his in his wife's freezer. Wrapped in paper like you would wrap meat and put [it] in the freezer but had no name on the package when all the rest of [the] packages was labeled. . . . He had money from ten different banks in his freezer.

"His wife, Mary, was one of the finest ladies I have ever met. She had no idea as to what he was doing. All she knew is he ran a big car lot in Cobb Co.

"What made her do what she done that day I will never know. She was defrosting the freezer and found the money. Thinking the money was legal, she took out 50 hundred-dollar bills and went to the bank to open her an account of five thousand dollars. She didn't need to do that because they already had a big bank account."

CHAPTER SIX

The money she took was from the Loganville bank, and the ninety-day hot list had not expired. When she handed over the money—all hundred-dollar bills—the clerk immediately checked the hot list.

The FBI was called in, and an agent asked Mary Davis where she got the money. She told him at home, out of her freezer. The FBI followed her home and confiscated the rest of the freezer money. Mary was not arrested, but agents set up a surveillance team at the Davis home.

Bill and the gang were in Alabama preparing to rob another bank when Davis called home to see if everything was all right. No, his wife said, you need to come home. She didn't say why, because an FBI agent was listening. The men called off the Alabama robbery, which was to have taken place the next morning.

When Davis got home, he was arrested and taken to the Hall County Jail in Gainesville. He was held for three weeks without bail, but Bill said he wasn't worried because Davis was solid as a rock.

"I sent him an attorney," Bill wrote, "and the lawyer told me all they could charge him with is possession of stolen money, which carried up to five years. There was no way they could identify us in the bank. We wore coveralls, ski masks and gloves."

It was clear to authorities that Davis was not going to talk, so they arrested his wife for questioning on the bank robbery. The law made sure Davis saw the arrest on television news.

Three days later, authorities told Davis his wife wanted to see him. On the way to the Cobb County Jail, where she was being held, the FBI moved Mary Davis to a mop room between two men's dormitories. This is where you'll stay the rest of your time here, she was told.

"When Billy Wayne saw his wife in that scum-room he was thinking she had been there all the time since she was arrested," Bill said in his letter. "She was crying and told him to please make them let her out of there."

That's when Billy Wayne Davis broke, Bill said. His wife would have been turned loose anyway, but Davis didn't know that. He agreed to turn state's evidence on Bill and Gaddis.

At their May trial in federal court in Athens, Bill and Gaddis took the witness stand and denied many of Davis's allegations. Bill said Davis never sold him an automobile and that he didn't owe him any money. But they were convicted. Davis's testimony was convincing. Bill and Gaddis were sentenced to twenty-five years in prison. Davis was given A-2 parole status for his part, meaning he could be paroled at any time instead of serving the customary one-third of his twenty-year sentence before being eligible for parole. Charges against his wife were dropped.

Of my five children, Norma Jean suffered the most from Bill's arrest on that fateful day in front of our house on Virginia Avenue. She was the one who saw it all, and, as she said, she was truly traumatized. She remembered that some of the law officers were wearing black jackets with "FBI" in big, yellow letters on the back.

Except for the times in school when she had to talk—"I probably spoke when I had to," she said, "but I don't remember"—my vulnerable, impressionable child was speechless. Instead of speaking, she ate.

"I went from a normal-child size to a whale," Norma Jean said years later. "And so many nights, I heard Mama crying, and I didn't want to upset her."

Norma Jean remembers the first and last time she got into a fight over something said about her daddy.

"It was probably the fourth grade," she said. "Mama always told us Daddy was at work. In my mind, I guess I knew where he was, but I didn't want to admit it. Kids repeat what their parents say. A child said to me, 'Your daddy is a murderer.' And I said, 'No, he's not.' She said, 'Yes, he's a murderer; he killed a bunch of people.'

CHAPTER SIX

"We were at lunch. I took my plastic lunchroom plate and I hit her across her head and broke her glasses. Of course, I got in trouble. That night, I heard Mama saying her prayers—we were living in the projects at the time—and she said, 'Lord, help me. I've got to buy that child a pair of glasses, and I don't know where the money is going to come from.'

"I decided not to ever cause my mother any pain again. So, if someone said something about my family later on, I just told them they were ignorant."

Norma Jean's sister Ann said she fought a girl at school for showing others a True Detective magazine that included her daddy's photo in a story about a murder. The principal sent her home, but she got the magazine. "Everything in my life is extraordinary," Ann said. "It's not just simple stuff. Nothing has been normal."

Later, after Bill's final arrest, Norma Jean usually went with me to see Dr. Laura McQuainy, a psychiatrist in Augusta. I was seeing Dr. Corbet Thigpen at the same time. Norma Jean knew that some people would criticize her for seeing a psychiatrist, but "I thought this was the best thing in the world," she said later.

Every time I took Norma Jean to see her daddy in prison, the trauma she first experienced in 1974 came rushing back when she heard the prison door slam shut behind her daddy. Seeing her daddy locked up behind bars was just too much for her.

I tried to be a good mother—and daddy—to the kids after Bill went to prison for good. I taught them to respect their daddy even though he wasn't there. As Norma Jean said, "God said to honor your father and mother, not honor them if . . ." When one of the kids misbehaved, I would say, "OK, when your daddy calls, I'm going to tell on you." I tried to give them a healthy fear of their daddy, to make them feel he was there, even though he wasn't.

If my children got in trouble and I thought they were in the right, I supported them. If they were in the wrong, they got a paddling. When an electrical storm hit at night, it wasn't unusual for some of the kids to pile into bed with me to feel safe from the thunder and lightning.

With Bill gone, I had to do everything. I made the decisions; I made the money; I paid the bills; I bought the groceries; I washed the car; I cut the grass; I coached a softball team and a cheerleading team; I served with the PTA (and became president); I served on a drug committee at one of the schools.

But I never complained to the children about their daddy's leaving me in such a fix. I tried not to argue with Bill when he called, even though I ended many of those calls in tears. I had forgiven Bill and even his girlfriends. Norma Jean wasn't as forgiving. She saw one of her daddy's former girlfriends eating at the Master's Table in town one night, back when Norma Jean was a waitress there, and she marched over and *accidentally* spilled hot coffee on the woman.

"You can't do that, baby girl," I told her.

"Oh, yes, I can, too," she said.

Bill had his baby dolls, some of them my friends, women I had sewn for. I had the misery. But I tried to live with it the best I could. Going around with hate and unforgiveness in my heart doesn't hurt anyone but me.

I understand why my children suffered from their daddy's bad reputation and sometimes rebelled. Just bearing the name *Birt* was reason enough to make them want to fight back. Ann remembers being stopped by a policeman one night when she was seventeen. She had received her driver's license, but had left it at home. She tried to explain that to the policeman, who was new on the force.

"When I told him my name," Ann said, "he had me spread-eagle against the car and then get in the back seat, hands first. The license was at home, but it wasn't showing up (when the policeman checked). Simply for driving without a license, one that was at home, I had to put both hands on the back of the headrest. Later, I went to court and showed my license, and that was it. Case dismissed. It all happened because I was a Birt."

CHAPTER SIX

Shane found that being a Birt was good and bad. It was good if you wanted to buy drugs—a Birt could get anything he wanted immediately if it happened to be illegal—but it was bad if you attended a local party of decent kids at someone's home. When the parents found out he was a Birt, sometimes he was asked to leave.

As I said, Shane was only two and a half years old when his daddy was arrested in 1974. He doesn't remember seeing Bill as a free man. One day, during a prison visit, Shane asked Bill, "Daddy, how could you have done all those awful things?" Bill said, "Son, to me, it was just a job."

Ann said she could talk to Bill about anything. She felt more like a son to him than a daughter. One day, she told him, "I don't know how Mama lived with you. I would have killed you in your sleep."

"Baby," Bill said, "that's why I married a woman like your mama and not like you."

If he had his time to go over, he told Ann, he wouldn't have left me and the kids. "But, you know," he said, "you can't go back."

To their classmates and teachers who didn't know better, my children would say their daddy was a businessman. That's what he told them he was, and they believed him, up to a point. They also believed he ate steaks every night in prison, because that's what he told them.

"I got to nineteen or twenty and realized he was lying to us," Ann said. "We thought prison was good." Bill didn't want the children knowing how bad prison was. "He never lied to us except for our own good." And he didn't want any fussing. He always told the children when they were grown, "You need to go by and check on your mama."

Shane added, "I can't remember a time (during a prison visit) Daddy would say, 'I'm going back to my cell.' He would say, 'I'm going back home.' We were going home, and he was going home." To Bill, *home* had become his cell.

"I don't know how he adapted to prison like that," Ann continued. "He adapted to whatever situation he was in, and he was in prison for forty-three years. He told me, 'Baby, if I ever get too old and can't take care of myself... I'm not coming out (of prison). I won't be a burden to y'all.'" Ann replied, "Daddy, we'll roll you out on a stretcher" if that's what's needed.

Ann telephoned me many times, often asking the same thing over and over: "Mama, how did you ever raise us?" If Ann had been the mother of Mama's five children, she said one day, she would have put everybody in a home.

Yes, Ann could talk to Bill about anything. "Baby, you should've been my son," he told her. But like the other children, Ann fell for her dad's charm. She said she did not see the bad side of her daddy, even when it was made public. Many people in Barrow County couldn't see that side, either. Bill had helped so many people—with money, groceries, correcting abusive husbands. As Ann put it, "We all saw what Dad wanted us to see, and we accepted it."

One thing Ann didn't accept, at first, was Bill's running around with other women.

But "after the fact, after he got locked up," she said, "I kind of accepted it because I put three of them to work for me and bragged about it." Ann was a distributor for Rainbow vacuum cleaners for several years. "I told Daddy, 'I got your whores working for me now.' He would laugh about it. 'They're not whores,' he said. 'They're just good old girls.' 'Well, I got some of your good old girls working for me now,' I told him. Mama ran my office and told them what to do.... Nobody held grudges because nobody spoke it. If you don't speak it, it ain't so."

Bill didn't volunteer any details about the murders to his two daughters, but he did answer sometimes, Ann said, if she asked specific questions about a killing. "I don't think you really want to know," he would tell Ann. But then he would say something like, "I had to kill him. He was a rat." For the daughters, his confessions always came with a generous amount of sugarcoating.

CHAPTER SIX

One time, Ann said, she told her daddy she wanted to marry a certain man, somebody Bill obviously didn't like. "Baby, I love you," her daddy told her, "but if you marry him, I'm going to put you and him both on the banks of the Mulberry River. And don't think I won't." Ann said she didn't believe he would actually kill her, but he made his point emphatically. And she did not marry the man.

As for me, well, I'll say it again: The Lord got me through all of this turmoil. The reality is, my children's daddy—my husband—was a murderer, a destroyer of buildings and families, a robber, a thief, a drug dealer, a philanderer. But I tried to keep everything together, even my kids' respect for their daddy.

My children and I didn't know much about Bill's illegal activities until he went to prison for the last time, in 1974. Bill didn't tell me what he did, but he did confide in the boys, Stoney, Montana, and Shane. They were about to find out just how ruthless he really was over his last years as a free man.

It hadn't been easy living with Bill—and without Bill—but God didn't promise us an easy life. He promised to be with us. We were poor, but I never let the children believe we were poor. We made it, thanks to God.

Hebrews 13:5–6 says, "Let your conversation be without covetousness; and be content with such things as ye have: for he had said, I will never leave thee, nor forsake thee. So that we may boldly say, The Lord is my helper, and I will not fear what man shall do unto me."

That's the reason I'm still here: a blessed woman.

Ruby in younger days.

CHAPTER SEVEN

When Bill went to prison for the last time, in April of 1974, I was given his personal belongings. They included thirty-five dollars in cash. I had five children to raise; I was getting welfare and food stamps from the government; eventually we would end up in public housing projects in Winder. And I had thirty-five dollars in my pocketbook. Bill had provided for his family, but in his last few years of freedom, he was strung out on drugs and left the providing up to me.

I had become dependent on Bill—I didn't know just how dependent until he was gone—but I was determined not to sit around and feel sorry for myself. What good would that do? I didn't moan and groan when I couldn't get the landlord to repair the bathroom where we lived. The toilet was literally falling through the rotted floor, but no one ever came to fix anything. So, I picked up that commode and set it out on the front lawn. Then I telephoned Paul Reynolds, an investigative reporter at one of the Atlanta television stations, and told him the situation. On the five o'clock news that afternoon, Reynolds interviewed me live while I stood beside that toilet on the front lawn of our home.

The brother of the owner of the place told me I had shamed him and his family by appearing on television and complaining about the bathroom. He cussed me. "I thought you were different from the others," he said. Bill found out about the incident and told me he looked forward to the day he would walk up and kill the man. Bill was in prison for good, and he'd never get the chance. But he never forgot.

The good news from that episode was, we didn't pay another dime of rent to the uncaring landlord. The bad news was, we ended up in the housing projects. Actually, though, it wasn't bad news at the time. Moving to Hardigree Terrace, what we call the projects, was definitely the right thing. In fact, it may have been a godsend, both financially and emotionally. Living there took much of the financial burden off of me, and it helped my children accept people as people, regardless of their color. Whites and Blacks lived peacefully beside each other, and friendships between my kids who grew up there and some of their Black neighbors continue to this day. My children did not learn tolerance of other races from my husband or his or my family. They learned it at the projects.

In the meantime, I had some changes to make in myself. I always said I would never ask my children to do anything I wouldn't do, and I wanted them to finish school. So, I had to finish school. I decided to attend classes at Gwinnett Technical College at night and get my GED, my General Education Diploma. My parents stayed with the children while I attended classes in Lawrenceville. As I said, I had finished only the fifth grade. Bill, I think, quit after the third grade.

I'll never forget the night I got that diploma. The stars were brighter than usual. They all seemed to be shining just for me. I looked up to the heavens and cried. I was a graduate. Finally. Maybe not a high school graduate, but I had my GED, and now I could do some things.

I went to the Barrow County school office and signed up to be a bus driver. Also, I passed a test to become a substitute teacher. I had kids in three different schools: elementary school, middle school, and high school. And one of those schools nearly always needed a substitute teacher. So, I ran my bus route in the morning, substitute-taught during school hours, and then bussed children home in the afternoon. The school system paid me for a full day's work. Later on, I bussed students to the Rutland

CHAPTER SEVEN

Psychoeducational School in Athens, where I worked as receptionist for many years.

At night, I sewed dresses for people and baked cakes, usually coconut cakes, my specialty. I underwent nearly a year of training at St. Marys Hospital in Athens to become a licensed practical nurse, an LPN, but I had to drop out when I heard the courts were setting a date for Bill's execution.

I'll tell you later about his sentencing.

And did I mention I also cleaned three houses for extra money?

After about five years in the projects, illegal drugs were becoming a problem in the neighborhood. It was time to get out. It was then I decided to add raising chickens to my resumé. Why not? *I can do that,* I told myself. I walked in down at Harrison Poultry Company and talked to Harold Harrison, the owner.

"Hi, I'm Ruby Birt," I said. "You don't know me, but I know you, and I'm going to grow chickens for you."

"You are?" he said.

"Yessir, I am. All I want is for you to give me a chance."

And he did.

Our family was ready to move from the projects to a house Ruth Chancey owned on Highway 124. As I said earlier, Ruth was mother of Harold Smith Chancey, one of Bill's partners in the illegal liquor business, and leader of the Chancey Gang. We worked to make the house livable and then started insulating and cleaning up the chicken houses we rented from Ruth. Shane, who was about eleven at the time, was my main helper. Finally, we got the houses acceptable to the poultry company's field representatives. Pretty soon, we had three houses and forty-eight thousand chickens to look after.

On a typical weekday, I would hit the floor at about four o'clock, go out and check the chickens, fix breakfast for everybody, run my bus route, take over as substitute teacher at one of three schools, run the afternoon bus route, and, after cooking supper for the children and me, I would sew and bake cakes. I didn't have time to dwell on my problems, or shall we say *challenges?* I just met them head-on.

I seldom was short of challenges. When Shane was a little boy, he needed a tonsillectomy, but I didn't have money for the surgery. I went to a local finance company, borrowed the money, and paid cash for the operation. Somebody told the Department of Family and Children Services (DFCS) that I obviously had a lot of money Bill stole from banks, because I had paid cash for the tonsillectomy. The department took me to court, claiming I had committed fraud and was ineligible for welfare assistance. A Legal Aid lawyer defended me. A DFCS caseworker took the stand in court and said she knew for a fact that I didn't have any money. I had borrowed the money. The case was thrown out.

I also had trouble with a batch of chickens that weren't gaining weight. My field supervisor advised that I destroy them and start over. I couldn't do that. I couldn't lose the money those chickens would bring in.

I started praying. "Lord," I said, "You know the work I've put out there. You know how bad I need the money."

I visited a longtime chicken man, Tom Gazaway, somebody who'd been growing broilers for decades, and asked him what I could do to save my chickens.

"When you're sick with a cold, what helps you?" he asked me. And then he answered his own question: "Liquor." The disease chickens had back then was like the flu that people suffered. Mr. Gazaway told me to buy some Golden Grain whiskey, which is a high-proof neutral grain spirit distilled from cereal grain. It's strong stuff.

I ran that whiskey and water through the chicken drinkers one day and Bayer aspirin the next day.

"You can't do that," the field man for the poultry company told me.

"Why not?" I said.

CHAPTER SEVEN

Well, I did it. I alternated mixing whiskey and aspirin in the drinkers and walked through the houses praying day after day.

"Lord, you know how bad I need the money from these chickens," I would pray.

The field man told Harold Harrison that Ruby Birt "is the prayingest woman I've ever seen." He'd look inside one of the houses, and there I'd be, walking back and forth, praying, "Lord, you know how bad I need the money from these chickens. Help them get well."

That batch of chickens, by the way, came out in first place among those of other growers. They outweighed them all. By the time I got through praying for them, I figured they were Christian chickens.

One thing I learned growing chickens is this: Treat the people who work for you right, and they'll treat you right. I always brought sandwiches, sometimes fried chicken, and tea for the chicken catchers, and some other growers would say, "You're crazy. That's their job." I said, "I know, but they're helping me." Because they were treated well, the growers volunteered to stay behind and close up the houses after all the chickens were caught and hauled away. "You go on home, Miss Ruby," one of them would say. "We'll take care of everything."

We experienced at least two other challenges in our early career as chicken growers. One of them slithered in on its stomach; the other walked on all fours.

One day, I was checking my chickens and spotted a snake trying to escape one of the houses through a crack between two cement blocks in the wall. I grabbed the snake by the tail—it was half inside and half outside the house—and I held on. I yelled for Shane to help. Shane found an axe, and when I pulled the snake out, he chopped its head off. It was a copperhead. This rascal could have killed a lot of my chickens, and, even though I'm terrified of snakes, I was determined not to let anything, snake or whatever, jeopardize my desperately needed income.

I was equally determined when we discovered a bear had visited one of our chicken houses and clawed some of the curtains to shreds. Assured that the intruder was a bear, Shane and I staked out the place the next night. Shane, armed with a shotgun, sat on top of a chicken house while I waited in a car, my headlights aimed at the house. About midnight, here came the bear. I started blowing the horn and flashing my headlights, while Shane fired a round of something.

"I didn't know if the gun had buckshot, birdshot or what," Shane said later. "All I knew was the gun went *boom*!" We figure the bear ran away laughing at us.

We grew six batches of chickens a year for about ten years, and sometimes our broilers would weigh six to seven pounds each. That's a pretty good-sized chicken.

Sometime in the 1980s, I took on another job: working at the Master's Table, a restaurant in town that became a catering business owned by Lynn Walls, my best friend and confidant. Lynn and I have spent many hours praying together for various needs and offering praise to God for His blessings. Today, at eighty years old, I still work occasionally at the Master's Table. I couldn't ask for a better place to work or a more faithful friend than Lynn Walls.

I never told Bill any bad news. I was working sixteen hours a day—sometimes more—to make ends meet, but he didn't hear it from me. I didn't want to worry him.

One day in the early eighties, Shane handed me a letter. "I want you to send that letter to Daddy," he said. "Don't read it. Just send it."

I did that, and not long after that, Bush Chancey came to the projects to give me a London Fog coat, which was top of the line at the time. Shane's letter, I discovered, said simply: "Mama needs a coat." Bill apparently called Bush.

Bush Chancey was a good man. He was a bootlegger, but he was good to me and my family. He would pick Shane up, buy him a biscuit, and then take him to school in the mornings. He took him home in the afternoon—after he bought him a hamburger, of course. When my car was repossessed because I couldn't make payments, Bush bought me another one. When he heard I was suffering from the flu, he came to my house to doctor me.

"Drink that down," he said, handing me a jar containing a few ounces of a clear liquid. "Then go to bed and wrap up real good." I drank that strong stuff—it burned all the way down—went to bed and woke up the next morning covered in sweat. Even the bed was wet with sweat. But the flu seemed to be gone. Bush's remedy, I found out, was moonshine, something he sold regularly from his barn on Highway 324 in Winder.

In fact, Bush was stocked and ready to sell booze any day of the week. On Saturday and during the week, he sold legal beer from his joint on Loganville Highway in Winder. On Sundays, customers would drop by his home on Highway 324 to choose their brand of beer—Pabst Blue Ribbon, Budweiser, or Miller, all of which was kept in a big cooler inside the residence. Only Bush could retrieve the hard stuff from the barn, but Shane actually helped with beer sales. For whatever reason, Shane was usually at Bush and Annie Chancey's home on Sundays in the late seventies and early eighties, when he was just a boy.

Bush would stand at the end of his driveway, take a customer's order, and yell out to Shane a color code for a brand of beer. "Blue" meant Papst, "red" was Budweiser, and "gold" was Miller. Shane would fetch the preferred twelve-pack from the cooler and take it to Bush. My boy was a bootlegger at nine or ten years old, but he didn't know it.

But Sunday sales ended promptly at 4:30, because Bush wanted to eat supper at 5:00. One Sunday, a man stormed into the Chancey home at suppertime wielding a pipe wrench, we're guessing to show authority. Shane and Annie stopped eating and watched the man as he walked back to the beer cooler. Bush never looked up. He kept on eating his crowder peas, his favorite meal. But as soon as the man walked out the back door with a twelve-pack, Bush got up from the table, grabbed a 12-gauge, double-barrel shotgun and unloaded both barrels into the man's rear end.

"The thing I remember," Shane said, "is seeing that man drag his butt along the ground like a dog with worms. Fortunately, the shotgun was loaded with rock salt. It wouldn't kill him, but it stung him real good."

Bush yelled out, "You can keep the beer."

Bush Chancey was a great friend to Bill Birt, and he believed his friend could do anything he said he could do. If Bill was betting with somebody on practically anything—racing down the highway, climbing a building in so many seconds, or whatever—Bush would say, "I'll take half of that," meaning the amount of money bet with the other person had just doubled. Bush wanted in on the action.

Shane said, "If Billy Birt said he could move Stone Mountain with a spoon in less than three minutes, Bush would say, 'I'll take half of that.'"

Bill and Bush looked after each other. Bush carried in his back pocket a .32 caliber pistol Bill gave him. As far as we know, Bush never shot anybody, but if got mad, he was known to grab his pistol and say, "You see this right here. Billy Birt himself gave me this pistol, and I ain't afraid to use it." He spoke with the same speech problem Bill had. Maybe he idolized him and wanted to be like him. Fortunately, he wasn't altogether like him.

In the middle of the night one time, after Bill and some of his buddies had been playing poker somewhere, they were driving home when they noticed a flashlight shining inside Bush's legal beer joint. The place was being burglarized. The men stopped to investigate, and two of the burglars cut out on foot. They escaped the wrath of Bush's friends. The third guy was trying to get his car started, but, in his panicked haste, he flooded the carburetor. Bill took the man inside the beer store and tied him to a chair. Then the guys started playing poker inside Bush's place.

"Daddy said they roughed the burglar up a little, but not much," Shane remembered. "But Harold Chancey added to the story.

CHAPTER SEVEN

He said the winner of each poker hand got to take a lick at the guy tied to the chair. A free lick. 'They beat the tar plumb out of that man,' Harold said. Daddy was hoping the guy wouldn't die."

After Bush arrived at his store, he noted several missing items, including a Philco eight-track tape player Bill had given him. After Bill and the boys finally got the unconscious burglar awake and coherent, they let him go with instructions to bring back all the beer, the tape player, and anything else stolen. He did that promptly.

"Daddy said he gave the man about a thousand dollars when he returned," Shane said. "He was doing his best not to get the man to sue them for whipping him so bad."

Bush Chancey came down with cancer in 1982 and eventually became bedridden. He had always been a heavy smoker, and he wasn't about to quit even though he lay slowly dying. "Daddy told me Bush was going to give me some money," Shane said, "and I was to use all of that money to go buy cigarettes for Bush. Well, Bush gave me a hundred dollars, and we got a hundred dollars' worth of cigarettes. I even lit them for him after he was unable to do that."

Bush was in a lot of pain, and since I'd been to nursing school, I knew how to give shots. So, I went by Bush's house fairly often to give him morphine for pain.

I helped his wife, Annie, obtain an apartment in the projects before Bush died in 1983 and then took her to a doctor to get her cataracts removed. Her vision was so bad, she recognized people by their voice. She couldn't see them.

As I said, Bush was always good to us, so we tried to help him out. He always wore overalls and a white shirt, and that's what we got him for Christmas and birthdays. He called me Gal.

"Gal," he would say, "I'll never forget you for being kind to me and my wife." I asked a preacher to go see Bush and tell him about Christ. "No," Bush told the preacher, "I've crossed too many bridges." He didn't think he deserved to be forgiven. Fact is, none of us deserves forgiveness, but God offers it anyway if we'll confess our sins, ask for forgiveness, and accept Jesus as our savior. Unfortunately, Bush couldn't do that. But I respected the man, and he respected me.

"You get what you give," I've always told my children. "If you give respect, you will get respect." Because of that principle, I believe, I have earned the respect of a lot of people in Barrow County. I was elected PTA president over a prominent citizen in town, and when John Mobley was running for mayor of Winder, he asked me to help with his campaign. I said yes. We were still living in the projects at the time. I want to thank Mr. Mobley for his confidence in me.

Many people have helped me out over the years. Yes, I was Bill Birt's wife, but I was not a criminal by association. People knew that and respected me. Well, most of them did.

When a piece of land went up for sale in a subdivision near the Winder airport, I was interested. I had driven by the property on my school bus route. A very nice lady at one of the local banks helped me get a loan to purchase the land. I never did anything with the property, and my friend Lynn eventually bought it. But we got everything paid off. I want to thank the bank official—she doesn't want her name used—for her kindness and her faith in me. And I'm thankful for her husband, who often bought tickets for me and my children to attend sports banquets.

Philippians 4:13 says, "I can do all things through Christ which strengtheneth me." I believe that wholeheartedly. I don't think that passage means, as some people believe, that you can actually accomplish *anything* in the world through Christ: climb the highest mountain, get the perfect job, make a lot of money. I think Paul was telling the Philippians they can bear up under any circumstance through Christ.

Paul was in prison and in poor health. But he was content despite his circumstances. That's what I found through my faith. I lived with a man who was not good to me most of the time;

CHAPTER SEVEN

he killed many people; he stole money; if he kept any of the ten commandments—with the exception of "honor thy father and mother"—I am not aware of it. But I made it through with Christ. And with the Lord's help, first and foremost, and with support from His servants on Earth, I have survived.

Bob Ingram.

CHAPTER EIGHT

It must have been Reid Oliver Fleming's nature to do his homework, because he was well-prepared to teach Sunday school on December 23, 1973, at his church in Wrens, Georgia. He had written an outline for the lesson. Here is the beginning of it:

> December 23, 1973.
>
> The Word dwelt among us. The Word became flesh. John 1:1.
>
> When a crime is committed in the United States, the GBI or the FBI starts to investigate at the beginning of the crime. They track down all witnesses. They get all information possible. Then they get pictures of how the crime was committed. They pick up all material, like a rug with blood on it, fingerprints. If a car was used in the crime, they find it. Putting all this together, they find the guilty parties. The GBI and the FBI must get the answers to the crime for no pay.
>
> If you and I want to know about this lesson and what it means to you and me, you must start searching the scriptures and living the Christian life.

Mr. Fleming and his wife, Lois, never made it to church on Sunday. Mr. Fleming never taught that prophetic lesson. The two were found dead in their home that very day, victims of a brutal murder. Robert "Bob" Ingram, an agent with the Georgia Bureau of Investigation, found the Sunday school notes during his investigation.

"This is beyond comprehension," Ingram said after reading the lesson outline from a paper he pulled from a file folder two inches thick. "This is absolutely almost exactly what happened."

Just as Mr. Fleming seemingly prophesied, GBI agents tracked down witnesses, got all information possible, photographed the murder scene, picked up all materials that might help in the case . . . and eventually found the guilty parties.

At the time, Ingram, in his twenties, was new to the GBI, working out of the field office in Thomson, Georgia, about twenty miles from Wrens, a quiet, little town where folks knew their neighbors and were generally cordial to strangers. On the day of our interview, February 6, 2019, he was chief deputy at the White County Sheriff's Office in Cleveland, Georgia, where he moved with his wife after retiring from the GBI and leaving Thomson.

Ingram sat in a conference room at the sheriff's office, occasionally pulling papers and photographs from his file, but speaking mostly from memory. The Wrens case was his first investigating a murder of such brutality. Forty-six years later, he remembered everything he witnessed in the Fleming home two days before Christmas. And sometimes, what he remembers about the Wrens case and other murder cases keeps him awake at night.

"I don't intentionally relive this," he said, "but how do you forget it?"

The Flemings had done everything right. They were home at night with their doors locked. They were law-abiding citizens, Mr. Fleming was retiring from an automobile dealership. His wife was a homemaker. "They were retired, trying to ease off into

CHAPTER EIGHT

the sunset," Ingram said. "They wanted to be left alone." But at least four men were hell-bent and determined to get what they thought they should have: the Flemings' savings.

On Saturday, December 22, 1973, two of the four men, driving a 1971 Cadillac, had visited the Flemings' automobile dealership on the pretense of purchasing a pickup truck. That night, three of them—according to a fourth suspect, who turned state's evidence—showed up at the Fleming home. One of them knocked on the door and asked about the truck. When Mr. Fleming asked them to come back later, the men forced their way inside.

The Flemings were not strong enough to resist. Mr. Fleming was seventy-five, his wife seventy-two. The men forced the couple into a bedroom and tied their hands and feet with a torn bed sheet. They demanded to know where the Flemings kept their money. At first, neither would say. The men began to ransack the house. Finding nothing of real value, they began to torture the couple. They slowly tightened strangleholds, probably taking turns, demanding again and again to know where the Flemings kept their cash. The couple had survived the Great Depression and had little confidence in local banks. They kept their money hidden at home.

Finally, one of the Flemings—officers believe it was Mrs. Fleming—revealed their hiding place. Officers said the men tortured Mr. Fleming severely while the wife watched, trying to get the wife to reveal where the cash was hidden. And when Mr. Fleming died, the men knew they couldn't leave a witness behind. They killed Mrs. Fleming. Who did the torturing is debatable within the Birt family. Some don't believe Bill took part.

Mr. Fleming's body was found lying face-up on the floor of the room. Mrs. Fleming's body was on a bed, her head almost hanging off, face down, as though she had been looking at her suffering husband two feet away. Coat hangers had been used to strangle them. An electrical cord also had been used on Mr. Fleming. Their legs and arms had been bound with strips from a bed sheet.

The men found the Flemings' money, along with adding machine tapes, sealed in numerous fruit jars and buried inside a smokehouse with a dirt floor. They got four thousand dollars. At least, that was the first estimate.

After performing autopsies on Mr. and Mrs. Fleming, Dr. Larry Howard of the State Crime Laboratory determined that Mr. Fleming's death was due to strangulation performed quite abusively. Howard found severe abrasions and contusions around the man's throat. He also observed two lines on Mr. Fleming's throat, lines caused by repeated applications of a ligature. There were multiple hemorrhages about the throat, face and scalp. Mr. Fleming's left thumb nail was split down the middle.

Mrs. Fleming died from strangulation, too, Howard said. Her eyes were bulging and hemorrhaged, and her tongue was pushed forward. He noted a bruise on her neck that had been caused by friction created by the rubbing of the coat hanger around her neck. Blood and fluid were found in Mrs. Fleming's nose and mouth.

Howard concluded that the deaths were not instantaneous, but resulted from prolonged episodes of abuse. He estimated the time of death as 10 p.m. to 11 p.m. on December 22, 1973.

During his investigation, which lasted about thirteen months, Bob Ingram came across a man named Carswell Tapley, who was employed by George Leisher on Leisher's farm in Washington County, Georgia. Leisher lived in Marietta and operated a used car lot. He made occasional trips to his farm.

Tapley hung out often at deer camps, Ingram said, and during one of his outings, in late 1973, he acquired information that the Flemings kept large amounts of money at their home. Tapley passed along the information to Leisher, who said he "knew some men who would look into it and pay twenty percent for help in setting up a job."

Once information is in certain people's hands, Ingram said, it becomes extremely dangerous. That's exactly what happened.

CHAPTER EIGHT

Leisher knew Billy Wayne Davis, whom Ingram described as "a known gambler, a thug, a hoodlum who had a used car lot in Austell (Georgia)." Davis got the information and passed it along to his partners. And it became extremely dangerous.

Jerry Hayman lived within a couple of miles of the Fleming home. He was preparing to go out of town when two men he didn't know showed up at his home, asking for information. Hayman saw them when they pulled up.

According to a report of the investigation by Jim E. West and Jack C. Berry of the U.S. Treasury Department, Hayman walked out to the car, and one of the strangers asked, "Do you know Harold Chancey?"

Hayman, who had lived years before in Bethlehem, Georgia, in Barrow County, said yes, he did know Chancey. Then one of the men said, "We are from up there, and Chancey told us you would probably sell us some whiskey so we could make a little Christmas money."

Hayman told them he had sold his package store but that he had a friend in Athens who would sell them whiskey at a good price. He returned to his house, telephoned his friend, and reported back that the whiskey would be available at a certain store in Athens.

The strangers obviously had no intention of buying whiskey to resell. They were casing the Hayman house.

Soon afterward, Hayman and his family left Wrens, headed to Texas to visit relatives. On Christmas Eve—Monday, December 24—Leon Hayman, Jerry Hayman's brother, discovered that the home had been burglarized. The men, authorities said, had cracked a safe. Items stolen included a pistol, shotgun, gold coins, binoculars, jewelry, some cash, and two cigar boxes full of pennies. Billy Wayne Davis told Ingram he left the Hayman residence and went back to Austell, located in Cobb County.

The men kept what they wanted from the burglary and left the rest in the trunk of the car, a Cadillac, they had used to commit the crime. Davis asked the man who cleaned up used cars for him, Elvis Larry Bethune, to dispose of the property left in the car. But Bethune didn't dispose of it. Instead, he telephoned Lieutenant Carlton Morris of the Cobb County Police Department. Morris recovered the stolen property and was able to determine that it came from the Wrens location. Ingram talked to Morris and Bethune and began to make a connection to the other men who burglarized the Hayman home and, afterward, murdered and stole from the Flemings.

Davis was easy to find. He had been convicted of robbing the bank in Loganville, Georgia, and was being held in a federal penitentiary.

"I began interviewing him," Ingram said, "and the more I interviewed him, the more I believed he had knowledge and involvement in the (Fleming) crime, and based on the fact that he gave Bethune the materials to dispose of. That was the link we needed." Finally, Davis told Ingram that he would unravel the whole case in exchange for immunity from prosecution.

While the other three men were at the Fleming home, Davis claimed he was waiting in a motor home parked at the intersection of Georgia Highway 11 and Interstate 20. This was in the middle of an energy crisis, and most service stations were closed on weekends. Davis said he drove a motor home, which held 60 gallons of gas, to furnish fuel for the other vehicles.

The three men, Davis said, had agreed to meet him at the motor home at one o'clock Sunday morning, December 23rd. But they were an hour late. When they arrived, they explained they "had some trouble in Wrens and had to kill the old man and woman," Davis told officers.

Davis said Bill Birt's account of the Flemings' deaths "sickened" him . . . "but I kept quiet," because he was afraid the three men might harm him.

While being interviewed by Ingram and Zollie Compton, then sheriff of Jefferson County, in which Wrens is located, Davis

CHAPTER EIGHT

said he could offer independent corroboration, co-defendants, and other witnesses who could back up his story about the Fleming case.

Davis, Ingram said, was the best hope for charging and convicting the other three and was granted immunity.

Billy Wayne Davis—now free from prosecution—named the other three men with him the night the Flemings were killed: Billy Sunday Birt, Bobby Gene Gaddis, and Charles David Reed.

After the three left Wrens and arrived at their designated location where Davis supposedly was waiting in a motor home, they discovered that a gun used in the Fleming home was missing. Concerned the weapon could be traced back to its owner, Davis, three of the men—Bill Birt, Gaddis and Davis—headed back to Wrens in the '71 Cadillac to find the pistol, while Reed left for Winder in a different car. (Bill said the pistol actually belonged to Reed, who was never at the Fleming home. "Reed was out doing something else," Shane said, "but Daddy didn't say what.")

On the way to Wrens, the three men stopped to urinate alongside the road, and afterward, their car wouldn't start. Two motorists, John Alley of Thomson and Edgar Chance of Wrens, who were leaving the nearby Huber Chalk Mine in separate vehicles, came to their rescue. Bill accompanied Chance and Alley to their place of employment to obtain jumper cables. Bill told the men that he and his friends were on their way to Florida.

Shane said this was no doubt the first time his father, angry about the foul-ups, spoke while committing a crime. Normally, he avoided speaking because he was easily identified by his speech impediment.

The men jump-started the car while Davis and Gaddis lay down in the back seat of the stalled car to avoid being seen. "I believe Daddy wanted them to hide," Shane said, "because he'd beat them to within an inch of their life" for screwing up a simple robbery, which, unfortunately, turned into two murders.

En route to Wrens, the car was still acting up—the lights kept dimming—so Bill suggested tightening the loose alternator belt with tools from the Flemings' garage. Back at the victims' home, Davis took care of the belt, while Bill looked for the missing pistol. It was not inside the Flemings' home, Bill told the others. He finally found it inside the Flemings' Ford automobile, which they had stolen and parked in a predesignated spot about two miles away from the home.

In January of 1975, about thirteen months after Bob Ingram and others began investigating the Wrens case, a Jefferson County grand jury indicted the three men—Bill Birt, Gaddis, and Reed—on burglary, armed robbery, and murder.

So now you've read Davis's story: that he was waiting for the others in a motor home parked at the intersection of Georgia Highway 11 and Interstate 20. "That's all a lie," Shane said. "He was there at the Fleming house, just like the others." But, as you read earlier, some in the Birt family, including Stoney and Ann, don't believe that their daddy helped strangle the Flemings. Stoney says his father was out burglarizing homes when the Flemings were being tortured and killed.

Here's what Shane said: "You'll never hear me say that Daddy was not there, and that he did not strangle the people. I do not know because Daddy would never tell me. What he did say is that he was one hundred percent responsible for the deaths. And the reason he didn't say anything was because, well, he was convicted, and he was not going to give Davis the benefit of watching him squirm."

In an interview on January 7, 2021, Bob Ingram agreed Davis was there in the Fleming house. "My gut tells me that Davis set this up," he said. "Davis set the Fleming case up. He drove the car. The thing of him waiting in a motor home is horse manure. He told me (in an interview on October 21, 2020) that he drove the car. When they stopped near the chalk mine, Davis was in the car."

CHAPTER EIGHT

The die was cast. Davis knew Bill Birt did not trust him anymore. He knew his former partner would eventually get his pound of flesh, and as soon as he got home from Wrens, Shane said, Davis started looking for ways to protect himself, one way or another. Ratting out Bill Birt eventually was his way.

So, in testifying for the state and against the other men, Billy Wayne Davis was not tried in the Fleming case. But Bill Birt would get his chance for revenge later on.

Bill in prison in Marion, Ill.

Jefferson County Courthouse.

CHAPTER NINE

To this day, forty-six years later, I can't get this one photograph, this horrible image, out of my mind.

Bill was being tried for the murders of the husband and wife in Wrens. The prosecution was passing around some photographs taken at the crime scene inside the couple's home. I was sitting on the second row of the courtroom seats, and I caught a glance at one of the photos.

It was a closeup of the woman's foot. She was lying on a bed, and her ankles had been bound with a piece of bed sheet.

I could imagine what had happened. Even though he denied it—and I thought he was innocent to the very end—I knew that my husband of twenty-one years, the man who was two people, could have been one of the killers of these decent, church-going folks, Reid and Lois Fleming. I was there to support Bill every minute of the jury selection and trial. Six long, hot days, I was there.

The trial was being held in Louisville, Georgia, the seat of Jefferson County and home of a market house where at one time people could sell just about anything, including slaves. The market still stands today, a cruel reminder of the suffering Black people experienced a century and a half ago. The murders took place in Wrens, about fifteen miles from Louisville.

Bill had been arraigned on June 7, 1975. On that day, the courthouse was surrounded by armed deputies from Burke and Jefferson counties, troopers of the Georgia State Patrol, and GBI agents. A sharpshooter with a rifle stood on the courthouse roof. Men in a helicopter watched from the air.

So here we were on June 23, 1975, listening to the defense and prosecution select jurors. Some were struck from the list, others approved. Finally, they had a jury: six men and six women, plus two alternates. The process took nearly seven hours.

Security for the trial was even tighter than it was for arraignment. One law officer said it was the tightest security he had ever seen for any trial in the region. A convoy of officers followed the car carrying Bill every day. Deputies carried shotguns and pistols. And this time, two sharpshooters, instead of one, were stationed on the courthouse roof. Visitors and officials alike were searched before entering the courtroom.

In the courtroom, one officer with a shotgun sat directly behind my husband; two officers stood at the side, each with a shotgun.

You would have thought Bill Birt was a dangerous man even in shackles. But it wasn't Bill the lawmen were worried about, I found out. They were afraid somebody—one of Bill's buddies—would try to swoop in and set him free. Bill had friends who would do whatever he asked them to do, and the law wasn't taking any chances.

I understood the tight security for Bill, but why follow me and Maxine Wade, a lady from Winder who became my good friend and accompanied me to court? Policemen—or whoever—tailed us to and from the courthouse every day. When we were leaving, they turned around at the city limits. But I wasn't upset. This was a quiet, little farming town, and folks there didn't want any trouble.

I was there for everything: the jury selection, the trial, the verdict. And I prayed the whole time: "Lord, help me get through this; give me the strength and will power. And be with the Fleming family."

Bill was charged with two counts of murder, four counts of armed robbery, and two counts of burglary in connection with the murders of the Fleming couple, and a burglary a night earlier at the home of Mr. and Mrs. Jerry Hayman, also of Wrens.

CHAPTER NINE

For the trial, Bill was wearing a light-colored sport coat and dark pants. He seemed relaxed as he talked and laughed with one of his attorneys, Eugene Reeves of Auburn, Georgia, who was married to my sister-in-law's sister. Gene was a fine man. Bill's family had taken up a collection to help pay Gene for representing my husband, and, at the end, Gene said he was overpaid and gave some of the money back. Gene was best known for representing Hustler magazine publisher Larry Flynt in an obscenity case more than four decades ago. Flynt and Gene were both shot while walking to the Lawrenceville courthouse in March of 1978. The shooting left Flynt paralyzed, but Gene recovered after about a month in a hospital. He later became a judge in Gwinnett County. He died in 2015.

I couldn't even imagine the fear and agony the Flemings went through that Saturday night in December 1973 when they were tortured and eventually killed. I couldn't imagine what went through the mind of their son, Hugh Fleming, when he went to check on them after they failed to show up for church. I don't have the right words to describe how he must have felt.

When he was indicted for murder, Bill was doing time in a federal prison in Marion, Illinois, for robbing that bank in Loganville. Marion was where some of the nation's most dangerous prisoners were sent once the federal penitentiary on Alcatraz Island, California, was closed down.

The kids and I had driven to Marion many times to visit Bill. One time, I remember, a cop pulled me over because my car was weaving in the highway. The policeman said, "Young lady, don't you think that with your precious cargo, you should get somewhere and sleep?" I had Shane in my arms at the time. He was nursing.

When we got to Marion, we went straight to a motel and got a room. I remember Shane was all over that room chasing a roach bug. Probably wasn't a classy motel. Anyway, this bug, trying to escape Shane's probing, scurried inside a power outlet. Not one to give up easily, Shane found a hairpin on the floor and stuck it inside the outlet, trying to get to the bug. The electrical shock knocked him plumb across the room. That was the last time he messed with an electrical outlet.

I'm not sure Bill appreciated all of us being there for him when he was in prison. He wasn't one for compliments. And I don't know how he felt about me being there for the murder trial, sitting behind him and his lawyers, hanging onto every word.

As the trial progressed, I was beginning to think it didn't look good for Bill. Still, I thought he was innocent because of the way he loved older people. In fact, I thought he might have been framed. My daughter Ann said she believed he was there at the scene, but didn't kill anyone. Stoney believes he was out burglarizing places while the others murdered and robbed the Flemings. Shane said he'd like to believe that, but he doesn't. Frankly, I don't know what Bill did.

As I said, Bill never revealed what he did after he left the house practically every night—unless it was to see one of his girlfriends; he sometimes slipped and told me about them. So, if he'd ever killed anyone, I didn't know it for sure.

Billy Wayne Davis told the same story in the court that he told to Bob Ingram, that he had not been present when the Flemings were killed. But who believes him? Just the same, the car dealer was granted immunity from prosecution and testified against Bill. The killers, he said, were Bill, Bobby Gene Gaddis, and Charles David Reed. Davis looked pale and nervous as he took the stand and told the jury his version of what happened on the night of December 22, 1973, when the Flemings were killed. He testified for nearly four hours. Reeves and Bill's other lawyer, O.L. Collins of Augusta, took up most of that time cross-examining Davis.

Two other men, Carswell Tapley and George Leisher, were granted immunity and testified for the state. Tapley told the jury he had identified the Flemings and others in the area as having

CHAPTER NINE

large sums money. Leisher, Tapley's employer, apparently passed along the information to Davis. Davis said he gave the names to Bill, who said "he would pay well for information like that," according to Davis.

Davis told the jury, as he had told Ingram, that he and Bill, along with the other two, Bobby Gene Gaddis and Charles David Reed, agreed to meet at about one in the morning at the intersection of Georgia Highway 11 and Interstate 20, where Davis claimed he was waiting in a motor home. But Bill and the others were an hour late. Their explanation, Davis said, was that they "had some trouble in Wrens and had to kill the old man and woman."

All of this testimony was hard to listen to, but I had no choice. Bill and his partners were accused of torturing these people, trying to get them to say where their money was hidden. And when the husband died, the prosecution claimed, they killed the wife so that she wouldn't talk. They hadn't planned on killing anybody—they just wanted to rob the couple, Davis testified—but it didn't work out that way. A husband and wife died in the worst way possible.

Bill denied it all, of course. He took off his tie and sport coat before walking to the witness stand to testify in his own defense. Like Davis, he looked nervous. Bill never liked to talk in front of a lot of people because of his speech problem. He had trouble pronouncing certain words.

A number of security guards watched his every move.

Bill testified that he had never heard of the Flemings before their deaths and that he had never been to Wrens before his arraignment was held. And he did not burglarize the home of Mr. and Mrs. Hayman.

"I want this whole town to know that I didn't kill no old people," he testified loudly. "I know Mr. (Hugh) Fleming hates me, but I didn't kill those people."

At one point, Bill told the jury he had been through hell the past four months. He said he wanted to tell "what has been offered me and how it has been offered." He was implying that the Cobb County district attorney had offered him immunity in the case. But that obviously didn't happen.

He also said a law enforcement agent told him he'd be shot if the jury didn't convict him. The judge, Walter C. McMillan, ruled out those comments, made without the jury present, and told Bill to respond only to questions from the attorneys.

I took the stand in Bill's defense. So did my mother. So did two friends. One of them was Brenda Wages, who eventually would marry Bill's attorney, Gene Reeves. We did not lie. We told the court that Bill had been with us on the evening of the slayings. And he had been. He was at home when Brenda came by to pick up some garments I had sewn for her. It was before bedtime. My mother, Nellie, had seen him that evening. We lived on Virginia Avenue, and she lived about a mile away on King Street. Bill often went by my mother's home to check on her.

Bill could have left later, after I went to sleep, but that wasn't unusual. He left most nights. He seldom spent the whole night at home.

As the trial wound down, the judge swore in two extra bailiffs for round-the-clock surveillance of the jurors' room. The jury had been kept at a local motel since the trial began.

My friend Gene Reeves motioned for a mistrial, noting that all of the security in the courtroom and outside the courthouse had influenced the jury, making a fair trial for Bill impossible. The judge overruled the lawyer. In fact, he commended the security force. If it had not been for heavy security, the judge said, "order would not have been possible."

On Saturday, June 28, 1975, my husband, Billy Sunday Birt, was sentenced to death after being found guilty of the Fleming murders. The jury deliberated two hours that day and four hours the day before. Bill also got two life terms for armed robbery, and the judge added twenty years for burglary. Bill was acquitted of

CHAPTER NINE

the burglary of the Hayman home. The prosecution apparently never proved he took part in that burglary.

Bill didn't show any emotion when he heard the verdict of death. I lowered my head into my hands and sobbed.

The judge sentenced him to die on August 24, 1975, between 10 a.m. and 2 p.m. A death sentence carries an automatic appeal to the Georgia Supreme Court, and Bill and his attorneys would come up with their own appeals later on.

It had been six grueling days, sitting in that courtroom, armed officers standing everywhere, Bill hopelessly trying to come up with alibis, testimony for the state going more and more against him. It was hopeless.

Today, I am a wiser woman. I am a forgiven woman. I know that Bill controlled me the same way he controlled those who worked with him, people who would kill for him. It was always his way or no way. I tried to be a good wife. I only wish he had tried to be a good husband, a good role model for his children, a good Christian, someone we all could trust to do the right thing.

But that was not to be. He was found responsible for the deaths of two fine people. And for what? For about four thousand stolen dollars. That's what the newspapers said. But Bill said it was more. "We didn't get four thousand dollars," former GBI agent Bob Ingram said Bill told him, looking straight at him. "We got forty thousand dollars." Four thousand, forty thousand—what difference does it make? You can't put a dollar value on a human life.

The death sentence changed nothing for Bill. He was already in prison; he would remain in prison.

But justice was done. Bill and his partners—all but Billy Wayne Davis, who received immunity from prosecution—were convicted. In later trials, Gaddis was sentenced to death and Reed to life in prison. Gaddis died in prison in 2007. Someone shot and killed Reed a short time after his release from prison.

Something happened after the Jefferson County trial that helped save my sanity. The Flemings' family members, obviously very forgiving people, came to me after the verdict was read and gave me a hug. I pray that they all have good memories of their folks before that horrible night in December of 1973.

For me, well, I am left with the image of that woman's bound ankle and foot lying on that bed. And a lot of bad memories.

Bill wasn't much of a drinker, but he hauled plenty of the stuff.

CHAPTER TEN

If Bill Birt had confined his illegal activities to hauling moonshine, he would have had all the illegal work he could handle, at least for several years. That's because Harold Chancey had liquor stills hidden everywhere. And Bill was his best tripper, someone who never got caught hauling.

Almost caught, but never arrested.

"At one time," Shane said, "Harold could've had ten, twenty or thirty stills all over the place . . . but if the heat ever got on one of them, Harold would have them blow that still up."

That's what happened in the late sixties or early seventies at a still site located off Highway 211, in the pristine area that now cradles the exclusive Chateau Elan resort near Braselton, Georgia. Chancey's men had used a tractor to dig into the side of a mountain, creating a cavern large enough for two-hundred fifty mash trays, Shane said he was told. "This was probably the biggest still Harold ever had."

Lawmen from the Alcohol Tobacco Firearms (ATF) division were hot on it, watching comings and goings at the site for some time. But they had not made their move; they were waiting on Chancey to show up. Very often, when authorities raided a still, they arrested the still hands, but seldom the owner, who was clever enough to stay away when he thought agents were watching. The ATF wanted the owner, Chancey.

Chancey got word through his network of informers that the site was being watched and that authorities had tapped his telephone. Word about the wiretap came originally from a woman who worked at the local telephone company. She notified one of Chancey's buddies, who in turn got word to Chancey.

The friend telephoned Chancey and said something like, "Harold, those boxes you ordered are in. Come up here and get them."

Chancey was quick to catch on. "Oh, yeah," he said, "the boxes I ordered."

Chancey then knew to be careful in what he said by phone, and he knew the huge still had to go. Shane picked up the story from here:

"My dad and my Uncle Bob drove up there one night and got out. They were in Mom's car. Both men were toting crates. Uncle Bob was toting a case of Mason jars. Every now and then he would shake them to make anyone watching think they were getting moonshine. Daddy was carrying dynamite and dynamite wire.

"They walked in acting like they were going to get some whiskey. Daddy set the dynamite up, and on their way out, they carried the same two boxes. Except this time, Daddy had the two wires set up so that they were rolling out as he was walking. The ATF could not see the wires falling out. They got back to the car, Daddy took the two leads and touched them to a battery, and it blew up.

"Uncle Bob swore that mash trays and stills went everywhere. And he swore to his dying day that he saw ATF agents go up in the air. They were laying all around, waiting on Harold. . . . They blew up stills all the time if the law was hot on their trail."

Chancey found the phone company employee who provided the tip and insisted she take money for her service. You saved me a lot of trouble, he told her.

Harold Chancey—who learned from the best, his parents, Hoke and Ruth Chancey—also had stills on his father's horse farm. One day, he and Shane were walking around on the farm, and Chancey asked, "Son, those back doors there, what do you

CHAPTER TEN

recognize about them?" He was pointing to a red horse barn on the back of the farm, one whose doors went all the way to the ground.

"You don't have to step over a knee wall to get in there," Shane answered.

"That's right," Chancey said, "and they're a whole lot wider. That's the reason you could tote a still or tote mash in and out without stepping over anything."

Moonshiners, especially the brains of the jobs, had to be smart and cunning. And Harold Chancey was smart. He loved animals as much as Bill did and always wanted to be a veterinarian. In fact, he was in veterinary school at the University of Georgia when his father was killed in a tractor accident. Chancey already knew something about moonshining; he had learned from Hoke. For his science project in high school, he built a miniature still. So, after his daddy died, he took over the illegal liquor business. He could have been a successful veterinarian who made animals well. Instead, he became a criminal who made moonshine.

Stoney Birt knows firsthand about some of his daddy's liquor runs because he went along for the ride, something his daddy regretted later.

"... Me and Stoney were always so close," Bill Birt said in a recording made in prison in December 1999. "While he was growing up, from the time he was a baby, he went everywhere with me. I'm ashamed to say this, but I even took him with me when I used to haul moonshine. His mama would have had a fit if she knew that back then. So there will always be a closeness between me and Stoney."

Bill Birt said he loved all of his children, but Stoney was the firstborn and his constant companion. "He kept me with him,

I mean, continuously," Stoney said in an interview with Karyn Greer, anchor for CBS 46 television in Atlanta, and crime scene investigator Sheryl "Mac" McCollum. "He would never take me on heists or let me hear about [crime] plans."

But he heard plenty in whispers at his daddy's pool room, the Winder Recreation Parlor, as some job was being planned. "I'd become conditioned," he said in the TV station's podcast called *CSI Atlanta*. "He'd tote a man in after a bank robbery and take a bullet out and just go to bed. And the next night, he'd be telling me 'Jack and the Beanstalk.'"

Speaking of moonshine, Stoney said his father "hijacked sugar trucks out of three states continuously just to keep the supply going. They serviced all the whiskey—the good whiskey—for Georgia, South Carolina and North Carolina for ten years. [The law] never could touch him. He was embarrassing the law."

Knowledge of whiskey-making, the interviewer noted, comes from a family legacy that dates back to 1810, through Prohibition and beyond.

If you ever had a chance to talk to ATF agents back in the late sixties and seventies, they might not admit that Bill Birt embarrassed them. But they would say it was not easy keeping tabs on trippers like him. Their job was hard and dangerous.

"I was afraid sometimes that he would not come home," Ann Holsclaw Hughes said of her husband, E.D. "Ed" Hughes, who at one time was senior special investigator with the ATF, serving the southeast region. "I would be expecting him to come home, but there was no way to find out where he was. When he was 'laying on a still,' as they called it, he could be there three days."

Ann Hughes said she didn't talk much about her husband's job. "We knew where the bootleggers lived (in and around Atlanta), and they knew where we lived," she said. Sometimes, on a Sunday, one of the lawbreakers would drive by an agent's home to see if his car was there, hoping to find out if it was safe to make a run.

CHAPTER TEN

And when arrests were made, it was usually the still hands who ended up in the slammer, people who had little or no money, prompting Ann Hughes to search her closets for clothes to give to the family's children. "The poor guys were the ones who got sent to prison," she said, "and their families suffered."

In 1967, Ed Hughes prepared a report, titled *Moonshining—The Real Story*, published by The Medical Times. In it, he wrote:

"Generally, a bootlegger brings havoc upon his family. Family life is utter chaos. Every stranger is a potential threat to their security, because he might be the law. Every strange vehicle arouses suspicion. It must be watched closely, lest it be an enforcement vehicle dropping off investigators to search for the moonshine still, or to await a load of liquor en route to a customer. This is part of their day-to-day existence; this is the price they pay for being criminals."

Hughes retired in 1983 and moved with his family to Gainesville, where he became a boat salesman. He died in 2006. In describing him in an obituary, *The Atlanta Journal-Constitution* newspaper quoted its own story, written in 1971 for the paper's Sunday magazine. "If you were directing a documentary sort of action drama for television," the article said, "E.D. Hughes is just the one you'd pick for the lead. He's a six-foot-six, 240-pound former end at Virginia Tech with just the right staccato style of dialogue. He's full of facts and figures about crime and extremism—in fact, he's written several monographs on police techniques relating to bombs. . . ."

Hughes was instrumental in setting up a task force of federal and state agents to deal with the Dixie Mafia during Bill Birt's era of tripping—the late sixties through the mid-seventies. Operation Dry-Up, the agents called it. After cleaning up much of the moonshining through Operation Dry-Up, the obituary read, he was put in charge of bomb investigation teams.

Andrew Hughes, Ed and Ann Hughes' son, recalled his father's talking about the danger of the agents' assignments. "He said there would be no less than four agents in a car at a time in between

Atlanta and Athens and Atlanta and Gainesville," the son said. "It was for safety."

The son said his father told stories about arresting people for moonshining and having dinner with the family before taking the defendant to jail.

"He had an incredible life besides being a giant in size," Andrew Hughes said.

Charles H. Weems, a retired special agent with the U.S. Treasury Department, wrote two books about the ATF and its agents. In his first book, *A Breed Apart: A True Story about U.S. Treasury Agents During the Moonshine Years*, he wrote:

"A lot of people who get into crime go most of their lives without doing anything more illegal than parking overtime or running a stop sign. Then something comes along that looks like a sure thing—little risk and a large payoff—so they take a chance. If they get by with it, they keep on and usually end up in larger and more violent criminal activity with disastrous results. Sometimes it's better to get caught on the first attempt. A good lesson is learned with no great loss."

To illustrate, he told of a man who owned an Atlanta bakery and had never been involved in criminal activity. Then he saw a chance to make money fast. "A confidential informant had been at the Farmers Market in Gainesville," Weems wrote, "and was told that this man could furnish all the sugar and materials needed to make liquor to anyone who was willing to pay."

Posing as a moonshiner who was willing to pay, Weems called on the man at his bakery, saying he wanted to purchase twenty-one bags—twenty-one hundred pounds—of sugar, but he didn't want anything reported. No problem, the baker said. I'll say I was using the sugar at the bakery. Later on, Weems called

CHAPTER TEN

to say he wanted another twenty bags of sugar, but this time the baker asked Weems to meet him at his home.

While the transaction was being made, other ATF agents showed up and arrested the baker. Weems wrote, "He lost a good pickup truck, two thousand pounds of sugar, lawyers' fees in excess of one thousand dollars, and even worse he lost his reputation as a law-abiding citizen and honest businessman. He was convicted and received probation. I feel sure (the man) never violated the law again."

Unlike most moonshine trippers, Bill Birt was a diversified criminal. He didn't stick to just transporting white lightning. He could haul illegal drugs from Mexico; he could rob banks; he could kill. And, as Stoney told the Atlanta TV interviewers, his daddy could rob poker games with ease. After holding up one game, ordering players to drop their pants, and making off with a pile of money, "that's when he got to know that his future was not in moving dirt or busting rocks," Stoney said.

Bill Birt couldn't be beat in poker, and Stoney himself learned from the pro, becoming proficient in the game. "How could you not be?" he said during the *CSI Atlanta* podcast. "I was the only kid in the first grade who knew the odds on pulling an inside straight on any hand you wanted to play."

Stoney said his daddy was good at poker because of his ability to read people. He learned it early. "When you're having to survive in life, in his situation—I can't imagine the poverty he came up in," Stoney said. "My situation, well, I never watched a football game or a basketball game . . . but what I do know is numbers, how to read people in pool, cards."

Lawmen eventually dubbed the Birt gang's illegal operations as being work of the Dixie Mafia. But, Stoney said, unlike the

Mafia that originated in Sicily and eventually gravitated to the northern United States, the Dixie Mafia was not organized. "What makes the Mafia is, if one of them ever turns, it would take the whole crowd down," he said. "Therein lies the power of the whole crowd to put the pressure on him. . . . They were just a group of guys who came to learn how to make a lot of money very easily compared to working."

Bill Birt became known as someone who could be trusted to carry out any crime, Stoney said. People started calling him after 1968, and he usually took the job, whatever it was. If it was a hit on somebody, his price for the killing was five thousand dollars if the contract involved someone in the inner circle. If the contract request came from a friend of someone in the inner circle, the price was ten thousand dollars.

Stoney told the interviewers he spent a lot of time "reconciling what he knew about (his daddy) as a father and what he eventually learned about (him) as a cold-blooded killer."

"There are people out there that you'll meet, and you'll think this is the grandest person on earth," Stoney said. "And he is. But a switch gets turned, and it comes to business or money or self-preservation, and you cannot believe what they're capable of doing. That was my daddy. He taught me better. He was taught better. My grandmother was a God-fearing woman, and she told him—if I heard it once, I heard it a million times—'Son, you're going to pay for what you do, seven-fold.' There ain't no lying in the Bible. There ain't no lying in God."

Several men Stoney considered as his heroes at one time should have heeded his grandmother's warning. They didn't. And they paid dearly on this earth, and then they had to meet their Maker, Stoney said.

"If any young person thinks Billy Birt is a hero, how wrong are you," Stoney said. "He's my hero and he's my daddy, and he's a hero as a daddy. But he's a cold-blooded murderer. He killed for self-preservation, for revenge, for money, and for hire. There ain't

CHAPTER TEN

nothing heroic about that. And if anybody is listening or reading this, I've got to ask you this: If you think it is cool to have that lifestyle, well, he has now met his Maker, and how would you like to change places with him? And I hope I got my point across."

Still, he said, Billy Sunday Birt was a good father. "I don't try to build him up as Superman," he said, "but as a father, there was no equal. There wasn't."

As dangerous as Stoney knew his father to be, he wanted to be like him as a teenager. "I had to become Billy Birt, because he was such a great man in my mind," Stoney told Sean Kipe in a podcast titled *In the Red Clay*, produced through Imperative Entertainment. "I had this romantic view of it all."

Stoney said he began robbing the same places his father hit and, at seventeen years old, convicted of several charges, he ended up serving time in the prison in Alto, Georgia.

During his imprisonment, believing his father was about to be executed, Stoney went berserk, psychotic, when the prison warden and others told him he couldn't be taken to see his daddy for what he thought would be the last time. He threatened to kill the prison officials and was placed in solitary confinement. Inmates call it the "hole."

One day, a prison chaplain overheard Stoney's ranting and raving from the hole and then persuaded the warden to change his mind. Two guards put Stoney into a paddy wagon and drove him four hours to the prison in Reidsville. He didn't know why. Maybe I'm being transferred down there, he thought. But, no, he wasn't being transferred. He was taken to see his father, and they got to spend eight hours together.

During their visit, guards brought them two chunks of ham, some bread, and two cartons of milk. "I believe that was the best meal we ever had together," Stoney told Kipe. When it was time to leave, Stoney kissed his father on the jaw, and Bill gave his son a "head kiss."

Stoney was taken back to Alto and thrown into the hole. He thought his father was to be executed at seven o'clock the next morning. But after he awoke, he was told at ten o'clock that his daddy had received a stay of execution. Everyone knew that earlier, but no one told Stoney. He was furious that prison officials let him suffer such mental anguish, all for nothing.

To pass the time in prison, Bill Birt sometimes made cloth, stuffed animals and mailed them to his sons. Inside some of the dolls the Birt boys would find crudely sketched maps to sites where their daddy had buried treasures—or stolen items not worth keeping or fencing. "Stoney must have thirty of those maps," Shane said. "Me and Montana gave Stoney our maps, too."

Kipe and Stoney wanted to see if they could find one of those buried treasures. First, though, they used Shane's heavy equipment to dig for bodies on the shore of the Mulberry River. They found nothing, Shane said. Then they scoped out one of Bill Birt's burial places for stolen items. Using one of the Birt maps and a metal detector, they found nothing but a piece of rusted metal the first time they dug into the earth.

But Stoney wasn't satisfied. On a second attempt, on another day, he and his son, Stone, went back to the site. They dug down with a shovel about six feet from the first digging. The shovel hit something hard. It could be money, Stoney said. What it was, though, was a thirty-inch, double-barrel shotgun wrapped inside a pair of handsewn, double-knit pants. Stoney gave Shane the pants, Shane brought them to me, Bill's wife, and I recognized them. I had made Bill those pants decades ago. As a matter of fact, I made most of his clothes back then.

CHAPTER TEN

Shane said he possesses the hammers and firing mechanisms for the double-barrel shotgun. He found them years ago in a hidden panel in the bottom of his parents' chifferobe, and he took them.

Other items, maybe treasures, maybe not, are thought to be buried out there somewhere.

In Stoney's pursuit to be more like his father, he never physically hurt anyone, he said. He mainly stole. But in a way, Billy Stonewall "Stoney" Birt carried on his family's legacy. In early 2020, Stoney opened his own legal distillery, Rock Solid Distillery, in Winder. But it closed to visitors a few weeks later because of serious contagiousness of the coronavirus pandemic.

His son, Billy "Stone," made the whiskey at first. "I'm good at running my mouth," Stoney said. The distillery opened back up a few months later. But it closed down again in the spring of 2021 because of a monetary dispute with investors. As this book went to production, the distillery was operating again.

CHAPTER ELEVEN

I MUST HAVE BEEN NAÏVE. Or maybe I had just closed my eyes and my mind and tried not to think of the terrible things Bill might've been doing when he went out at night, leaving the kids and me alone in the house.

My surprises were just beginning. One by one, murder by murder, bombing by bombing, robbery by robbery, I was learning the truth. My faith in God was as strong as ever, maybe even stronger because the Lord had been with me all during some really tough times. But my faith in Bill—what little I had—was shattered.

Since the trial for murdering the Wrens couple, I had learned of other killings Bill and his notorious friends had committed. I'll tell you about them later. First, let's go back to 1975 in Marietta, Georgia. That year, Bill confessed to killing two prominent physicians in Marietta (Cobb County), Georgia, a crime that generated a lot of publicity.

The murders happened moments after dawn on May 7, 1971, at the home of Warren and Rosina Matthews. Just as it was nearly three years later in the Wrens murders, Bill and his partners hadn't planned on killing or hurting anybody. They just wanted money.

Seven people had been convicted of the Matthews murders in five separate trials from 1973–1975. But they were all innocent. They were accused on false information provided by a South Carolina prostitute named Deborah Ann Kidd, being held on unrelated charges. In July 1972, authorities in South Carolina told officers in Cobb County, Georgia, that the woman could give names—nine in all—of people involved in the murders. She was promised immunity from prosecution for her cooperation.

Seven of the nine were convicted in the widely publicized case. The "Marietta Seven," they were called. But, on September 2, 1975, all charges were dropped and the convictions reversed because of gaps in the woman's story. She later admitted to perjury, but because she had been promised immunity, she was never tried.

Bill confessed to killing the couple in a letter to *The Atlanta Constitution* newspaper. Essentially, he said that he, Billy Wayne Davis and Willie Hester went to the physicians' home to rob them, but something went wrong and they had to kill them. The newspaper published the letter.

"I think publication of Billy Sunday Birt's letter helped knock down what appeared to be a house of cards that (Judge) Luther Hames, (former district attorney) Ben Smith and others built around that fake confession of Debbie Kidd," said David Morrison, one of the newspaper's writers who covered the Marietta Seven debacle. "With a heated election campaign for district attorney underway and one of the most heinous crimes in the county a year unsolved, they had latched on to what amounted to a sketchy tip from a prostitute who was trying to get out of a drug bust in another state and changed the whole direction of the real investigation."

Morrison said he had doubts about Kidd's story from the start.

After Bill fingered Billy Wayne Davis in the Matthews murders, Davis went on trial in October of 1979. My husband again entered the picture, not as a defendant this time, but as a witness for the prosecution. This was his chance to get back at Davis for testifying against him in the Loganville bank robbery case and on the Wrens murders. Davis was serving twenty-five years for the bank robbery, but he got off scot-free in the Wrens murder trial. It was Davis, a car dealer from Austell, Georgia, who furnished a

CHAPTER ELEVEN

1971 luxury automobile for the trip to Wrens. But because Davis was cooperating with prosecutors, he could say anything and not be tried.

Now it was payback time in Marietta, Georgia, scene of Davis's trial for murder. Bill got his chance to testify against Davis when the trial entered its fourth day. Several Cobb County sheriff's deputies led Bill into the packed courtroom the afternoon of October 25, 1979. Other armed officers stood in different sections of the courtroom.

Bill Birt had Billy Wayne Davis right where he wanted him, and Davis's defense attorney knew it. One day during the trial, one of Davis's lawyers got on the courthouse elevator with me and said, "Oh, by the way, Billy Wayne Davis fell in the shower and has amnesia and doesn't remember anything. He has nothing to say." He was suggesting to me that Davis didn't plan to testify anymore against Bill, so maybe Bill wouldn't testify against him. But that wasn't going to happen.

When Bill's time to testify arrived, Davis's attorney objected, claiming that Bill was an atheist and could not swear to God to tell the whole truth as required by law. But he was allowed to testify after he said he did believe in God, "but I don't live it now."

Bill spoke the truth there. He certainly didn't live a godly life. Anyone who took the lives of innocent people. . . . Well, I don't need to say anything else.

But at least Bill attempted to look after me and the kids when he made an agreement with members of the families of some of the people convicted in the Matthews case. He telephoned one day and told me to call Bobby Lee Cook, a well-known defense lawyer, now deceased, and say this: "Do you want to know where the gun is that killed the Matthews couple?" Cook was attorney for three of the seven convicted earlier.

Bill's sister Jody and I met with Cook to discuss the agreement. Cook promised twenty-five thousand dollars if Bill's testimony led to indictments and convictions. During the trial, Cook said

I had been paid five thousand dollars, but that the rest of the money was withheld after we could not produce a gun used in the Matthews murders.

I don't remember the amount of money paid, but I know what I did with part of it: I bought cemetery lots. I also thought the gun was found behind a service station. But, when contacted by email, Cook said otherwise. He said no gun was found.

Whatever the case, the trial of Billy Wayne Davis was underway, and Bill was there to tell it all, his way. "I am testifying here today," Bill said in response to questions from Cobb District Attorney Tom Charron, "because that man there (motioning toward Davis) once was my best friend. We robbed banks together, we done everything together, and he testified against me." As long as the bond of friendship has been broken, he said, "all the truth should come out."

Here's some of what Bill testified after he was brought to the Cobb County trial from Reidsville, where he was imprisoned on death row:

Davis had telephoned him in Winder on the night of May 6, 1971. "I've got pigs ready for sale," Davis told Bill. "Pigs" meant robbery or burglary, and "hogs" meant murder. Figuring the cops had bugged their phones, Davis and Bill were careful not to use incriminating words. So they devised mysterious messages about pigs and hogs to disguise their plans. The signals told Bill what he needed to take on the job. Robbery required masks and gloves. No shooting was planned, but, of course, the men always took their guns. Their goal was to rob the couple of forty to fifty thousand dollars believed to be kept in the couple's safe.

But the robbery was botched. And Bill blamed Davis. Actually, Bill said, the robbery was Davis's idea.

As usual, I was sitting in the courtroom with my friends as Davis's trial progressed. Sometimes Bill would look toward me, sometimes he glared hatefully at Davis, the traitor. Davis was sitting there smiling. One time, Bill looked straight at me, and

CHAPTER ELEVEN

I silently mouthed, "Take him." He'd already testified against Davis in an earlier case in Douglas County, Georgia, and now it was time to do it again. Davis saw me mouth those words, "take him," and just shook his head.

"We had a rule between us," Bill testified. "If anyone could identify either one of us, they had to die." You never leave witnesses behind. Another rule was that Bill was to never open his mouth to speak, because if he did he could be identified by his speech impediment.

So what was supposed to have been a robbery, Bill said, turned into a double murder, Here's what he testified: He, Davis, and the third accomplice, Willie Hester, were waiting outside when Warren Matthews opened the garage door of his home, preparing to leave for work the morning of May 7. The men, each one wearing a mask, approached Matthews, and the doctor "went wild," Bill said. Davis "throwed a gun on him," and Matthews reached for Davis's mask and snatched it off.

"I went ahead and pulled my mask off, too," Bill said. "I knew what had to be done. He wasn't going to be alive when we left."

After a brief struggle in the garage, Matthews took off running down his driveway, and Bill shot him twice in the back as he ran. After Rosina Matthews appeared in the doorway holding a .38 pistol, Bill said the two exchanged gunfire in the garage. He wounded the woman. But it was Davis, Bill said, who chased her to the backyard patio, held her down with his knee and shot her in the back of the head with her own pistol, which she had dropped.

The three men fled the scene in Warren Matthews's small Mercedes automobile and returned to Bill's car, which had been left parked down a side street.

On Friday, October 26, 1979, Cobb Superior Court Judge Luther Hames said he had doubts Davis was even present when the Matthews were killed. He told Cobb District Attorney Charron he had been "pondering the charge of the crime of conspiracy," because "you've got enough evidence with his confession to show he (Davis) may have been a party although not present." Charron had introduced into evidence a handwritten statement Davis gave to police in August 1975. The statement indicated that Davis had some involvement in the crime: that he was supposed to have driven Bill and Willie Hester to the Matthews home, but decided at the last minute not to go. He said he learned of the killings later that morning, May 7th.

On the stand, Davis testified that the statement "is a complete fabrication, made by me and (former district attorney) Ben Smith and others who may or may not have known what was going on." Smith testified earlier that he had helped Davis draft the confession in August 1975 while Davis was being held in jail in Forsyth, Georgia.

"I had nothing whatsoever to do with that occurrence (the murders)," Davis testified. "I didn't kill either one of those people, and I don't know anything about it." In cross examination by District Attorney Charron, Davis said he had been "framed by my own stupidity" in formerly confessing to the crime. "I was in jail with Birt in 1974, and he told me then that if I testified against him in the Jefferson County (Wrens, Georgia) case, then he would implicate me in the Matthews murder."

When the trial ended and the jury began deliberating, I didn't have any idea what the verdict would be. I knew that Bill hated Davis, and I knew he wanted this used-car dealer to pay for testifying against him in the Wrens murders and the Loganville bank robbery case. But who can predict what a jury will do?

And the jurors weren't sure, either. They were deadlocked six-six—six for acquittal, six for conviction—after four hours of deliberation. Their indecision was understandable. Bill had admitted in court that he held a grudge against Davis. How would the jurors know if he was telling the truth about Davis's involvement? Besides, they were considering a transcript of the testimonies of more than forty witnesses, along with more than a hundred exhibits presented by the defense and prosecution.

CHAPTER ELEVEN

In his final argument, defense attorney William Holley asked the jury, "Must we build this mansion that the state has set out to construct, on the word of a brutal killer, Billy Sunday Birt, who is faced with the eventual day when he would walk down a corridor and have his life removed by the law?"

District Attorney Charron countered. "Who brought these two assassins to Cobb County?" he asked the jury. "What could two country fellows be doing in a fashionable east Cobb subdivision if the mastermind hadn't given them the word?" Davis, he maintained, was the mastermind.

On Saturday morning, November 3, 1979, the jury finally reached a verdict, ending the trial after eleven days. The jury found Billy Wayne Davis not guilty of the 1971 slayings of Warren and Rosina Matthews. Davis, flanked by his attorneys, William Holly and Gary Walker, wept when the verdict was read.

District Attorney Charron immediately stalked out of the courtroom, refusing to answer reporters' questions. Later, however, he said, "The jury spoke—that's our American system of justice—and we accept it. We had an excellent judge, an excellent jury, and no one should have any regrets about this trial."

The one who had regrets was Bill Birt, my husband. His plan to put Davis away, a second time, had failed. The judge was right: Billy Wayne Davis was not present when the Matthews were murdered, Bill told Shane a few years ago. He had concocted the whole lie to get back at his former friend and partner.

So who was there? Bill said it was him, Willie Hester, Bobby Birt, Bill's brother; Otis Reidling, and another person we will not name because he was never implicated in any crime. (He is now deceased.) This is what really happened at the Matthews home, according to what Bill told Shane:

Both physicians came out of their home with guns blazing. It was a real shootout right there in the garage and driveway. Who ended up shooting the couple? We don't know. Bill didn't say. But he did say this: The unnamed person broke an ankle jumping over a wall, and Willie Hester was shot in the shoulder. Bill brought Hester to our home in Winder to remove the bullet. Bill asked me to boil some hot water. I did that and then left the room. I don't know anything else.

When Bill concocted his scenario in court, he figured there was no reason not to name Willie Hester as one of the would-be robbers. He was dead. But he didn't want to rat on the others—his brother Bob, Otis Reidling, and the unnamed fifth person. He left them out of the made-up story. He named Billy Wayne Davis instead.

You may be wondering what happened to Willie Hester, implicated in the Matthews murder but absent at Davis's trial. Hester had been missing for several years when his body was finally found near Athens, Georgia. Bill believed that Hester had started turning on him. He had four or five jobs lined up, Bill told Shane, but when he telephoned Hester, he always had something else to do. One time, when Hester couldn't go on a job, Bill drove by the Barrow County Sheriff's Office, climbed up a wall and looked over. There sat cars from the Georgia Bureau of Investigation and the Drug Enforcement Administration.

"The cops were sitting there waiting on me," Shane recalled his daddy saying. Bill believed Hester ratted on him.

At 12:15 a.m. on August 24, 1971, Hester left home, telling his wife he was meeting Billy Birt. He was driving a blue Oldsmobile that he purchased from C.W. Royster in Winder. The next morning, the Olds was found parked in Royster's car lot, Winder's Belk department store had been burglarized, and Hester was missing.

ATF investigator Jim Earl West's informant said Bill devised a scheme to make it appear Hester held out on him and Reidling after the three of them burglarized the Belk store, where Hester's wife worked. According to West's informant, Bill told Hester to

CHAPTER ELEVEN

keep some of the stolen money in his back pocket. "Later, when they divided the money," West said, "Billy Birt shot Hester and made Reidling shoot Hester, too, and told him to look in Hester's back pocket for the money he was holding out on them."

Turned out, Hester told Harold Chancey he had actually talked to federal officers, "but he hadn't told them anything," the investigator's report said. But just talking to officers—whether or not he revealed any criminal activities—was enough to get him killed.

The story of how and where Willie Hester died will change later on. Just be patient.

Like Davis, Bill had been indicted on two counts of murder in the Matthews case, but he was never tried, apparently because he had already been convicted of murdering the Fleming couple in Wrens. District Attorney Charron said because of Davis's acquittal, he was "not sure it would be fair to try the co-defendant (Bill Birt)."

The district attorney said Judge Hames, who presided over the earlier Matthews trials, had asked him to look again at two other charges against Davis and Bill: the shooting death of Samuel Thompson of Mableton, Georgia, in November 1971, and the slaying of Lewis James House of Toccoa, Georgia, in April 1972. The two killings were included in the indictment returned by a Cobb County grand jury that named Bill and Davis in the Matthews case. We never heard anything else about those alleged murders.

As I said earlier, another chance to rat on Davis had presented itself in Douglas County, Georgia. Bill was under indictment for murder in the county seat, Douglasville, where he testified in a trial in 1976. As it turned out in the Matthews case, Bill was a witness for the prosecution against Davis. He said Davis had contracted him to kill Charles Mack Sibley, a gambler in Lithia Springs who wanted money Davis owed him from poker games. Davis was convicted, but Bill's case never went to trial.

Davis, Bill said, had lost fourteen thousand dollars to Sibley playing poker and was forced to give the winner an IOU. My husband apparently came up with the idea of robbing Sibley and paying him back with his own money. But Davis said he had a better idea. You kill him, Bill, and we'll keep the money. Bill testified that he, Davis and Otis Reidling carried out Davis's plan the next night after they talked. Bill and Davis entered Sibley's house and waited while Reidling cruised by every fifteen minutes, watching for Sibley's car. When Sibley came home, the two robbed him of several thousand dollars. Bill put him inside a closet and shot him. The body was discovered the next day.

For his service, Davis gave Bill four thousand dollars in cash and a car.

Bill ratted on Davis, telling investigators that he ordered the hit on Sibley, and eventually then-GBI agent Bob Ingram and Sheriff Earl Lee of Douglas County drove to Marion, Illinois, where they got Bill out of prison to testify against Davis in his trial in 1976.

"We talked with Birt and were able to convince him to testify against Davis in retribution for Davis's testifying against him (Birt)," Ingram said. "Billy Birt was a dangerous man, with or without a gun. We were able to get Birt to testify against Davis and convict Davis. You can imagine how Davis felt toward us. He got life in the Sibley case."

At one point during the Douglas County trial, Bill told the judge not to feel bad about any sentencing because "me and that man may have killed more people than you can imagine." He was referring to Davis.

CHAPTER ELEVEN

Besides the Fleming case, Bill was convicted of one other murder—and believe it or not, he knowingly set himself up to be tried. Here's Shane's explanation:

"Daddy couldn't initiate this hisself. He couldn't be the author of a rat. So what he had to do, he had to come up with a ruse and let somebody else play that part. And that was Bobby Gene Gaddis. He told Bobby Gene what he wanted to do, and Bobby Gene took that information and did exactly what Daddy said.

"Daddy already had everything set up with the law. The law knew what was going to happen. Daddy worked out a deal to get Stoney out of prison. He would get word out that he committed a certain murder—and be tried—in exchange for Stoney's release from prison. So Stoney was in prison a few years, rather than several."

After the deal was approved, Bill was tried in Winder and found guilty of killing Donald Chancey—and perhaps for the same reason he murdered Hester. He thought Chancey was working with the feds on moonshine cases. Harold Chancey, Donald Chancey's cousin, said that every time he set up a still, it wouldn't be a month before somebody would be there busting it up. Like Bill, Donald Chancey was a tripper—or a runner—of moonshine. If Chancey was tipping the feds, Bill wanted him out of the picture. And, according to former GBI Agent Ronnie Angel, Bill was right about his suspicions.

"We were going to put him (Chancey) in the witness protection program," Angel said. "He was supposed to testify against Billy and others about the liquor business."

At one point, a GBI agent interviewed Bill, Angel said, and tried to play on his sympathies. We want the Chancey family to have closure, the agent told Bill. It won't affect you, so give us an idea where we might look for his body. Chancey's family would like to give him a decent burial.

"Billy had a smirk on his face," Angel said, "and then he said, 'What makes you think he hadn't already had a decent burial?'"

123

This was a murderous time in Barrow and surrounding counties, mainly Jackson and Walton. About a dozen people disappeared between 1967 and 1974, when most of Bill's contract jobs were carried out. He didn't always do them alone; sometimes he had help.

Donald Chancey, a welder in Atlanta, left home for work at 6 a.m. on July 31, 1972, but he was driving in the wrong direction, his wife told authorities. He always drove to the right, toward Atlanta. But on this day, he turned left. Mrs. Chancey said she didn't think much about it until her husband didn't come back home that evening. She never saw him again.

Chancey's body was found October 9, 1979, buried beside a creek in Barrow County. He was facing charges in a federal liquor case when he disappeared.

Bill had already been sentenced to die for his part in the Flemings' murder, so what was one more murder conviction? He went on trial in February of 1980, and the key witness for the prosecution, of course, was Bobby Gene Gaddis, who had been promised immunity for his testimony. Gaddis told the court that Bill and Charlie Reed came to his house on the day of the murder, and Bill asked him to "help take care of something." Gaddis testified that he rode with Bill and Reed to a street near Chancey's home, and then he and Bill left Reed with the car. In the meantime, Bill and Gaddis watched Chancey's house. As Chancey was preparing to leave home, the two walked up to his car—one report said they were hiding behind the car—and Bill told Chancey he wanted his help in getting away from the law.

They drove in Chancey's car to a dirt road in a remote area of the county, where Bill told Chancey to get into the trunk of the car. The two got out of the car, went around to the back, and Gaddis said he heard two shots. Bill and Gaddis then went to meet Reed, and the three of them drove to an area near Chicken Lyle Road, where they buried Chancey's body in a ditch.

CHAPTER ELEVEN

Bill had told an informant that Chancey was eliminated, but he didn't say how or reveal where Chancey's car was ditched.

An investigator from the state crime lab testified that Chancey died from two gunshot wounds to the head.

Among personal effects found with Chancey's remains in October of 1979 were boots, clothes, a pocket knife, and a lighter inscribed with the names of Chancey's children on one side and "Chancey loves Carol," his wife, on the other. Chancey's former dentist identified the man's body using dental records.

Bill's attorney, Bud Siemon, argued in his closing statement that Gaddis, who already was facing a death sentence in the Wrens case, had nothing to lose by testifying. In fact, he said, he hoped to have something to gain. "He believed he could get help," the attorney said. "He wanted to bargain his way off death row."

But District Attorney Nat Hancock told the court, "Nobody promised (Gaddis) anything except me—immunity."

On February 19, 1980, after deliberating almost four hours, a jury of four women and eight men found Bill guilty. After the jury announced the verdict, Bill thanked the county sheriff, John Robert Austin, and deputies for treating him "so nice" and told Superior Court Judge James L. Brooks to not worry about the life sentence since "one more won't hurt."

Apparently, Bill had a reason behind every one of his killings. "Some people were plain evil and killed people for the heck of it," Angel said. "Birt had a weird sense of justification about him. He killed a lot of people, but he didn't kill those people because he enjoyed killing people. He killed them for a reason."

Before he went to prison for the last time, Bill was a bit paranoid. I told you that. Well, he also was a little nervous about people snooping around the Mulberry riverbank. One day, he was a passenger in a car traveling down Highway 211, when he spotted a car in a sand flat along the river.

"I don't know what to make of that," he told the driver, Billy Wayne Davis, who related the story to Jim West. Bill had Davis turn around and drive back to the river. "You drop me off and let me walk in there and see what's going on," Bill said.

"Why you so upset?" Davis asked.

"I've got some bodies buried in there," Bill said.

Bill walked down to the river. When he returned, he told Davis, "It's okay. It's just a boy and girl parked down there."

We don't know what year this incident occurred, but we can tell you this: Later on, Davis knew that at least one body was buried on the Mulberry, because he helped bury it.

In April of 1974, an official digging took place. Acting on a tip, law officers from several agencies gathered along the floodplain of the Mulberry as earthmoving machines from the state transportation department dug into tons of the sandy soil near the Hall-Barrow-Gwinnett county lines. Inmates from the Hall County work camp did some of the hard labor. The FBI was there; so was the GBI, along with federal alcohol and tobacco tax officers, and sheriffs and deputies from nearby counties.

They were looking for bodies, maybe as many as seven or eight, said Angel, who was in charge of the operation as head of the GBI's major cases squad. The rumor mill in the county was even more imaginative: As many as a dozen area residents, missing or dead over the past two or three years, might be buried alongside the river, some residents believed. A second digging on the sandy riverbank took place in October of 1978, but former GBI agent Stanley Thompson said nothing was found.

In 1974, the ATF was investigating a number of murders and disappearances connected with liquor cases. Some of the deaths, sources said, probably resulted from fights among the Dixie Mafia and other gangland packs that dealt in stolen clothing, illicit drugs, car thefts, and moonshine.

CHAPTER ELEVEN

"There are about nine million rumors" about the digging operation, one officer said at the time. "Everybody has a sandbar they saw some dog diggin' in."

The 1974 digging lasted ten days and drew widespread attention, although the operation was supposed to have been under wraps. Even school children knew about the digging. Occasionally, one of the big, yellow school buses would slow down as it passed the riverbank on Georgia Highway 211, and one of the students would lean out of the window and shout, "Have they found any more bodies?"

Newsmen from all over the country stood and watched from a distance. The news editor from the local weekly newspaper, *The Winder News*, was arrested and charged with "interfering with police officers" for venturing too near the search area, which covered about three acres and several hundred feet of soil.

Another newsman, Johnny Solesbee, then editor of *The Winder News,* said he "spent many hours with crews who were digging for remains of Billy's victims in mostly isolated areas in the woods and once along the bank of a small creek. John Robert Austin always took everybody involved to John's Barbecue, which he owned, for lunch on the house."

After four days of digging and shoveling along the Mulberry, searchers came up with only one body: that of Otis Robert Reidling, twenty-four, of Winder, one of Bill's best friends. The only other significant find was a pair of panties, Angel said.

Reidling had been shot, his hands crossed over his face, and his body buried under four or five feet of ground. He had been missing about five months, since November 4, 1973. Driving a 1968 Oldsmobile, he left that day from a Winder service station bound for Gainesville to pick up his family. He never arrived.

James Reidling, Otis's uncle, spoke about the investigation at the dig site.

"How come nothing was done about this before?" a newspaper reporter asked, referring to the crime ring in Barrow and nearby counties.

"Because there was no one in Winder to do it," the uncle said.

"How come?"

"Because people were scared."

"Are you scared?"

"No, I'm not scared."

James Reidling might not have been scared, but I agree with Bob Ingram, the agent who investigated the Wrens murders. He said everybody, including Bill's family, was afraid of Billy Sunday Birt. And that includes me, his wife. I also was afraid of other people who might want to get back at Bill for something he did to them or to a family member. Law officers came to my home one day to warn me not to let strangers come in. Billy Wayne Davis's wife had been found dead in bed, they said, and the cause of death was unknown. So be careful, they said.

Elaine and Randall Holland were afraid to do anything at all after Bill stole their son's pony out of their yard and brought it home to our kids.

"It was grazing in our yard," Elaine Holland said by phone, "and then our pony disappeared, and it was grazing on their front lawn."

"Did you try to get the pony back?" she was asked.

"No," she said, "it wasn't worth it. . . . It wasn't funny, but we just laughed about it, because we weren't about to go get it. It was a nice-looking pony."

When friends asked Randall why he didn't go get his kids' pony, he responded, "I didn't want to end up in the lake."

Just before Shane was born, I saw a Chevrolet Kingswood automobile with wood sides, and I commented to Bill how pretty it was. "I'd like to have one like that," I said, not thinking I'd get one. When I got home from the hospital after birthing Shane,

CHAPTER ELEVEN

a Kingswood was sitting in our driveway. I thought Bill had bought it. I found out much later he had killed somebody on a contract, and his reward was that car.

Whatever Bill wanted, he apparently thought it was his right to take it, whether it was a pony, an automobile . . . or a life.

I didn't tell you the circumstances surrounding Otis Reidling's death. Actually, there are two very different stories about why and where that murder occurred. ATF agent Jim West learned one version of the story from his informant.

Bill, West said, borrowed a car from Billy Wayne Davis and then picked up Reidling and a girl. He had planned on killing Reidling, but now that a girl was with him, he would have to eliminate her, too. With both Reidling and the girl in the back seat, Bill drove a short distance "and pulled over to the side of the road and stopped and shot both of them." This, West said, happened November 4, 1973.

Bill told a different story when several authorities showed up at his prison on April 13, 1978, to get information about five murders that occurred in Hall County, two counties over from Barrow County. That version, we are convinced, is the truth. I'll tell you about it later.

But West was right about one thing: Otis Reidling had no promising future hanging around Bill Birt. In fact, West and Walton County Sheriff Frank Thornton warned Reidling that it would be just a matter of time before Bill would turn on him or kill him because he knew too much or for some other reason.

Reidling, however, was loyal to his friend. He said he wanted to talk to West and the sheriff, but he wouldn't say anything that would incriminate Bill Birt. He said his kinfolks didn't care about him and that he had been sent to reform school twice. After he got out the second time, Bill looked after him.

Another time Bill came to Reidling's defense was after his young friend was caught wearing an expensive ring taken in a burglary of The Jewel Box in Winder. Bill, Reidling, and the unnamed accomplice hit the jewelry store in 1972 and stole a bagful of jewelry—its worth estimated at between twenty and thirty thousand dollars. Most of it was fenced in nearby Athens, but Reidling kept one of the rings for himself. And he made the mistake of wearing it while walking through a downtown store in Winder. Larry Evans, owner of the jewelry store, spotted Reidling and his expensive ring and contacted the law. Reidling was arrested.

When the case went to trial, Bill told Reidling to blame him. You need to testify that you bought the ring from me, he said, and I'll testify I bought it from Willie Hester, who, unbeknownst to the jury, was dead.

In a letter to Stoney, Bill said Reidling would've been better off without his testimony. Bill, who was high on pills, was Reidling's only witness. Here's a portion of the letter:

> "Nat (Hancock), the DA (District Attorney), asked me where did I work. Well, I didn't work anywhere. So, I told him I was a farmer.... Nat asked me what did I farm. I couldn't think of nothing else right then. Like I said, I was pilled to the gill. So, I just said, 'Pigs.' Nat said, 'You're a pig farmer, huh?' and I said, 'Yes.' He said, 'How many pigs do you raise on your farm?' I was afraid to tell him a hundred or more for he might have sent someone to check me out. And I did have a few pigs I had turned a loose in my pasture where I lived down at Statham just in case he did send someone to look. So, when he asked me how many pigs

CHAPTER ELEVEN

did I have on my farm now, I counted on my fingers while he waited, and he looked like he was about to bust.... I think I said eleven. Might have said ten, but anyway it was real low. Damn, the whole room started laughing. Judge too. Nat asked me was I married. I said, 'Yes.' He asked me did me and my wife have any kids, I told him we had five kids. He said, 'You mean to tell me you feed and clothe your wife and five kids by raising eleven pigs. I said, 'Yes.'

"The jury and everybody in that court room busted out laughing, and the Judge turned around in his chair, put his hand on his head. I really felt like a fool sitting there."

But his glorious testimony was all for naught. Reidling was convicted of possession of stolen goods and sentenced to seven years in prison. But Bill got Alfred Quillian to appeal the case to the Georgia Supreme Court, and the sentence would be overturned, eventually. "But," Bill wrote Stoney, "it would take six months for the court to rule on his case so in the meantime Otis had to stay in jail for the judge wouldn't set him no appeal bond. So they sent Otis to Stone Mountain prison."

Several months later, Bill and three friends visited Reidling in prison. As they were leaving, Bill saw Reidling peering out a prison window "with that look on his face [and] telling me he couldn't stand it, to get him out," Bill wrote. A couple of nights later, Bill couldn't sleep. He and Reidling had buried the body of a man who had been snitching to the feds about moonshine stills, and Bill was worried that Reidling would squeal to get out of prison. He knew where the body was buried. So Bill got up in the middle of the night, drove to the Mulberry River, finally located the remains about a mile from Moon's Bridge, put the body in a sack and carried it, on his shoulders by himself, about a mile down the river and reburied it. Then he washed himself—clothes and all—with lye soap in the river.

"But all that work was for nothing," Bill wrote. "Otis stayed in prison for six months and kept his mouth shut. When the appeal court heard his case, they overturned his sentence. . . . But by being paranoid I sure did put myself through some hell. There ain't no amount of money that would make me do something stupid like that today. Hell, I would be afraid to even be down on that river by myself today, must (sic) less carry a dead body over my shoulders. But I guess that was just the way it was back then."

After Reidling got out of prison, he and Bill were constant companions.

By the way, Bill told Shane he burglarized The Jewel Box to prove he could commit a crime right under the noses of the law and not get caught. The FBI and GBI had set up shop in the Peskin Building, located across the street from the jewelry store.

It's true, Bill looked after Reidling, but in the end, Jim West and Sheriff Thornton were right: No one was safe around Bill Birt if he got angry or just upset. And the word is he found a reason to kill one of his best friends, someone he called Otie, a rock quarry worker who was only twenty-four years old.

But Bill said he wasn't the one who pulled the trigger.

J.C. Mathis with wife Dianne.

CHAPTER TWELVE

Because I was married to Bill Birt, I guess I knew him as well as anybody could. But I'll never understand him. People have asked me, "What happened to your husband to make him turn out the way he was." All I can say is what I've always said: "He was two people in one."

On May 13, 1996, when Bill was on death row, he scribbled several messages to God on a newspaper clipping about a family of five from Cobb County, Georgia, who were killed in an airplane crash as they were returning home from a weeklong Caribbean vacation.

"Why?" Bill wrote in large letters at the beginning of the article.

"Please Father keep this family together in heaven—5-13-1996," was another message.

And: "God take care these kids up there and their mom and dad."

And: "I guess wanting these kids with him God. Feel so bad tonight."

The clipping was signed "Billy Sunday Birt Death Row."

This was one person in the body and mind of Bill Birt. The good person. The one who couldn't understand why—why this lovely couple and their three precious children had to die. The one who would scold anyone hurting a butterfly. The one who handed out money to people he didn't know at the county fair. The one who would buy groceries for someone in need. The one who would trip and kick down a man who abused a mama dog.

But then I have to ask "why" to the other person in that same body and mind. The bad person. Why would he be part of a plan to kill a decent, God-fearing couple in their quiet, little community of Wrens, Georgia? For money? How much is a life worth? A hundred dollars? A few thousand?

Why would he shoot his own brother?

Why would this man run around with other women when he had a good, faithful wife—me, his Pretty Woman, he called me? Why wouldn't he be there for his kids when they needed him most? Why?

I don't know why. Still. After all these years. I know what the studies say. One of the main studies, one done by Edwin H. Sutherland, says that criminal behavior is learned, not inherited. I believe that. Bill Birt and I had five children who are proof of that theory. Yes, they got into trouble in their younger years. But they all turned out to be good, responsible, law-abiding citizens, for the most part. The King James Bible says we should "train up a child in the way he should go: and when he is old, he will not depart from it." The key word is "old." Our children straightened up in their later years. What happened to Bill Birt?

If he was abused at home, I never heard about it. His parents were pretty good people. And even if they weren't good people that's no excuse for bad behavior. We can overcome our past. We can't go around blaming our childhood troubles for our adulthood evil. I could blame my problems on my daddy, an alcoholic and a sometimes-thief. But I don't do that.

I know this about Bill: Two of his sisters, Jody and Frances, said he was made fun of in school sometimes because of his speech problem. They recalled Bill's telling about being put on a stage and told to read part of a book out loud to the rest of the students. He was up there reading, they said, and everybody started laughing. Bill stood up and cussed them out, but no one knew it—they couldn't understand his cuss words. That certainly could damage a young boy's self-confidence.

CHAPTER TWELVE

Uncle J.C. Mathis was one of Bill's boyhood friends. He knew Bill long before I did. His explanation for Bill's behavior as he grew into an adult: "He was a good boy who got in with the wrong crowd."

I wish I had known young Billy Birt when he was an average little boy who liked to play marbles and ball and splash around in Walnut River with J.C. At that time, Bill lived on Duck Road in Jackson County, and J.C. lived at the Hall County line, near Macedonia Church.

"We'd run up and down that river," J.C. remembered. "Gainesville Midland Railroad ran through there. And I used to bale cotton with Billy and his daddy, Claude Birt. We took pitchforks and put hay in the haybaler and tied it up with wire. . . . He was a good boy. We came up together."

I can believe Uncle J.C. Mathis. Our blood runs thick together. We're double-related. He is my mama's brother, and his late wife, Pat, was my daddy's sister. So if J.C. says Bill was a good boy, then he was a good boy.

If you talk to my uncle long enough, however, you'll find out the boys did get into a little trouble every now and then. One time, on a pretty Sunday afternoon, J.C., Bill, and some other boys "borrowed" a handcar from the Gainesville Midland Railroad. They planned to ride to Belmont, pumping those handles up and down to cruise down the tracks and enjoy the day. They had planned on returning the handcar undamaged.

But things didn't work out too well. They met a train coming right toward them. They grabbed the handles to try to stop the handcar, my uncle said, "but it beat us to death. Billy said, 'Only thing we can do is bail off.' So we did." They jumped to safety near the trestle on Highway 60 that crosses White's Bottoms. They rolled down the hill, leaving some of their hide behind on sticks and weeds.

"We were running up the river, but I stopped to watch," my uncle said. "I wanted to see the train hit that handcar. The cowcatcher on the front of the engine caught that thing—it wasn't anything but lumber and old wheels—and it threw it up in the air. The wheels are still laying in that swamp there. We cut off through White's Bottoms and hit Duck Road. Then we scattered out and went home."

Bill wasn't mean back then, just mischievous, Uncle J.C. said. He liked to have fun, sometimes at J.C.'s expense. Many times, when they were loading hay onto a truck, Bill would throw a bale hard against J.C.'s calves, causing him to fall. Bill obviously got a kick out of that kind of thing. But, at the same time, he was a hard worker. "When I had to haul hay," my uncle said, "Billy was the one I hunted."

The two of them still hung around together after they were grown and married. Bill sometimes helped my uncle pack up his old wood-shavings truck to move a family's belongings from one place to another. And both of them loved motorcycles. Bill owned a Harley-Davidson that he would share with J.C. after he got tired of riding. "He'd pawn it to me for a hundred dollars," my uncle said, "and then, six months later, he'd come back, give me a hundred dollars and take the Harley. We swapped around like that for several years."

J.C. occasionally was shocked by Bill's harmless adult pranks. Literally shocked. What happened was this: Bill went by J.C.'s home one Sunday evening, presumably to tell him about a fine motorcycle he found for sale. Bill was driving an Oldsmobile, and he was laughing when Uncle J.C. sat down. "I set my butt down on that car seat, and he turned a shocker loose on me," Uncle J.C. said. He had connected to the coil of the spark plug wires and then to the passenger's seat. "It was setting my butt on fire," J.C. said. Bill just laughed.

Apparently, Bill learned to pull practical jokes at a young age. When he was eight, nine or ten, he and three or four other adolescent boys decided to move the church's outhouse a few feet back while a night revival was going on. The nasty receptacle the

CHAPTER TWELVE

outhouse covered was completely exposed. Well, the first person to visit the privy on that dark night was Booty Granny, a nickname the kids gave Bill's mother, Eunice. Booty Granny fell into that pit. And after she crawled out—or was pulled out—she didn't waste any time seeking vengeance, relieving God of his responsibility. "Daddy said she beat them within inches of their life," Shane said.

Bill was always tight with my brother Clarence. They hung out together sometimes. One night, they stopped at a store not far from my parents' home and tried to buy a Coke from a machine out front. But they didn't get a drink or their money back. "Put more money in it, and it'll give you a drink," the storekeeper said. Well, they weren't going to do that, so they left. The next night, after the store closed, they tied a chain around that Coke machine and hauled it to J.C.'s sister's backyard. Leaned it up against a pecan tree. Broke that machine open and got everybody a drink.

By this time, Bill was thirty years old, and he was heavily involved in criminal activity. But Uncle J.C. didn't know about it. They were just buddies, he and Bill, ready to help each other with anything. I certainly didn't know what was going on with Bill.

But I did know about one thing that happened early on—actually, I told you about it earlier—and my uncle knew, too, because I stayed with him and Aunt Pat part of the time when my parents, Mack and Nellie, along with Bill, went to jail for stealing, I understand, a well pump. Bill actually served seventeen months, from May 4, 1959 to October 9, 1960. The Georgia Central Registry of Convicts said Bill was sentenced on "larceny from a house"—that could have been for stealing the well pump—and "larceny of auto." So Bill apparently served extra time for car theft.

How did they get caught on the well-pump deal? Well, they sold the pump to another fellow, and they took a check for it. "How do you want this check made out?" the buyer asked. And my mama said, "Nellie Lee." That was the wrong thing to do, take a check—with your real name on it—for a stolen well pump. "I think Nell Granny did what she had to do to put food on the table," Shane said.

It was my daddy, Mack Lee, you had to watch, Uncle J.C. said. "If Mack was around," he said, "I watched everything I had. It didn't matter what it cost you. If he could get a half-gallon of liquor for it, he'd steal it."

My daddy once stole J.C.'s battery out of a 1940 Ford coupe he owned, but everything backfired. "Somebody's fooling with your car," Pat told her husband, looking out a window at their home. It was Mack. He was stealing J.C.'s good battery to replace a dead one in his truck. "Just watch him," J.C. said to Pat, "and I'll swap them back after he goes to bed." J.C. sneaked over to Mack's home nearby, put the dead battery back in Mack's Ford truck and recovered his good battery. The next morning, Mack's vehicle wouldn't crank, so Nell came out and gave him a shove to crank his truck.

One thing Shane says he missed growing up was being around his daddy when Bill was pulling some of his daredevil stunts. Bill was in prison nearly all of Shane's life, but Shane would have reveled in watching his dad climb a power pole backwards and walk across a cable spanning Tallulah Gorge up in the North Georgia mountains. Uncle J.C. witnessed both of those feats.

The pole-climbing came after a man bet Bill he couldn't do it. "I'll bet you a hundred dollars against your fifty that I can climb that pole backwards," Bill said, according to my uncle. And he did it.

J.C. also was there at Tallulah Gorge when Bill trotted across a cable like he was taking a quick walk in the park. That was the same cable that German daredevil Karl Wallenda walked across on July 18, 1970, while about thirty thousand people watched. Wallenda no doubt made a bunch of money for his stunt, and he used a long pole to balance himself. He also stood on his head in the middle of the span. Only J.C., his wife Pat and a few others watched Bill do the same thing, but without a pole. He just held out his arms for balance.

"He pulled his shoes off first," J.C. said. "He went across and then trotted back across. Then, he wanted me to bet my

CHAPTER TWELVE

Harley-Davidson motorcycle that he would stand on his head in the middle. I wouldn't bet him because I knowed he'd do it. And he did. He got out in the middle and caught the cable around like that and stuck his feet up in the air. He didn't get his legs straight, but he stood on his head."

It was probably in the late 1960s when Bill decided he wanted to fight a monkey. He and his brother Ray had fought everybody else, so why not a monkey? Here's what happened:

Bill and his brothers Ray and Bob, along with several other friends, were taking in the Northeast Georgia Fair in nearby Gainesville. One of the attractions was a monkey in a cage. The deal was, if someone would stay in the cage and fight with the monkey for five minutes, he would get twenty dollars as a prize. If he caused the monkey's shoulders to touch the floor, he'd get fifty bucks. Folks were standing around the cage. They had paid their fee to see a fight, but no one was brave enough—or crazy enough—to take the dare. Then Bill and Ray walked up.

Ray wanted to fight the monkey—which really was a chimpanzee—but Bill insisted that he fight him first. He handed Ray his pistol and went inside a trailer to get suited up. His outfit included a football helmet for protection.

"While they were putting pads on Daddy," Shane remembered, "Ray knocked on the door of the trailer and yelled, 'Billy, don't go out there. It's a trap. It's a gorilla.' Bill said, 'I don't care if it is King Kong. I'm going to fight that monkey.'"

Well, the man in charge had taken the chimp out of the cage and run in a ringer—an orangutan. Bill said Ray was almost right. That orangutan was big as a gorilla. Bill told the rest of the story—what happened after he entered the cage—in a letter to Stoney:

"I turned around and started banging on the door and hollered for the man to open the door, but he wouldn't. I turned around and looked at the monkey. He was still sitting on his stool. So I went to the other stool to get as far away from him as I could and sat down on that stool. I wasn't going to mess with the monkey if he didn't mess with me.

"We sat there looking at each other for about a minute. I guess it was a minute. Might have been ten seconds. Then I heard a bell ring three times. That monkey came over there and dragged me off that stool. I had to fight then, or the monkey would have beat me to death. But I really didn't have a fighting chance. That monkey was as hard as a rock. I hit him in the stomach with everything I had. Felt like hitting a brick wall. Almost broke my hand. Plus, the monkey had me at a disadvantage to start with. The cage had monkey bars overhead for him to hold to and swing on.

"The monkey reached up and got ahold of the monkey bars with his hands and put me in a headlock with his legs. But I still had a football helmet on, so it wasn't hurting me too bad. So I got ahold of both of his legs and pulled on them as hard as I could. I was just going to hold him there until his hands gave out and he turned loose of the monkey bars and his shoulders would hit the floor. Then I would have got paid fifty bucks.

"All the time I was pulling on the monkey's legs, he had his head throwed back just looking at the people standing outside. My arms were giving out from pulling on him. I guess he got tired of me pulling on him. He drawed up his legs and kicked me across the cage so hard I thought it had broke my back when I hit the bars on the other side of the cage.

"Well, he turned the monkey bars loose and was standing on the floor like he wanted to box. He would make a motion with his hand like he was fixin to swing at me. So I was watching his hands. All at once a big foot slapped me upside the head so hard it broke the strap that held my helmet on and almost knocked me out. I landed on the floor on my stomach with my face right up against the bars. I was in a daze, but I remember Ray had his face up next to mine saying, 'Bill, get up. Bill, get up.' But I couldn't get up. The monkey was on my back jumping up and down. He

CHAPTER TWELVE

just kept it up. I had left my pistol with Ray, and I was telling Ray to shoot the damn ape.

"I remember seeing this girl that I went to school with in the third grade while this ape was jumping on my back. Reba Elder had her hands over her eyes.

"I don't know why the monkey did this, but while he was jumping on me, he messed all over me and it stunk real bad."

Finally, Bill said, the man pulled the orangutan off of him and told him he stayed in the cage only four minutes. But he still got twenty dollars, which did not compensate for his headache and stinky clothes. When Bill looked toward his car, he saw Ray with two policemen. One of the cops was holding Bill's .30-30 rifle. They had caught Ray running back to the trailer with the rifle.

"Ray had told the police he was taking the rifle out there to show it to some man who wanted to buy it," Bill wrote. "But they still wanted to charge Ray and take him to jail, but I talked them out of it." They kept the rifle to run a check on it, but Bill didn't get it back. It had been stolen.

"When we got away from the police," Bill continued, "I asked Ray why he had got my rifle out of the car. He said, 'Hell, Bill, you told me to shoot the ape while he was jumping on your back, and I was afraid to shoot it with your pistol. That would have just made him mad. Then he would have killed you."

Bill said his back and head were hurting really bad, he had lost his rifle for good, and he smelled like monkey poop. A woman who had witnessed the fight told Bill he was a fool for fighting the monkey.

"I know that now," Bill said. The woman walked away, probably because of the odor.

Bill was always tempting death, and, obviously, death meant nothing to him, because he took the lives of many people. Uncle J.C. was astounded when Bill went to prison, first for robbing a bank and later sentenced to death for murder.

"I couldn't believe it," my uncle said.

I couldn't believe it either. I knew Bill was capable of stealing; he'd proven that several times. But I never thought he was capable of killing people, and for money—"blood money," he called it. Did he have a conscience in those days? If he did, his trigger finger didn't know it. He told Shane he lost his conscience after he shot his brother Ray. I guess he did. I'll tell you about that shooting later.

Grover is another man who knew Bill growing up. (Grover is not his real name. This friend did not want to be identified.) Bill was seven years older, but he didn't mind this young sprout hanging out with him and his buddies. They would run the creeks around Chicken Lyle Road, kill snakes and catch turtles.

"Back in his young days," Grover said, "Billy was just another person. He would do anything in the world to help you."

He helped Grover one night without being asked. Grover, then a teenager, had drunk a bit too much—"In fact," he said, "I was real drunk"—and somebody he didn't know beat him up pretty badly. Following the fight, Grover was sitting at a service station near the old bus station in Winder when Bill drove up.

"Man, what happened to you?" Bill asked the bloody, red-faced Grover.

"Well, I just got the hell beat out of me," Grover said.

"Who was it?" Bill said.

Grover didn't know the man, but one of the other guys in the crowd gave Bill the name.

CHAPTER TWELVE

"OK," Bill said, and he left.

"About thirty minutes later," Grover said, "he drove back up and he had this guy with him."

"Is this him?" Bill asked.

One of the other boys said, "Yeah, that's him."

"What do you want me to do with him?" Bill asked Grover.

"I don't know," Grover said, "whatever you want to do with him." Bill drove off. And that was the last time Grover ever saw or heard from the guy who roughed him up.

"I don't think he did him in," Grover said. "Billy hadn't done a whole lot in the early sixties." He may have just taught him a lesson he wouldn't forget.

Bill Birt, Grover found out, didn't like to lose. One night at Tooney Royster's beer joint in Winder, Grover was bragging about Shoats Doster's 1964 Chevelle powered by a Chevrolet 396 V8 engine. "I went to ride in it," he said, "and, boy, it will pull your face back. . . . That's the fastest thing I ever rode in."

"Bet it won't outrun my Mercury," Bill said, referring to his 1970 Mercury Cyclone. Grover accepted the bet: a hundred dollars Doster's Chevelle would outrun Bill's Mercury in a drag race down Interstate 85. "There wasn't a whole lot of traffic on I-85 back then," in the 1960s, Grover said.

Each man put up a hundred and let Shorty Harris hold the money. The two drove to Braselton and got on the interstate heading toward Atlanta. Sonny Lee flagged them off. Grover said Doster won the race, but Bill said, no, he didn't, I won. The fan belt on Doster's car had slipped off at the end of the race, and by the time they got it fixed and arrived back at the beer joint, Bill had collected the money and left.

About two weeks later, Grover's father came home and handed his son a hundred-dollar bill. "Billy Birt said you'll know what this is for," he said.

"OK, but where's the hundred I won?" Grover said to himself. Oh, well, at least he got his hundred back.

Bill would bet on anything, Grover said, but it wasn't gambling if he knew he'd win. One time, Grover said, a man from Monroe bet Bill he couldn't climb a telephone pole to the top and come down a guy wire in forty-five seconds.

"Billy kicked off his shoes and went up that telephone pole barefooted, like a monkey," Grover said. "He grabbed that guy wire, slid down it, and stopped close to the ground."

"How much time have I got?" Bill asked, hanging onto the wire.

"You done done all that in fifteen seconds," Grover answered, "so you got thirty seconds to drop to the ground.... The man from Monroe just shook his head."

Like Uncle J.C. Mathis said, Bill was mischievous when he was a young man. Just like a lot of boys, he loved to show off. But when he got into killing and stealing, well, I was devastated when I found out about it.

I get no pleasure in recounting all the bad things my husband did. I'd like to say that he was a great man all of his life, a deacon in the church, a Sunday school teacher, an honest, responsible man who loved me faithfully, a father who was always there for his family. But I can't say that. As I told you before, one reason we're writing this book is just to set the record straight—and to give God the glory for getting my kids and me through some horrendous years. Truth is truth. There's been enough romanticizing about Billy Sunday Birt.

Bill often told our children, "If you see money on the ground, don't pick it up. It belongs to somebody else." My daughter Ann said there was not a kinder, sweeter man than her daddy—when everything was going his way. Bill wanted our kids to obey the laws and do the right thing. And yet he robbed and stole and burned and murdered.

I don't expect every family whose lives were shattered by this man to forgive him. All I can hope for is that he asked our loving God to forgive him. And that God granted that forgiveness.

Billy.

CHAPTER THIRTEEN

By now, you surely want to know: Just how many people did Billy Sunday Birt kill? And the answer is, I don't know. I only know what I've been told. My kids know more than I do. So do some law officers.

Frank Thornton, sheriff of Walton County back in the late seventies, was quoted in a newspaper: "We have put together the facts that tie him to as many as twenty-eight killings. . . . Anybody that participated in a crime with Birt got missing."

The sheriff was partly right. Bill did kill several of his partners in crimes, but not all of them. Look at the Matthews murders in Marietta. He protected two of the men—his brother Bob and the man we don't want to name—who took part in that botched robbery. He protected others, too.

Other lawmen heard different death tolls. Former GBI agent Ronnie Angel said Bill had been tagged with twenty-three murders. Another former agent, Bob Ingram, said Billy Wayne Davis claimed he could link Bill to fifty-two slayings, at least fifteen of them from Barrow, Walton, Jackson and Oconee counties. Tim Pounds, sheriff of Douglas County, Georgia, said his former boss, the late sheriff Earl D. Lee, got the number fifty-six from Bill himself.

Former GBI agent Stanley Thompson said Bill told him he took out fifty-six people.

Jimmy Terrell, former chief investigator for the Barrow County Sheriff's Office, said he heard numbers ranging from fifty-five to eighty-five, but more likely it was about fifty-five.

"I think Billy at times had visions of grandeur," Angel said. He embellished his ill deeds to make himself look better, or worse, depending on who was judging. "Most (criminals) wouldn't tell the whole truth. Birt was the same. But he was pretty honest with me."

Bill may have been experiencing one of his visions of grandeur when he told Shane during a prison visit he had exterminated "either 158 or 168 lives." Sounds unbelievable. But, Shane said, "Dad never lied to me."

Bill was also honest with me, his wife. Sometimes. But he never talked about his contract jobs or the killings borne of his urge to get even. I saw that one flash of light I assume came from a gun outside our home that strange night, and then, on another day, I overheard a woman hiring him to kill her husband for five thousand dollars. Other than those two instances, I know nothing personally. Stoney, Shane, and Montana know a lot more, but Bill seldom revealed to our daughters, Ann and Norma Jean, anything about killings.

I do know, however, that Bill wasn't the same person after he was released from federal prison in 1973 after serving time for possession of a weapon by a felon. Not that the former Bill was anyone to brag about as a husband. But he was even worse after he completed his term, which began in July of 1972.

Bill had been on drugs for some time. He had run a pool room—the Winder Recreation Parlor—from 1966 to 1971. Later on, he bought the Winder Truck Stop, where Bobby Gene Gaddis worked at night. I don't think he was taking drugs when he had the pool room; in fact, that may have been the last honest job he had. But it's a fact that truckers used to take amphetamines—also known as black beauties or RJSs—to stay awake. And plenty of the pills were available at the truck stop.

Bob Ingram thinks Bill was definitely taking RJSs. "Billy would use and stay awake two days, three days, five days," he said. "When you haven't had any sleep and you're high, you're crazy and wild.

CHAPTER THIRTEEN

Couple that with mean. . . . As a result, Birt was involved in a great deal of illegal activity."

Bill was tight-lipped about most of it. "How do you think I got away with everything?" he said. "I didn't talk about anything I did." But he wasn't shy in expressing his hatred for Billy Wayne Davis and his illegal activity. Okay, he said about Davis, you did that to me; you testified against me. Now it's my time. He would do anything to get back at Davis, even make up a crime he didn't commit.

I don't know, but I suspect Bill was taking more than RJSs. Bob Birt, his brother, said at one time he was taking PCP, a drug developed as a pain reliever but also sold and taken illegally. As I said, Bill almost never spent a full night at home. In our last months together, he was always restless. He was paranoid. He kept looking out the window when he was home. He talked in his sleep. He had nightmares. Most nights, he didn't even come home. He was not a pleasant person to be around.

After Bill was imprisoned for the last time, the children and I began to hear stories of disappearance that turned into stories of murder. Bill was tied in some way to nearly all of them.

In November of 1971, Harold Chancey's stepfather, James O. Daws, sixty-seven years old, was reported missing from his home in Monroe, Georgia, where he operated a small grocery store, Quality Food Market. Daws was married to Chancey's mother, Ruth, but was in the process of getting a divorce. I'll tell you more about the Daws saga later.

On February 12, 1972, Mrs. Carolyn Baird Cooper, former wife of Fred Cooper, who had been charged in a liquor case, disappeared from the AMVETS club in Athens. Her brother, Joe Baird, was expected to testify for the prosecution in the case.

A fisherman found Cooper's pocketbook on high ground in the Mulberry River at the Jackson-Barrow county line. Certain that she had met with foul play, investigators said they "obtained the services of an old-timer familiar with the old homeplaces and wells in the area" and began looking for her body. They started in area near where Cooper was living.

Her body was eventually found in a dry well in Barrow County. She had been shot under her right eye and in her back. A load of garbage had been dumped on top of her. Bill apparently went back to the well after "the odor became a problem," an informant said. He suspended a charge of dynamite five or six feet from the top of the well, set it off, and blew a large cavity in the side, covering Cooper's body with dirt. Barrow County Sheriff Howard Austin and a crew dug through the debris and found the body.

Bill told an informant he killed Cooper for Harold Chancey, according to Jim West.

Actually, there are two other versions of how Cooper died. Bill told Shane and Ann that he killed her because she wanted to tell police about a shooting of four Black people in Atlanta. Here's that story:

Four men were sitting on and around Bill's car when he and Cooper came out of a theater—one with a porn shop on the first floor and a hotel area upstairs—and the men would not leave peacefully. They challenged Bill to do something about it. He shot and killed three of them; the fourth man escaped with a serious wound. Cooper freaked out on the way home. We need to tell the police what happened, she argued. Finally, Bill pulled out his pistol and shot her.

"Baby, I had no choice," Bill told Ann when she asked how Cooper died. "I had to shut her up."

Bill's brother Bob told a different story. He said Bill and Billy Wayne Davis had robbed a bank and were counting their take at Tooney Royster's pool room in Winder. Carolyn Cooper showed up while the counting was going on, and the men warned her to leave. "Just walk away and there'll be no trouble," one of them said. She refused to leave, Bob Birt said. Davis then pulled out his pistol and shot her.

CHAPTER THIRTEEN

"I don't know which story is true," Shane said. "But Dad told both me and Ann about the Atlanta incident. . . . I believe what Uncle Bob said. He had no reason to lie about it, at all. He (Bill) may have told us the Atlanta story to soften it. . . . That was a way he could tell Ann and it didn't make him sound like a bad guy. Daddy wouldn't tell the truth when it came to Billy Wayne or anybody else (involved), because that would make him a rat. He didn't trust Ann or the girls not to repeat what he said."

However Carolyn Cooper died, one thing is certain: Bill hid out for a time following her death. He even faked his own death. He shot three holes in a door window of a pickup truck he owned, cut himself, slung blood inside the truck cab, left the truck abandoned on Highway 53, and continued to stay out of the county and out of sight. The local newspaper reported that the blood-stained truck had been found; people speculated that Bill had been killed.

But, several days later, Bill telephoned Sheriff Austin long distance to say he was alive and well. He just wanted the law to *believe* he was dead.

The killings continued. Another state's witness expected to testify in the liquor case also disappeared. An investigator said Charles Edward Martin, who worked on a maintenance crew at the University of Georgia, had contacted Sheriff Howard Austin to say "he could take him to the place and put him within a hundred yards of where Willie Hester's body was buried." Word must have gotten back to Bill, because the night Sheriff Austin and Jim West were to meet Martin in Arcade, Georgia, Martin didn't show up.

An informant said Martin had asked Bill for a sketch of where Hester's body was buried. Bill reportedly said he couldn't draw him a sketch, but he could show him where. Later, Martin's body was found in a shallow grave in Barrow County.

In April of 1972, a number of seemingly random dynamite blasts were reported in Barrow County. But they were not random.

A policeman's car, a package store, and an insurance agency were among the property destroyed.

The policeman's private car was dynamited, Shane believes, because a local lawman stopped Stoney for driving without a license when he was thirteen. The car Stoney was driving wasn't just an ordinary car. It was a muscle car: a 1968 Chevrolet Camaro Supersport 396. Stoney was forced to turn in his keys and apologize to the officer. He did that. And he obviously told his daddy what happened.

Statham Package Store, owned by Wade Grizzle, was destroyed when someone broke a window and threw dynamite inside. The store was located on Highway 29 at the intersection of Highway 324. If dynamite was used, no doubt Bill was the culprit. Few people used dynamite to destroy buildings, but Bill became an expert blaster working at a rock quarry.

At 5:10 on the morning of September 8, 1971, Bill dynamited the Farm Bureau insurance office—or had it dynamited—after the agent, Tom Locke, refused to pay off on a claim. Bill wrecked his Ford Torino during a race with Harold Chancey and showed up at the insurance agency on Athens Street in Winder to file a claim. Following some haggling between Bill and Locke, the agent said he couldn't pay because Bill was racing when the car was damaged.

Jim West's report said Bill was spotted in town a few minutes after the office exploded. But here's what Shane recalled from a conversation with his father:

Bill arranged explosives at the office, and then established an airtight alibi for himself. He got one of his partners to touch the battery leads together, setting off the dynamite, while Bill and a friend were having breakfast at about five o'clock in the morning at a gas station miles away from Barrow County.

"Yes," Shane said the proprietor of the gas station told authorities, "he was here early this morning."

The explosion awakened the sheriff, Howard Austin, who told news reporters that the blast blew glass across the street and

CHAPTER THIRTEEN

damaged nearby homes. Force from dynamite placed in the back of the building launched bricks from both sides, destroying the main part of the structure.

Later on, Shane said, the insurance agent ended up dead at his office after he pulled a gun on Bill, apparently intending to kill him. Bill grabbed the man's arm, the gun fired, and the bullet went through the ceiling of the office. Bill was able to turn the barrel toward the attacker, and the gun went off again—apparently three times, because investigators said Locke had been shot three times. According to Bill's account, however, the gun never left Locke's hands, and Bill's fingerprints were not on it.

Shane said his dad told him that Locke earlier had tried to hire a couple of Bill's comrades to kill him. And that's why he went to see him a second time.

Locke's death was ruled a suicide.

On June 20, 1972, J. Marion Kilgore and his wife, Beulah, both seventy-four years old, were found dead inside their Winder home, which had been built onto a store they owned. Suspects were Bill Birt and Bobby Gene Gaddis. According to an informant, the two intended only to rob the Kilgores, but after they got inside the building, Mr. Kilgore grabbed a double-barrel Derringer pistol from under a counter and barely missed shooting Bill in the chest. Bill forced Mr. Kilgore to open his safe, where he found twenty-two thousand dollars, and then choked the couple to death with his hands.

Apparently hoping to prevent investigators from finding out the two had been strangled, Bill poured gasoline into their mouths and set them on fire, the informant said. He then set fire to the house and store.

At 4 a.m. on June 20, Mrs. Kilgore's body was found face-up on a bed, and Mr. Kilgore's body was lying face down about eight feet from his wife. Their badly burned bodies were taken to Wise Funeral Home, where autopsies were performed. Investigators determined the fire had been set.

155

"Our information on this," an investigator said, "is that this was just a burglary-robbery deal, and Billy's idea was not to leave anybody alive who could testify and send him to prison."

More than anything, even death, Bill feared spending the rest of his life in prison.

Shane said Bill had contracts for killings in other states: Florida, Louisiana (at least four there), Texas, Montana, somewhere north of the Shenandoah Valley. Shane is named Billy Shenandoah. Bill thought that valley was the prettiest he'd ever seen, so he told me he wanted his last child named for the valley. Montana is named Billy Montana, I guess because Bill liked Montana the name and liked Montana the state, although he was shot during an incident there. Bill said he almost died after being shot with a shotgun in his left shoulder and arm. He still had pellets from the blast in his skin, "and he would sometimes point this out to people," Shane said. Bill did not elaborate on how he was shot.

Bill had dynamite hidden all over the county, most of it taken from a rock quarry in Buford, where Bill operated a crane. One of his hiding places was in an abandoned house across Highway 53 from Rockwell Church. The explosives, caps and all, were stuffed behind a chimney in the attic. One night, Bill and Otis Reidling were together at the pool hall when fire trucks roared through town. The two got into Bill's Mercury Cyclone and followed. The abandoned house was on fire. Bill parked close to the burning house. After seeing the fire slowly move toward the chimney, Bill said, "We need to go."

"Go where?" Reidling asked.

Bill didn't answer. He drove to the church yard across the highway and, minutes later, watched the old house explode into hundreds of pieces.

CHAPTER THIRTEEN

I don't like talking about Bill's girlfriends, but I need to tell you one story. Bill and one of his many sweeties were taking a shower together in a motel room when Sheriff John Howard Austin walked into the room—the proprietor had given him a key—snatched back the shower curtain and told Bill he wasn't welcome there. You need to move on.

"Fine," Bill said, "that's what we'll do."

The next night, Bill entered a storage building behind the motel, set a case of dynamite in the middle of the floor, put four or five cement blocks on it, pulled the battery leads out and away from the building, touched them together, and set it off. Damage to the motel was repaired. The storage building was never rebuilt.

Bill was not always a respecter of persons, even kinfolks. He got mad at my mother one time and took serious action. He was angry because she had sworn out a warrant for Bill's brother Jimmy. She charged him with assault—it's a long, confusing story, and I won't get into details—but Bill said Jimmy was innocent. He had not assaulted anyone. Bill warned his parents-in-law not to press charges, but Nellie—Nell Granny, as the kids called her—didn't listen. "Now Jimmy is not going to prison for something he didn't do," Bill told my daddy, Mack.

When the case went to court, my mother was on the stand testifying, and Bill was listening in the back of the courtroom. He sneaked out of the courtroom, and his brother Bob took his place, wearing a coat similar to Bill's and holding his head down to avoid being recognized. Bill drove to my parents' home, set fire to the place, and rushed back to the courtroom to replace Bob. The house was destroyed.

A few minutes later, someone ran into the courtroom and yelled, "Mack, your house is on fire."

"Billy, you didn't have to burn my house," my mother hollered out. "There he is, Judge. That's the S.O.B. who burned my house, and he's sitting back there eating smoke links and drinking a Pepsi. And that's my smoke links and my Pepsi."

My parents decided not to push the case against Jimmy any further, and the charges were dropped.

Bill took up for his brother that one time, but another time, Jimmy was being a smart-mouth, according to Bill, and he locked him up in a room. Bill threatened to kill my brother Freddie, but was talked out of it. He wrestled with my daddy in the pool room for showing off a photo of me, his baby. He took the picture away from him. When our daughter Ann underwent surgery, a preacher brought her flowers. Bill wouldn't let me take the flowers home.

I know I'm repeating myself, but Bill was a complicated man. He shot his own brother, Ray, six times, leaving eleven bullet holes in him, after Bill went to his home and they argued over a woman. It apparently was self-defense. Ray survived, but his recovery time was long. After Ray was shot and killed on January 27, 1973, at the May Street Tavern in Winder, Bill was determined to go after his killer. It apparently was all right for Bill to shoot his brother, but not for anybody else to shoot him.

At Ray's funeral, Bill and his brother Bob talked about taking out Ray's killer. One of them would do the job. But Bill decided they couldn't do that "because all roads lead back to us." Ray's killer was still alive and well when Bill went to prison in 1974.

Years later, Bob was talking to Shane and his son Jackson, and "something was gnawing on him," Shane said. He had promised Bill that he would eliminate Ray's killer, but he had not done that. "Bob started crying in front of us," Shane said, "because he had not fulfilled his promise."

Shane told Bob the man had died, "so your promise does not need to be carried out." Bob raised his hands into the air and said, "Thank God." Bob had become a Christian—he was baptized in Shane's church—and Shane's news about the killer finally brought him peace.

CHAPTER THIRTEEN

"This," Shane said, "showed me how important the word between two brothers is. Bob considered killing Ray's killer more important than his own salvation."

Bill wasn't an every-night, big-time poker player, although he was known to bet on anything. He played poker occasionally to pass the time—and to win spending money, of course. But he was choosy about when to play. If he felt jinxed, he wouldn't gamble. And he wouldn't do anything else illegal.

Better than playing poker and *maybe* winning, Bill figured, was robbing high-stake games and *definitely* winning. Gambling was illegal, so no one was going to report a robbery. Bill couldn't rob all of the big games, because moneyed people would stop gambling altogether. He would rob every fifth or sixth big game.

At a big-stakes game one Friday night in Colbert, about thirty-four miles from Winder, Bill won big, got up to about five thousand dollars. When he announced he was playing his last hand, he felt threatened—you don't want to leave with all our money, do you?—and he was outnumbered. So he played until he lost down to five hundred dollars, the amount he started with, and got up and left. He told the crowd he'd be back. This is what happened when he went back the next Friday night:

Wearing ski masks, Bill, armed with an automatic shotgun and a .45 pistol, and Willie Hester, carrying a double-barrel shotgun, knocked on the door of the poker hideout and, after someone answered the knock, forced their way in. Bobby Gene Gaddis was outside pulling coil wires off car engines. Hester, the spokesman, told everybody to get up against the wall and drop their pants. One big dude refused and started walking toward Hester. Told to stop, he kept coming. Hester told him to stop a second time. He kept coming. Bill shot the man in the thigh with a .45 pistol, and he stopped—lying on the floor about ten feet from where he had been standing.

Hester was collecting money and money belts in a plastic trash bag when one of the men begged him not to take his cigarettes. Bill told Hester to take the cigarettes, too.

The trio left with about twelve thousand dollars. Inside the man's pack of cigarettes were seven rolled-up one-hundred-dollar bills.

At one poker-game robbery, Hester was wounded with a .38 Derringer when he tried to relieve a guy of his diamond ring. Hester was supposed to only collect money, but he also coveted the man's ring. The victim pulled out his little pistol and plugged him. "That knocked Willie across the room," Bill said.

Bill was a multi-faceted criminal. He could kill. He could rob. He could burglarize. He could haul liquor. He could explode buildings. He could haul drugs across the U.S.-Mexican border. He could con people.

And, believe it or not, he could break into Barrow County's courthouse. He and three of his buddies did just that in late October of 1972. He told me to make him a backpack, and innocent, naive, obedient me, I did it. I didn't know why he needed a backpack. He needed something to carry his small acetylene torch, his scuba mask, and an oxygen tank—everything a thief would need to break into a safe or vault. Oh, yes, he also had a big pasteboard box, all folded up, once used for shipping a refrigerator.

The men entered the building through a bathroom window and then tried to get into the clerk of court's office through District Attorney Nat Hancock's office, which was located directly above the clerk's area. They cut the carpet and began drilling into the floor. They hit concrete. Bill then used his torch to cut a hole in the metal door of the clerk's office.

Once inside the office, he unfolded the pasteboard box and put it in front of the walk-in vault to hide the light from the torch. He

CHAPTER THIRTEEN

put on his mask to protect his eyes, hooked up the oxygen tank, got out his torch again and started cutting. He got the vault open.

Inside, Bill found evidence and indictments of four men he knew, plus evidence in a number of other cases. He rifled through the papers and pieces of evidence, put most of them back into the vault, and struck a match. In all, the sheriff's office said, the men lifted or destroyed eighty-six indictments and fifty-five accusations. They also made off with more than twenty-eight hundred dollars in cash and stole a revolver believed to have been used in a hit in nearby Athens, Georgia.

The next day, or maybe it was another day later, Bill showed up in court, sat in the gallery, and waited for the session to begin. Most of his face was very red, practically blistered by heat from the acetylene torch. The area around his eyes was lily white. He looked like a man who had worn dark glasses and lain out in the sun too long. Actually, he looked a little clownish.

The judge, Mark Dunahoo, took his position at the bench and announced that some scoundrels had broken into the court's safe and destroyed a bunch of indictments and evidence. But don't think you're going to get away with it, he said to no one in particular, because you can't escape the long arm of the law.

Bill was never caught, and cases for everybody scheduled for trial that week, including a couple of Bill's buddies, were delayed for several months. Or maybe they never came up again.

Also in 1972, Bill, his brother Bob, and Bobby Conners, their driver, stopped at a restaurant in Atlanta. It was no accident that Bill and Bob chose this particular restaurant. Conners, who knew nothing about his riders' plans, went inside to order several hamburgers. While he was waiting in a long line to place his order, Bill and Bob left the car, hurried to an area where they had hidden coveralls and masks, changed clothes, walked across the street and robbed a bank. They took the money back to their hiding place—Shane believes it was a big culvert nearby—changed clothes again and got back into the car.

Bobby Conners, innocent as a newborn kitten, came back to the car with the hamburgers, and the men began eating. Lawmen showed up to investigate the robbery, and Conners commented, "Somebody must have robbed the bank." The cops spotted and recognized Bill. They approached the car and questioned him. "No," Conners said, "they've been right here with me the whole time." Conners was their alibi.

Sometimes, though, things didn't work out as planned. One night, Bill and his gang planned a heist at a company in Winder that made top-grade clothing. They went to the plant, broke in, and changed into plant uniforms. Local lawmen showed up, wondering what was going on. One of the uniformed would-be thieves walked out and calmly chatted with the officers while others transferred goods to a truck at the back loading dock. Then someone got the bright idea to steal the company safe, which was on wheels. The men pushed the safe to the loading dock and then onto the truck. Suddenly, the truck went straight to the ground. It was not capable of taking on five thousand to six thousand pounds of steel at one time. The burglary was over.

Another aborted crime happened when Harold Chancey and Bill were hauling moonshine. They would usually flip a coin to see who would drive the fast car—the chase car—and who got the big Oldsmobile Delta 98 loaded with liquor. Bill lost the flip. His job was to drive the heavy liquor car while Chancey engaged police in a chase, diverting their attention.

In the meantime, Bill motored along to his destination, not able to run more than seventy miles an hour because of the extra weight. The front seat was full of illegal cargo; the back seat had been removed to make space for more jugs. The Olds, Shane said, was like a tank—slow but able to push away anything that got in its way.

Chancey roared through Barrow County all the way to Dawson County, the law right on his tail. Bill and the Olds lumbered along behind him. When Bill came to a big, green bridge that

CHAPTER THIRTEEN

crosses Lake Lanier, he had a decision to make: jump and swim a long way or risk getting caught. He had to do something because lawmen had blocked off the bridge entrance with their cars and set up a roadblock on the other end. Bill got out of the liquor car as the cops ran toward him.

If he jumped off the bridge and stayed in the same area, he'd be caught. But if he swam way out to a sand bar in the lake, he had a chance to escape. He jumped off and swam as fast as he could. After some time went by, he swam to the shore and made his way back to the road. He heard the Ford, the chase car, coming. The car slowed to a stop, and Bill snatched open the back door and crawled in. He was freezing. This was February.

The car took off slowly down the road, and Bill asked in a cold, shaky voice, "Harold, where you been?"

A voice from the front said, "By Harold, would you mean Mr. Harold Chancey?" The cops had taken the diversion car, and Bill was riding with them. Bill opened the back door and rolled out of the moving Ford, which had reached about 25 miles an hour. He shook himself off, ran to a nearby tree line and stumbled over something. He thought it was a log. He hit the ground and heard, "Umph!" Logs don't make sounds.

"Harold, is that you?"

"Yeah," Chancey said, "they got my car."

Bill responded, "Don't you think I know it?"

Shane said he knows the event happened that way because Chancey told the same story.

Bill has been in the doghouse with me countless times because of his running around with other women—even though I couldn't do anything about it—but one time he ended up in a real doghouse on one of his jobs. Here's how Bill told the story:

He and Harold Chancey had run into a bit of pushback from a deputy in one of the Northeast Georgia counties. Some lawmen could be paid off, but this one walked the straight and narrow. It was time to teach the deputy a lesson. They would dynamite his house.

After casing the place, Bill told Bobby Gene Gaddis how much dynamite and wire to get for the job. If you want to be one hundred feet from the blast scene, you need two dynamite wires one hundred feet long; two are needed because there's a positive line and a negative line. Unfortunately, Bill didn't know it until he had placed dynamite at the deputy's house, but he had only one hundred feet of wire, meaning he could take cover only fifty feet away from the explosion. At one hundred feet, he would've been protected by big trees. At fifty feet, there was only a big doghouse.

Bill crawled into the doghouse with his two wires. He touched them together. And that's the last thing he remembered doing that night. The next thing he knew, Harold was slapping him in the face saying, "Wake up, Billy. Wake up." The doghouse was nowhere to be seen.

We began this chapter by asking: Just how many people did Bill Birt kill? I'll say it again: I don't know. And, frankly, there's no way to know the names of all the people Bill killed, or how many he killed. He didn't talk about everything he did, even with the kids—and, as I said, they heard more than I did. As Bill told Shane during a visit in prison, "Son, to me, it was just a job." Killing people was just a job. I don't understand that, and I don't expect you to understand it. *It was just a job.*

But, thankfully, his job ended on April 3, 1974, when he was arrested for the last time, sentenced first for robbing the bank

CHAPTER THIRTEEN

in Loganville, Georgia, and later for murder after he and Billy Wayne Davis started telling on each other about killings. I'm glad no one else would lose his or her life because of Bill's "job." If he hadn't been arrested and put away for good, I suspect at least three more people would have died by his hand.

The night before he was picked up the last time, he told me that four people would be going on a trip, but only one would return. That one would've been him.

"You're going to hear a lot of things," he said that night, "but when I get back, don't let me find out that you've done something to get even with me."

I'm not sure what he meant by that. I don't know what I could have done to get even with Bill. There was no way to get even with him for all the pain he caused me over the years we were married.

Bill was angry and paranoid in his last months as a free man. Someone had ordered a hit on him—three men were planning to ambush him—and he found out about it. He was ready to kill everybody, even his friends. "That was the beginning of the end," Shane said. Bill's being arrested saved a lot of lives.

My husband knew what I had been through. But I survived, thanks first to God and second to my children and good friends.

I have to believe that God even gave Bill a second chance. And if God could forgive Billy Sunday Birt, He can forgive anybody. Anybody at all.

CHAPTER FOURTEEN

Bob Ingram kept referring to my husband as a mean criminal, so, finally, we had to ask: On a scale of one to ten, with ten being the meanest, where would Bill Birt rank?

Without hesitation, Ingram answered, "Ten. If there was an eleven, he'd be eleven." Of all the murderers he has interviewed in his forty-eight-year-long career in law enforcement, Ingram said Bill Birt was the meanest and the most dangerous. And he's including people like Carl Isaacs, who, along with three other men, killed a family of six, the Aldays, in Seminole County, Georgia, in May of 1973.

There's no way, Ingram said, to compare Bill with Isaacs, whom he interviewed fourteen times. "Isaacs was a punk. He killed six people, but he was a punk, nineteen years old and trying to be a big shot.... But Billy was a tough hombre. I have dealt with some tough ones, but he's number one. Billy Birt was the deadliest man in Georgia."

Certainly not a title to pursue, nor a husband to admire.

Besides the degree of meanness, there was another big difference between Isaacs and Bill. Isaacs bragged about what he did, Ingram said. Bill seldom even talked about his *jobs* with anyone who wasn't involved. That's how he got away with killing dozens of people before he was found out.

Bill was clever, smart, mean, and dangerous—a deadly combination—and he knew how to avoid detection by police. He didn't smoke, never had, and investigators knew that. So to throw them off, he would burn cigarettes at a crime scene, holding the smokes with a filter clip so as not to leave fingerprints, and drop the butts onto the ground or in a house.

He wore a size ten shoe, but sometimes on a job he would wear a twelve or thirteen. He stuffed paper into the front and back of the shoe to give it the right roll and a believable footprint. He sometimes ran a file down the barrel of his gun to change the rifling on a bullet. On most jobs out of state, he traveled and worked alone. Often hyped up on drugs, he would drive to another state, take care of business, and drive home, going sleepless for days. He never stayed in a motel, avoiding any kind of record showing he had been in the area of a crime.

If there were witnesses, he eliminated them.

Bill had a hair-trigger temper, and it took only a slight pull to set it off.

"You tell Billy a lie and you don't say 'excuse me,' you're dead the next day," Ingram said. People in Barrow County knew that. Even his friends knew that.

Bobby "Bogey" Brown, a really good guy who lived in Winder, told Shane that "at the end, everybody dreaded to see your daddy pull up in the yard. If you left with him, you didn't know if you would be coming back. If you said no, there was a one hundred percent chance you're dead, because your daddy couldn't trust you."

Brown said Bill Birt asked him to go riding around with him one day. "Listen, you can't see where we're going," Bill said. "I'm going to have you ride in the trunk." Bogey became sick to his stomach. He told Bill before he closed the trunk lid, "If you're going to kill me, do it looking at me." He thought Bill would shoot him through the trunk. "Make sure you kill me; don't let me bleed out in this trunk."

"Son," Bill said, "why would I kill you? You're the only true friend I've got."

How many true friends Bill had, I don't know. Nobody, not even I, his wife, was immune from punishment, possibly death, if Bill sensed he'd been offended or misled.

CHAPTER FOURTEEN

"Actually," Shane said, "he didn't see anything wrong with what he did. He had regrets later on—many of them—but not at first. And he was good at what he did."

But Bill had this strange code about him. He wouldn't hurt an animal, and he didn't like to hear a man use bad words around women. He killed a few women, but he wanted everyone else to respect them at all times.

He even went to their rescue sometimes.

When Shane was in Athens one day getting his driver's license renewed, the woman behind the counter said, "Are you kin to Billy Birt?"

"Yes, ma'am, that's my dad."

"When you see him again, you tell him I still love him," she said, and went on to tell her story. One night at the VFW (Veterans of Foreign Wars [building]) in Athens, a man who was not her date asked her to dance. She obliged. When she returned to her table, her date reached across and slapped her. Hard. "Nearly knocked my teeth out," she said.

Bill checked on the woman—"Hon, are you okay?"—and then took care of the abuser. "She said he got hold of her date and flipped him back and forth like a doll and then ran him out," Shane recalled from her story.

Years after Bill had been imprisoned for the last time, that same woman was still going to the VFW, ordering drinks, and putting them on her rescuer's tab, just as Bill had told her to do.

"Nobody was paying his tab," Shane said, "because everybody was still afraid of him."

While playing cards in prison in Marion, Illinois, Bill was deeply offended when one of the prisoners bragged about raping a woman, killing her, and cutting her baby out of her womb with a car key. Bill had had enough. He grabbed the man and threw him off a high ledge and onto the concrete below. Bill said he didn't remember what happened, but witnesses claimed the man jumped to his death.

When our daughter Ann was in a bad marriage, Bill told her to come see him in prison. "When you get back home," he told her during their visit, "your divorce papers will be there."

"No, Daddy, he won't give me a divorce."

"Yes," Bill insisted, "when you get home, you'll find your divorce papers."

Sure enough, the papers were lying on her kitchen table when she arrived home. Shane asked his daddy how he got that done. "Son," he said, "I worked for a hundred people, and all those people owe me everything they got now." The truth was, no one could say no to Bill Birt. If they did, even though he was in prison, they'd be gone after Bill made a phone call.

Bill looked after his kids, to a certain point. But I was the one worried about Shane living in Ruth Chancey's house, and I told Bill. Shane wouldn't leave for me; he had it made there: nice house, free rent, extra money from Chancey, leader of the notorious Chancey Gang. But his daddy knew how to get him out.

It all came to a head in 1992, while Shane was divorced from Jill, one of the nicest women you'll ever meet. Bill apparently arranged for the two of them to be at the prison in Jackson, Georgia, visiting him, at the same time. Stoney brought Shane; Norma Jean delivered Jill. Bill was trying to do the good-daddy thing and get them back together. But he also had a message for Shane . . . and for Ruth Chancey.

"Shane," he said, "what time will you get home from here?"

"About three o'clock," Shane said.

"OK," Bill said, "when you get home, get your stuff together and out of that house." Shane tried to convince his daddy he had it made there.

"Well, let me put it to you like this," Bill said, grabbing Shane's knee. "If you're not out of that house by seven o'clock—if you're still there, I'm sorry, but I'm going to have it blowed from one end of the county to the other. I'm not going to let your mama worry no more."

CHAPTER FOURTEEN

Conversation over.

Bill handed Stoney a letter for Ruth Chancey. It said basically the same thing: that Shane would be out of her house by seven o'clock that evening.

"It'll be done," Chancey said after reading the letter.

Shane was packed and gone well before the deadline. "It didn't matter that I was his son, his own blood," he said. "Daddy would've done what he said he would do if I hadn't left." All it would have taken was one phone call from prison.

Bill's explosive of choice was always dynamite. That's what he would've ordered used on Ruth Chancey's house if Shane had not left. That's what he used on a policeman's private car after the officer stopped Stoney while driving at the age of thirteen. That's what he used on a package store after someone there refused to allow me to park my car there after I had a flat tire. That's what he used on the Farm Bureau insurance office after the agent wouldn't pay for damage done to the car he wrecked during a race. That's what he used everywhere when an explosive was needed for a job.

Ruth Chancey loved Shane like a son, but she shot at him at least twice. Once, when Shane entered Ruth's chicken house without announcing himself, Ruth pulled out her pistol and fired. "It's me!" Shane yelled. Better announce yourself, Ruth said.

Another time, Shane, Bobby Chancey, Bebo Pardon and two other guys were working on Shane's car inside a pole shed on Ruth's property. Ruth didn't know who was there and started firing. "We hit the ground spread-eagled," Shane said. Bullets were zipping and zinging everywhere. Better announce yourself next time, Shane, Ruth Chancey said.

When Shane turned sixteen, his daddy began telling him bits and pieces of his criminal activities. That went on for thirty years. He talked about his jobs when the two of them were alone, never when either of his two daughters was present. It was part of his code: Don't upset the ladies.

Norma Jean certainly didn't know everything her daddy did for a living. While she was a county commissioner in Barrow, she went to the parole office to plead his case. Surely he wasn't guilty of the crimes he was accused of, she thought.

"Do you know who your dad is?" one of the parole officers asked her.

"Sure," she said.

Parole officials began to bring out box after box of information about crimes her daddy was believed to have committed. She couldn't believe what she saw. She telephoned Shane on her way home from the parole office.

"She asked if I knew all Daddy did," Shane said. "I said, 'No, and thank God, I don't know. What I do know has scarred me.'"

"Well, I didn't know anything," she said.

"You're a girl," Shane said.

"I'm going to see him," she said, "and he's going to tell me everything."

"Good luck with that," her brother said.

Bill told Shane that Norma Jean wanted to know everything he did, "But, son, I can't remember everything I done." As far as the daughters were concerned, when they were young, Bill was a businessman or maybe a farmer. That's what he said in court one time when he was asked about his occupation. "It's farming," he said.

My husband told our sons about a number of murders, even though his famous words to law officers were always, "I ain't killed nobody," said with a smile. "I usually didn't get the whole story," Shane said, "just bits and pieces." Bill usually didn't volunteer any information, but if one of the boys already knew some of what went down, he would fill in a few details.

CHAPTER FOURTEEN

What he did reveal was fairly easy to remember, frankly because of his speech impediment. When he would talk to you, he would pronounce a word and then he would ask, "Do you understand what I said?" Sometimes, Shane said, he would make his listener say the word back to him. It was like practicing for a spelling test. The listener remembered. (His brother Bob had the same speech problem. So did Montana at a young age, but as an adult, he speaks clearly.)

Although Bill denied it in a letter to Stoney, authorities insist my husband had killed for a number of people, including C.W. Royster, Reece Spencer, Lee Gilstrap, A.D. Allen, Harold Chancey, and, of course, Ruth Chancey. Within that circle of people, Bill was a contract killer. He killed for them and for acquaintances they trusted, authorities said. "So it's fair to say," Bob Ingram said, "he killed a lot of people."

Bill also looked after his friends—as long as they didn't cross him. Harold Chancey was severely injured in a car wreck and put in a body cast before he went to prison on illegal liquor charges. Bill would take my station wagon to Chancey's home, pick him up like he was a baby and put him in the back of the car. Then he and Chancey would ride around.

But "when it came down to the hard stuff," as Shane called it, Bill didn't trust anyone. That total absence of trust, combined with his suspicion of nearly everyone wearing a badge, served him well in prison. After Bill was convicted on charges of carrying a concealed weapon by a convicted felon, he was sentenced to eight months and sent to the federal penitentiary in Atlanta, the same prison that held Harold Chancey. Normally, a prisoner wouldn't be lodged in a federal pen for carrying a concealed weapon. That's not a federal crime. But prison and court officials wanted Bill and Chancey in the same place, where their cells could be bugged in case they talked about past crimes.

Officials listened for six months, but neither Bill Birt nor Harold Chancey said anything worthwhile for their listeners. If they needed to say something they didn't want the prison officials to hear, they wrote in the dirt when they were outside in the yard, and then rubbed out the message.

Shane was about nine months old when his daddy went to the federal pen. He was about two and a half when Bill went to prison for the last time. I had to be mother and daddy to the five children, but especially to Shane, who never really knew his daddy out from behind bars. But I didn't want them to forget Bill. Bad or good, he was the kids' daddy. So when a birthday rolled around, I always had a gift from Bill sent to the house. I would meet our mailman somewhere and give him a package. The return address was Bill's, and as far as the birthday boy or girl knew, the present was from Daddy.

Daddies don't forget birthdays.

Ruby with Bible.

CHAPTER FIFTEEN

I CAN HEAR YOUR WORDS now: "Why didn't this woman leave that man, move to another city, and start a new life, a life without all the crime, fear, deceit, and turmoil?" You're not the first to ask that question.

A Barrow County detective made that very suggestion one day. He came by the house and said to me, "Why don't you leave Barrow County and go somewhere the kids will have a chance?" He had some of his fellow officers with him. I told him that we hadn't done anything wrong, my kids and I, and I was going to show Barrow County what we were made of.

They all just laughed.

I got the same advice from none other than Dr. Corbett H. Thigpen, the psychiatrist who co-authored the famous book, *Three Faces of Eve*, which later was made into a movie. My doctor in Barrow County, Dr. Ed Etheridge, and some law officers were worried about my state of mind; living with a murderer and egomaniac like Bill would stress out anybody. So they got me an appointment with Dr. Thigpen in the Augusta, Georgia area. Norma Jean, who had been traumatized when she saw her daddy arrested in 1974, had sessions with Dr. Laura McQuainy.

"They contacted me and wanted me to talk to you," Dr. Thigpen told me during our session in his office. I didn't know why he was asking me so many questions. I really didn't know why I was there.

Finally—I guess it was in our last session—Dr. Thigpen said, "My advice to you is to leave that man and take those children somewhere and raise them. You might remarry and get those kids a father. And change your name."

I told him, "Look, I'm a married woman, and I'm staying that way." The doctor got up, shook my hand, and said, "You've got it all together."

But there's another reason I didn't leave Bill Birt. I was afraid of him. My most fervent prayer to God was that I would live long enough to raise my children. And if I left Bill, I'm not sure I would have.

One night, Bill was shaving, getting ready to go out on the town, no doubt with one or more of his women.

"Bill, why don't you stay home with me and the kids tonight?" I pleaded.

"Can't do it, Pretty Woman," he said without hesitating. "I gotta go."

"One day you'll want me and I won't be here," I said.

"And one day you'll die, too, Pretty Woman."

Would he have tracked me down and killed me? I think so. No one crossed Bill Birt, not even his wife.

I know it's strange, what I'm telling you. I know Bill loved me, in his own weird way, but remember what I said: I wasn't just his wife; I was his possession. He owned me. I couldn't go against him, if I wanted to live.

Actually, I understand why a person who has been kidnapped sometimes develops empathy and sympathy toward her captor. She may even have positive feelings toward him, sometimes to the point of defending him and identifying with him. The textbooks call it the Stockholm Syndrome, or capture-bonding. I guess I had it with Bill. He was my captor, and I defended him, even empathized with him. I lived with Bill's confused sense of love all of my married life.

One day, Bill and I were going to Athens for something, and we talked about the place where a car had run off into a creek, and a mother and her children had drowned.

CHAPTER FIFTEEN

"If that happens to me," I said to Bill, "you'd better go for the children first, not me."

"Pretty Woman," he said, "I'm going for you. I can live without the kids, but I can't live without you." He was dead serious at the time. And yet, I think he would have killed me if I left him while he was still a free man. If the truth be known, I didn't feel safe even when he was in prison. If I did something he didn't approve of, he'd know about it immediately. Even behind bars, he still controlled me. A lot of people owed him favors because he had killed for them, or burned a house for them, or forcibly collected rent for them. All he had to do was make a phone call and collect on one of his IOUs. He was a mover and shaker, but in the worst way possible.

It wasn't just Bill I was afraid of. I was afraid of someone retaliating against me for something Bill had done, maybe a family member or friend of someone he had murdered. One night, the children and I had just gone to bed. Everything was quiet. And then I thought I heard something moving overhead. Somebody was crawling around in the attic. No, it must be my imagination. Then I heard it again. The sound was coming my way, toward my bedroom.

I yelled out, "Kids, get up! I forgot something over at Paw and Granny's. Let's get up and go after it."

"Mom, you go get it," one of the kids said. "We'll stay in bed."

"No," I said, "we're going together. And we'll come straight back."

I got them all in the car, and then I walked back to the porch and found a wide push broom leaning against a wall. I placed it against the screen door, and then we left. We spent the night at my parents' home and returned to our house the next morning. That sweeper I had pushed against the screen door was back against the wall. When I looked inside, I saw that somebody had fallen through the ceiling and onto my canopy bed. Debris from the ceiling was everywhere.

Now, I don't know that whoever was sneaking around in the attic would have been a threat to me and my children. It could have been someone checking out the rumor that Bill had a lot of money from bank robberies lying around the house. Little did most people know that Bill spent bank money almost as fast as he stole it.

So it could have been someone after me or someone after stolen money. I don't know the answer to this day. But I do know it was a scary night.

My job, I've always known, was to protect my kids. They hadn't done anything wrong—at least nothing like Bill's wrongs—and they didn't deserve to live in fear and shame because of their daddy. During the height of his criminal activity, he was on television news all the time. When another news report about him was about to be announced, I would change the channel or turn off the television. The kids didn't need to hear that stuff.

I've always been there for my children, and God has always been there for all of us. With Bill or without him, God has protected me. He protected me and the family when our home caught on fire. Shane said Bill ordered the house burned to collect insurance money. "If Daddy had insurance on a place, it went down," Shane said. I always thought our home on Picklesimon Road was struck by lightning. Whatever the case, we got out of that burning house alive and well.

We were all asleep at the time. Well, Bill might not have been asleep. Suddenly I smelled smoke and awoke. I couldn't see anything for the smoke. Bill grabbed Stoney, and I grabbed Rubyann, a baby at the time, who had crawled under the bed. I grabbed her by a leg and pulled her out. We rushed outside. No one was hurt. The house was practically destroyed, but a Bible that always stayed on the headboard shelf of our bed was not even scorched. Nor was a necklace bearing a Christian cross.

God had protected us and his Word.

He has always been there. I owe Him for everything, even life itself.

Stanley Thompson.

CHAPTER SIXTEEN

On the morning of August 8, 1973, a Wednesday, Fred C. Jones, Jr. was found dead in the garage of his Chevrolet dealership on the public square of Dahlonega, Georgia. The mayor of Dahlonega and former state legislator had been shot in the head.

According to a report compiled by Jim Earl West of near Monroe, Georgia, and Jack C. Berry, both of the U.S. Treasury Department, Billy Sunday Birt was a suspect.

"I understand that they thought it was murder, then listed it as suicide, and I don't know," West wrote in his report, "but this is still Billy Birt's type of operation and he did deal in cars and C.W. Royster and Birt dealt in cars, and Birt was operating in that area at the time and he was needing money for his lawyer at the time."

That one long, rambling sentence says a lot about Bill Birt. Everything, said West, seemed to fit Bill: Jones could have been a hit; Bill didn't trust many car dealers; he knew how to get blood money without being caught.

But did Bill ever talk about Fred Jones to his family?

"No," Shane Birt told Bob Ingram on the morning of April 30, 2019. "I haven't heard anything about that."

Ingram had requested the meeting with Shane, along with Michael Walsingham, assistant special agent in charge for the Georgia Bureau of Investigation, and writer Phil Hudgins, to talk about a number of deaths included in West's report.

The four men had gathered in an interrogation room at the White County Sheriff's Office, located not far from the picturesque town square of Cleveland, Georgia. Ingram's reason for the meeting was simple: If Shane could shed light on murder cases still on the books—more than four decades after Bill was imprisoned for the last time—then Ingram wanted his help. And if a case had been ruled a suicide—and it wasn't—the family of the victim surely would want to know that.

At the time of the April 30 interview, Ingram was chief deputy for the White County Sheriff's Office. He had retired as a GBI agent in Thomson, Georgia, moved to the mountains with his wife, taken the chief deputy's position, and was awaiting his second retirement in about a year.

Robert Franklin "Bob" Ingram is the kind of law officer who commands respect. Now in his seventies but still lean and muscular, he sits ramrod straight and focuses like a laser on the person in front of him. His whole demeanor says he's still a United States Marine—as he was at one time—everything from his closely cropped hair, to his starched and pressed uniform, to his spit-shined shoes. Ingram fits the image of a disciplined law officer/Marine, one who knows the techniques of good interviewing. He investigated a number of high-profile cases, including the Atlanta child murders of 1979-1981.

He was the one who interviewed Billy Wayne Davis about the murders of the couple in Wrens, Georgia, at Christmastime in 1973. Bill Birt, Charles David Reed, and Bobby Gene Gaddis were convicted of those murders on Davis's testimony.

Now, Ingram wanted to know about other deaths that Jim West listed in his report. Twenty-four cases and thirty-eight victims, the document claimed. All of them in north Georgia except one in Dublin, Georgia, about 135 miles southeast of Atlanta. Bill apparently told West's informant that he could count fifty-two murder victims, but he named only a few and described how Bill Birt killed them.

Was Fred Jones one of Bill's victims? West's report on the death was brief, just one paragraph. Reports from investigators on the scene were more complete.

CHAPTER SIXTEEN

At about 7:30 on the morning of August 8, 1973, Carlton A. Sisk, a mechanic at Fred Jones Chevrolet Company, discovered Jones's body lying on the floor of the dealership garage. He had been shot once. The bullet entered slightly behind the left ear and exited below the right eye. A .38 caliber pistol was found on the floor several feet away. Jones's billfold, which contained some paper currency, was nearby.

A witness said that after Larry Howard, head of the Georgia Crime Lab, arrived, he looked down the barrel of the pistol, smelled it, and said the gun had not been fired. He apparently didn't smell powder in his initial inspection. The revolver contained three shells, two empty chambers, and one spent cartridge. It turned out, however, the pistol had been fired once that very morning, according to a ballistics test conducted later. A projectile that later was determined to have been fired from the revolver was found in a tool box several feet away. The revolver actually belonged to the City of Dahlonega, but Jones, as mayor, was known to keep it with him.

Jones, fifty-two years old, may have encountered enemies during his lengthy career in politics and as an automobile dealer. He had served in the Georgia General Assembly for fifteen years and was in his third term as Dahlonega's mayor. Kenneth Seabolt, local sheriff at the time, said he knew of about four times the mayor had been threatened. But probably none of the threats resulted from Jones's presiding over city court. He had never been known to be harsh to violators in court, the sheriff said.

He may have had a few enemies, but no doubt he had countless friends. And they turned out in droves for his funeral at First United Methodist Church in Dahlonega on Sunday, August 12, 1973. Dr. Jesse Warwick, one of the officiating ministers, told the packed congregation that Jones's strongest characteristic was to help people. Another minister, Dr. Robert Green, said the mayor was a good man who had a compassionate heart.

At first, investigators were fairly certain Jones had been murdered. Over the next few weeks, five GBI agents were sent in to investigate. A friend who had served with Jones in the legislature pressured investigators to find out what happened. Jimmy Carter, Georgia governor at the time, offered a thousand-dollar reward "for information leading to the arrest and conviction of the person or persons who took the life of Honorable Fred Jones. . . ."

Jones's wife told investigators that she took two telephone calls for her husband the night before he was found dead. One came in about 7:30, the other one at 8:10. Both calls came from the same person, who said it was urgent that he talk to Jones, the investigators' report said.

Mrs. Jones said her husband got home about 8:20, ate supper, and went to sleep. She woke him sometime later, and at 12:15 a.m., they talked. She went to bed about 1 a.m., and later he came to her room and asked about their dog. She didn't notice whether he was dressed or at what time he left the house.

On August 22, 1973, a coroner's jury was impaneled, even though R.C. McCracken, regional GBI supervisor, said he thought the inquiry was premature; all crime lab tests and investigative leads had not been concluded. At that point, between twenty and twenty-five people had been "closely investigated as suspects in the case." But the jury of five convened anyway, and Larry Howard of the crime lab and GBI special agent Stanley Thompson testified.

The coroner's jury concluded that "the deceased's death had been the result of a gunshot wound fired by person(s) unknown (murder)."

Shortly after the ruling, Agent McCracken contacted Coroner Forrest Sisk and Sheriff Seabolt and asked them to reopen the inquest, naming the same five people as jurors. The Jones family objected.

A second inquest appeared to be imminent, but then on September 14, 1973, Bill Beardsley, then director of the Georgia Department of Investigation, said the case had been completed.

CHAPTER SIXTEEN

"It has been concluded that the death was a suicide contrived to appear as a homicide," Beardsley said.

The position of the gun, found five feet from the body, and "other things at the crime scene initially indicated murder," he said. But further investigation indicated the fatal wound was self-inflicted and "there was no probability of outside causation."

One factor that delayed the final determination was a crime lab examination that later showed "nitrates from gunpowder in a position that would confirm the suicide theory," the September 1973 statement said.

The county attorney, in the meantime, advised that a second inquest would not be legal.

Stanley Thompson agreed with the conclusion. "Fred was fixing to lose his Chevrolet dealership, and he was needing money," Thompson said in an interview. "He apparently gathered up car parts and stacked them around, and then he sat down like he had surprised a burglar and shot himself, is my opinion."

So why did Bill Birt turn up as a suspect in the case? He was, after all, mentioned in a long list of murders he was believed to have committed. The cases were compiled by West and Berry, agents with the ATF, which had investigated Bill in a number of liquor, firearms, and dynamite cases.

Bill Birt's name came up because there appeared to be a murder in Dahlonega, Georgia, and "at that time," Thompson said, "anything that happened, Billy Birt was a suspect."

It was as simple as that: If someone had been murdered, you looked first at Billy Sunday Birt.

About three months following Mayor Jones's death, a man and his sister were found shot to death just south of Dahlonega—in the Wahoo community of Hall County, off Highway 52 and just across the Lumpkin County line. Police reports identified them as James Crump Moon and Ollie M. Taylor, who looked after chicken houses for the owner of the property. West's informant said Bill had information that the elderly siblings, who lived in rental houses on the property, were working alone and that the woman "carried her money in her bosom with a string around her neck, and she had a lot of money." If free money was available, Bill Birt, Billy Wayne Davis, and Otis Reidling were there to get it.

But Thompson and Ingram said the main reason they were there was to intercept a load of illegal drugs they expected to be delivered to Moon and Taylor's stash house—a place to hide drugs. The owner of the property had no involvement in the illegal activity, Thompson said.

West's report on the murders was sketchy—and the date was wrong—but Bill Birt laid it all out for authorities when they visited him in prison on April 13, 1978. Present were Ron Attaway, chief deputy of Hall County; Fred Perra, chief investigator for the district attorney's office; GBI agent Stanley Thompson; and Douglas County Sheriff Earl Lee, who was the recording officer. They were there to ask Bill about five murders believed to have occurred in Hall County. District attorney Jeff C. Wayne had agreed for Bill to plead guilty to the murders and to waive the death penalty in those cases.

Here's what Bill said happened in the Moon-Taylor case:

Otis Reidling had his eye on a Mustang that sat in Billy Wayne Davis's used car lot in Austell. So Davis agreed to give him the car and some cash if he would help with the Moon-Taylor heist. Reidling agreed.

On Sunday, November 4, 1973—the last day Reidling was seen in Barrow County—Davis drove to the Birt home and told Bill he "had a job up in Hall County." He expected a shipment of about two-hundred thousand pills, probably RJSs, to be delivered to this house in the Wahoo community. Bill, of course, said he'd help. Davis and Bill picked up Reidling, and the three drove to

CHAPTER SIXTEEN

Hall County to check out the house, which was a shotgun-style structure with three chicken houses across the road. They waited in their car all night, but the deliverer of drugs never showed up. So Davis and Bill designated Reidling as the lookout. They gave him a sleeping bag, a pair of binoculars, and a bottle of thirty to forty pills to keep him awake, and they left. Reidling set up camp on a hill so that he could see the comings and goings at the house.

In the meantime, Bill Birt and Davis drove to Athens to check out a future job and then to Mansfield, southwest of Athens, to look at a bank they planned to rob. They drove back to the Hall County house on Friday, and Reidling told them the drugs delivery man had pulled in about twenty minutes earlier. Five boxes had been taken from the trunk of a car and into the house.

The three men pulled up to the front of the house, and one of them raised the hood of the car. Davis walked to the house, knocked on the door, and told the man—James Crump Moon—that his car had broken down and asked to use his phone. Davis went inside. Bill told Reidling to close the hood and back into the driveway. By the time Bill arrived inside, Davis had his pistol out and Moon and Taylor tied up and lying on the floor of the front room.

The two men demanded to know where the pills were stashed, but Moon said he didn't have any pills. Bill went into the bedroom and found the boxes under a bed. Davis and Bill each carried two boxes to the car, and then Bill went back for the fifth box. He found a .22 caliber rifle in the bedroom and, holding the rifle in one hand, shot Moon and Taylor in the head two or three times. Bill went out and threw the rifle into the car.

Sitting in the driver's seat ready to leave, Bill heard another gunshot inside the house. He went to investigate and met Davis coming out the door. Davis told Bill he was slipping—"that woman wasn't dead"—so he shot her again.

The men took about twenty-eight hundred dollars in cash contained in a small sack, somewhat like an old tobacco sack, that hung around Taylor's neck.

Traveling through Gainesville, the seat of Hall County, on the way home to Winder, Bill said he had to stop the car to get Reidling calmed down. "Otis Reidling had never seen an out-and-out murder like that," Stanley Thompson surmised, and he freaked out. Seeing two cold-blooded killings, going without sleep for several days, and taking drugs combined to make him go berserk.

He was hollering, screaming, and crying. Davis wanted to shoot Reidling right then, but Bill said no, the young man meant too much to him.

Farther down the road, on Highway 53 toward Winder, Reidling panicked again, and this time, Bill agreed with Davis: Reidling had to die. Davis pulled a gun from the glove compartment, turned around and shot Reidling three times as he ranted wildly in the back seat. (Jim Earl West, remember, reported totally different circumstances that led to Reidling's death. Authorities believe Bill Birt's and Agent Thompson's version.)

Bill or Davis had already thrown the Moon-Taylor .22 rifle into Lake Lanier and then, closer to home, they stopped by Mulberry River and hid Reidling's body under some brush, afraid to bury him in broad daylight. They went back later and buried the body, which authorities found in April of 1974 when they dug up part of the riverbank near the Hall-Barrow-Gwinnett county line.

Bill's and Davis's killings were not over yet. The woman who tipped Davis about the drugs to be delivered to the Moon-Taylor house was complaining she had been gypped. She thought 200,000 pills would be delivered, but the count was about 110,000. Bill and Davis must be cheating her, she thought.

Davis got a date with the woman, who lived in Austell, and drove to South Carolina. They were headed back home on Interstate 85, in the middle of the night, when they spotted Bill standing by his car with his car hood up. He was pretending, again, to have car trouble.

Davis stopped, Bill asked for a ride, Davis said sure, get in, and they took off down the interstate. How much would you

CHAPTER SIXTEEN

charge me to take me home? Bill asked. Davis agreed to take him and turned off the interstate and onto a side road. Bill, sitting in the back seat, put a rope around the woman's neck and strangled her. They buried her body near where Reidling's body was interred.

Some time after the Moon-Taylor murders, a truck driver arrived at the Murrayville farm to collect eggs the brother and sister had gathered. He couldn't find anyone. He left a note over the door at a chicken house, explaining how many cases of eggs he had picked up. And he notified someone that the two were not around. Their bodies were found later inside a rental house.

Stanley Thompson, by the way, possesses a .38 caliber pistol he believes Bill Birt used in some of his killings. Told by his supervisor, R.C. McCracken, to go pick up the gun, Thompson met a man named Herman Rice at Toto Creek Bridge in Dawson County. It was midnight. Thompson was alone. He held a shotgun beside his leg as he approached the man in the dark, just in case. Fortunately, there was no trouble.

"That could be the murder weapon," Thompson said, pulling the pistol from his brief case. "(Sheriff) Howard Austin had the gun at one time, and then Jim West got it. Somehow it got back to Dawson County, and I was sent to get it." The pistol would have been destroyed as needless evidence, but Thompson has held onto it for more than four decades.

Being a government law enforcement agent was more dangerous forty or more years ago. Back then, Bob Ingram said, you often went alone on investigations, even at midnight on a lonely, desolate road. Today, the agency sends a team of investigators into a dangerous situation.

Shane doesn't believe the .38 pistol Thompson possesses belonged to his father. The barrel was the regular length. Bill always shortened the barrel of his pistol, Shane said.

Thompson, by the way, has had more than his share of close calls. In high school in Gainesville, Georgia, in the 1950s, he was accidentally shot in the stomach by a friend and taken to the local hospital, where he underwent an eight-hour surgery and spent thirty-one days recovering.

As a GBI agent in the mid-1980s, he was cutting down a chicken-wire fence surrounding a marijuana field in Oglethorpe County when he hit a yellow jackets' nest. He was stung from the waist up more than two hundred times and eventually airlifted in a helicopter to a hospital in nearby Wilkes County, where he spent four days in an intensive care unit. His son, Kevin, at that time a state trooper in Thomson, Georgia, rushed to the hospital to see his father, but didn't recognize him.

"It was a pretty rough time," Stanley Thompson said.

During the April 30 meeting in White County, Bob Ingram began by asking Shane about a killing—the first one in Jim West's report—that reportedly took place in Dublin, Georgia, shortly after Bill got married. This one may have been in the late 1950s. The informant told West that Bill was angry with the man "about something (Bill) had stolen—some boat motors or something relating to boats—in north Georgia." So he killed the man with an axe. Officers arrested Bill and held him in jail for some time, the report said, but they lacked enough evidence to charge him. He was turned loose.

I know that Bill and my parents, Mack and Nellie Lee, went to jail after stealing a well pump somewhere. That happened not long after we married. But I'd never heard anything about the

CHAPTER SIXTEEN

Dublin case. And neither had Shane. Shane and I wonder if the report is confusing two different cases. We'd never heard that Bill stole boat equipment. But one thing is certain: The GBI checked out the informant's claim, and a man was axed to death in Dublin, Georgia, about the time and in the manner described. Surely Bill was not the killer.

Now then. We might as well reveal who Jim West's informant was if you haven't already figured it out. West never said, but it's obvious it was Billy Wayne Davis, who would rat on Bill more than once. West wrote near the end of his typed report that Bill "went to the informer's car lot in Austell, Georgia" to talk about killing a man. Who else could it be? Davis owned a car lot in Austell and was one of Bill Birt's closest associates. They had robbed banks and killed several people together, and Bill apparently trusted this car dealer at one time. He may have told him about a number of murders, robberies, and other crimes. Davis no doubt was a party to some of them.

But whether Davis told West the whole truth is debatable.

West himself was criticized, even in his own ranks, for being heavy-handed in his investigations, willing to go to any length to get his suspect. The criticism heightened after Annie Mae Daws, the unmarried sister of the murdered Jim Daws, willed a 270-acre farm near Monroe to West. The farm, which belonged to Jim Daws until his death, was said to be worth several hundred thousand dollars.

On Friday, February 27, 1981, reporter Paul Lieberman asked in an article in *The Atlanta Constitution* newspaper: "How was it that the federal investigator who challenged the so-called Dixie Mafia, may wind up owning the property of one of his witnesses, a witness who himself had operated on the fringe of the criminal organization?" Jim Daws was to have been the witness in a liquor case involving Harold Chancey, but was murdered before he could testify. Jim West retired to Florida after his retirement. Annie Mae Daws also lived in Florida.

Despite questions about the believability of Davis, West's report, based on Davis's information, was the most comprehensive account of Georgia murders produced at the time. West claimed he could tie Bill Birt to at least twenty murders on his list, which was prepared just months before West retired.

West himself was to have been one of Bill Birt's hits. As the story goes, Davis didn't know, or didn't remember, Jim West's name when he was telling about Bill's plans for future hits. So he didn't realize that the man Bill wanted to kill was the man he, Davis, was talking to, Jim Earl West himself.

Davis told West that Bill had come to his car lot to talk about a "job." Harold Chancey had offered him twenty thousand dollars to kill Jim West, federal officer, near Monroe, Georgia, and I need your help, Bill allegedly told Davis. *Wonder if West flinched a little when he heard his name mentioned as a future hit.*

"Well, how would we do it?" Davis asked.

"I've already gone out and looked at his house and place there," Bill said. "Where he drives into the highway there is a drain, and I've got a case of dynamite, and we could put the case of dynamite in the drain tile and run the wires on down below it there about a block. We could park a truck there and raise the hood up like it was broken down and then watch and just as soon as he started to drive across there, why, I could touch this wire with flashlight batteries, and we could blow him up, let the hood down on the truck and drive off."

Sounds too risky, Davis is said to have told Bill. What if someone came along about that time?

Bill agreed. "Well," he said, "he's got a barn right across the road there. . . . If you'll drop me off, I'll hide in that barn with a rifle, a .30-30, then when he starts to drive on the road, I'll get him and I'll go back through the woods and you can pick me up."

CHAPTER SIXTEEN

Davis said, "I would still be afraid to do that since he is a federal officer."

"Well, listen," Bill said. "West knows my car. How about letting me borrow that convertible there? I've got another fellow who would drive for me. We'll catch him on the road there and I'll just drive by and shoot him with a shotgun."

"I'll let you have the car," Davis said.

Davis said he thought every day he would hear over the news that somebody had shot West. But then, about two weeks later, Bill brought the convertible back to the lot. He never could catch West on the road.

Fortunately, the hit never happened, and Jim West lived to investigate again.

John Latty at 18. John Latty today.

CHAPTER SEVENTEEN

John W. Latty of Gainesville was thought to have been murdered in 1970. But he lived to tell his story. Here it is:

It was the middle of summer. Latty was eighteen, just a month past high school graduation in 1970, and working at the Mar-Jac Poultry Processing Plant in Gainesville to help supplement his family's income. His father, Raymond William Latty, had died from cancer the summer before.

Latty lived with his mother, Frances Toney Latty, and two younger sisters, Hilda and Harlie, on Candler Road, directly across from Fullenwider Road in southeastern Hall County. His older sister, Harriett, had married and moved away.

It was a Friday night. There'd be no handling of live chickens for two whole days, and the weekend was open. His mother and younger sisters were spending the night with his maternal grandmother, Ruby Stoie Hall Toney, who lived in Gainesville. This was going to be a relaxing evening, Latty thought to himself. Just kick back, watch the Atlanta Braves on television, and enjoy the time.

Latty wanted a little company, though, so he drove about a mile up Calvary Church Road to pick up his friend, Robert Lee West, an avid baseball fan who understood the game. And he was always fun to be with.

The two of them settled down at Latty's home and watched the Braves until the game was over. It was late, about two in the morning, because the game was being played on the West Coast. Rather than driving his friend home at such a late hour and awaken his friend's mother, Latty suggested that Robert spend the night in an adjacent bedroom and go home the next day. So they went to bed, Latty to his bedroom, Robert to his. It had been a long day—Latty had worked that day—and he fell asleep quickly.

The outside doors were unlocked. "It was a quieter, simpler time in rural Hall County," he said, "so I hadn't bothered to lock any outside doors." There was no air conditioning, so the screened windows were raised to allow a gentle breeze and distant noise from chicken catchers down the road to waft inside.

"In what turned out to be a short time later," Latty said, "I was roused from a sound sleep by what sounded like the front door opening and closing." After a hard day at work and a long night watching baseball, he was groggy. He thought it was daylight and his mother and sisters were returning home. He went back to sleep.

More time passed—he doesn't know how much—and he awoke a second time. Now, he was more alert. Even startled. It was dark. He glanced at his clock with fluorescent hands and saw that it was four o'clock. He heard what sounded like whispering and footsteps in the grass outside his open window. His first thought was that somebody was trying to steal his 1965 Chevrolet Chevelle parked in the yard.

He jumped out of bed, clad only in gym shorts, picked up a dumbbell—there was no functional firearm in the house—and headed toward the front door.

"As I exited my bedroom and entered the very small hallway that opened into the kitchen, I saw him standing there," he said.

The house was configured so that three bedrooms, a bathroom, and the basement doors opened into a small, roughly square hall that led into the kitchen. Latty's daddy had planned and built the house in the mid-1950s, but, reluctant to go in debt, he never borrowed money to finish it. Because of that odd configuration, Latty was face-to-face with the intruder about eight to ten feet away. The man was silhouetted against a kitchen window, and he could see the glow of a lit cigarette in his left hand, extended

CHAPTER SEVENTEEN

downward by his side. He was standing completely still. He must have heard Latty's approach.

Latty realized later that the intruder couldn't see him, because he was standing in the square hallway in total darkness. Next to the man was a low table against the kitchen wall. The telephone was on that table. Maybe this was a chicken catcher from down on Fullenwider Road who wanted to use the phone. He needed to run him off.

"There was a brief period," Latty said, "when we were frozen in place confronting each other."

But then Latty summoned the courage to ask, "What are you doing in here?"

The silhouette of the man seemed to tense up when Latty spoke. The man took a step backward.

"He appeared to try to locate where I was as I could see his head move slightly from side to side," Latty said. "I gripped the dumbbell tighter and thought of lunging at him and attempting to strike him with it, but I was unable to muster the courage."

So Latty demanded in a louder voice a second time, "What are you doing in here?"

The intruder turned suddenly and ran. He bolted through the kitchen and into the living room through the connecting door without running into anything. Latty thought about chasing him, but managed only a couple of steps and stopped.

"I heard a loud 'bang' which I took to be the front door slamming violently," he said. The noise was loud enough to awaken his friend, Robert West, who ran into the living room and yelled, "What the hell is going on?"

That's what Latty wanted to know, too. He thought the door had slammed shut and then popped back open. It was open when he and West walked through it and onto the front porch. The chicken catchers down the road had completed their dusty, noisy work, and except for katydids singing in the bushes, everything was quiet.

Latty looked for headlights and listened for the sound of a vehicle being started. Nothing. Latty and West re-entered the house after a few minutes, locked the outside doors and went back to their beds.

Latty slept soundly until his mother woke him up about mid-morning that Saturday. She was not happy. She ordered her son to come to the living room, pointed at her piano and snapped, "I have told you and told you and Tommy about lifting weights in my living room. Y'all have knocked a hole in my piano."

Sure enough, there was a gaping hole beneath the piano's keyboard. But he and Tommy Collins, his best friend, had not damaged anything lifting weights.

"I immediately realized," Latty said, "that it was a bullet hole."

Latty told his mother about the incident from earlier that morning. She was skeptical at first, but then Robert West corroborated his story.

Nothing was done for a couple of weeks. Then, while cleaning under and around the piano, his mother found what she thought was a lead sinker for fishing. But Uncle O'Dell Toney, his mother's younger brother, was visiting at the time, and he said, "No, that's not a sinker. It's a bullet."

A few days later, Latty's brother-in-law, Harold Edmonds, took the flattened lead ball to the Hall County Sheriff's Office where Lieutenant Ron Attaway confirmed it was indeed a bullet, one from either a .38 or .357 caliber handgun.

That was the end of the matter. As far as Latty knew, no official report on the incident was ever made, and no one knows what happened to the bullet.

Latty told the story of that scary night several times over the next eight years, still wondering who walked into his mother's house and tried to kill him. During those eight years, he spent three years in the army, married his childhood sweetheart, attended college, welcomed his first child, and began a career in law enforcement with the Gwinnett County Police Department. His first day on the job was February 27, 1978.

CHAPTER SEVENTEEN

In mid-April of that year, Latty was summoned to a meeting with agents from the Georgia Bureau of Investigation. "What in the world have you done, son?" his captain asked him.

Latty was directed to a room where several GBI agents and investigators from the Hall County Sheriff's Office were waiting. One of the main interviewers was GBI agent Walt Stowe of Gainesville. He and others started asking him about a reported shooting incident at his mother's home in the summer of 1970. "Did it happen?" They wanted to know.

Latty said yes, and he told them every detail. He had not forgotten anything that happened that night. The men looked at each other and nodded knowingly.

"That has to be the one," one of the officers said after a brief period of silence.

"There's no doubt," another one said.

The officers then asked Latty a number of strange questions:

Did the man say anything?

Have you been running around with anyone's wife or girlfriend?

Did you spend time around Winder?

Have you had trouble with anyone who you thought might want to harm you?

Do you have any idea who shot at you?

The answer to all of those questions was no.

In early 1978, his mother had talked about seeing two official-looking cars pull into her driveway on Candler Road. Several well-dressed men got out of the cars and walked around in her yard. She thought they were there checking her property because it had been rezoned to light industrial, and she had petitioned to have it returned to agricultural/residential just in case she needed to replace her house for some reason.

One of the men in her yard was Lieutenant Ron Attaway.

No, Mama, Latty told his mother. The sheriff's office would not be involved in a routine rezoning request. Those men were there for another reason. That reason, it turned out, was to investigate a claim by Latty's assailant that he had killed somebody in a house on Candler Road.

Finally, the officers asked Latty if he'd like to know who tried to kill him?

Of course, he said. He'd been wondering who it was for eight years.

"Have you ever heard of Billy Sunday Birt?" one of them asked.

"My knees wobbled just a little bit," Latty said. Yes, he had heard of Billy Sunday Birt. Who in law enforcement had not heard of him? (Initially, Attaway thought Bill Birt had gone to the wrong house, but Latty determined later that he was at the right house. The correct target was him.)

Bill Birt had directed officers to the Latty home and told them, "I killed somebody in that house." That's why sheriff's officials were walking around in his mother's yard that day. Bill was with them, and "that's when he was confessing to all those murders," Latty said.

"He has confessed to killing you," one of the men said.

"He was convinced that he killed me, or somebody," Latty said, "so he never came back."

Bill told officers he killed—or, he found out later, *attempted* to kill—John Latty as a favor for someone. In describing his actions that night, Bill said he was dropped off at the location and entered the house. He had been told that only one man was inside, but then discovered two men sleeping in separate bedrooms. He didn't know which one to shoot, so he went back outside to ask. When he entered the house again, he heard someone—it was Latty—leaving one of the bedrooms. And he saw him coming toward him. He thought Latty was holding a gun. It was a dumbbell. So he fired at the man "who was hit and killed," he told officers. Actually, he had killed Frances Latty's piano.

But who would want to harm or kill John Wilbur Latty, an eighteen-year-old kid who had no known enemies? Latty thinks he knows who ordered the job, but the person really wasn't an

CHAPTER SEVENTEEN

enemy. He was someone close to him, someone he'd angered in an argument about a month before the shooting, someone who said he would "take care of" him. He also thinks this someone wanted Bill Birt only to scare him, not kill him. But Georgia's most notorious hit man specialized in killing, not scaring.

John Latty, remember, had never seen Bill Birt's face. All he saw that predawn Saturday was the silhouette of a man standing in his mother's house. But he got a chance to see his assailant in October of 1983.

His wife, Rebecca, was in Northeast Georgia Medical Center in Gainesville awaiting surgery. Latty was with her. He had read in a newspaper that Bill had been stabbed with a shank multiple times while in Lee Arrendale Prison in Alto, Georgia, and he noticed a uniformed correctional officer posted outside the second-floor room next to his wife's. Latty wanted to see the man who shot his mother's piano.

"Over a period of two days," he said, "I frequently spoke with the correctional officers posted there, explaining who I was and that my wife was next door, offering to run errands for them—mainly fetching coffee, Cokes, etcetera. I could hear Birt's voice, usually bitter complaining, and realized he had a severe speech impediment, hence the question in 1978 as to whether he had spoken on that night in 1970."

Latty had gotten a couple of brief glimpses of Bill Birt in the hospital bed, and he could see that his left eye was bandaged. Bill had lost that eye in the stabbing attack by another inmate.

On the last day of his wife's stay, Latty was leaving for the night, going home to get ready for work the next morning. He decided to check with the officers guarding Bill to see if he could help them in any way. He approached the door and saw two uniformed officers inside. Thinking they knew him, he entered the room.

The officers, it turned out, were new on the guarding job. They didn't know Latty; nor did they know he was a police officer.

They challenged him and ushered him outside. Latty identified himself, showing his badge, but the officers asked him to leave immediately. Latty apologized.

The next morning at work, he received a telephone call from Steve Howard with the Georgia Department of Offender Rehabilitation, as the unit was called then. He had known Howard a long time. But their acquaintance with each other did not soften Howard's anger. He was irate.

He asked Latty if he had entered Bill Birt's room the previous night. The answer was yes.

"I knew it was you," Howard yelled. "After my officers called me and reported what had happened, I went to the hospital and checked the patient list for that floor. As soon as I saw Rebecca Latty was there, I knew it had to be you. Do you know how much trouble you put me through last night?"

Latty admitted he made a mistake by visiting Bill Birt's room. He apologized, again. And then he told Howard he had done a poor job of protecting a hit man. Newspapers told everybody that Bill Birt was in the Gainesville hospital, and there he was on a floor between two entrances with only two lightly armed correctional officers guarding him. Latty said he could have taken out all three of them with one fragmentation grenade. And he didn't appreciate being dressed down by a fellow officer.

"He calmed down," Latty said, "and we laughed roundly together. Steve then told me that he had removed Birt to a safer and secret location. From that day onward, he has ribbed me about Birt, thinking he saw a ghost in his room that night."

Latty was never formally introduced to Bill Birt, but he met his younger brother, Homer Bobby Birt—the Birt kids' Uncle Bob—in the summer of 1982.

CHAPTER SEVENTEEN

As an investigator in the criminal investigation division of the Gwinnett County Police Department, Latty was dispatched to a multiple shooting incident at a place called Flat Rock, on the Gwinnett/Walton county line. One person had suffered several gunshot wounds, two had been severely pistol whipped, and five others had been shot at inside their vehicle. Members of the Walton County Sheriff's Office had apprehended the shooter, but the incident took place inside Gwinnett County.

Here's what Latty's investigation revealed:

Several people were at Flat Rock swimming, some drinking beer. Bobby Birt had gone there with another man who was driving since Bobby had been declared a habitual violator due to previous convictions on driving under the influence. Shortly after their arrival, Bobby Birt was confronted by a man named Carlton E. Criswell, who asked, "Are you Billy Birt's brother?" When Bobby said yes, the man began cursing Bobby and attacking him with a hawk-bill knife.

After fending off the assault, which resulted in a laceration to his right hand, Bobby fled, entered his vehicle, and was driven to his mother's home in Winder. He retrieved his mother's .32 caliber Rossi revolver and a box of ammunition, then was driven back to Flat Rock, where he found Criswell.

"Do you want some more of me?" the man asked. Bobby Birt immediately fired four rounds into him. He then sought out Criswell's wife and pistol whipped her and a male in a vehicle with her.

As he walked away from his three victims, someone in a vehicle occupied by a young couple and their child stopped and asked if Bobby, bleeding from his hand wound, needed help. Bobby fired into the vehicle, having reloaded his revolver after shooting Criswell. No one was hit.

Bobby grabbed a beer from a cooler inside a parked vehicle and drank from it until law officers arrived. He surrendered meekly.

Later that evening, Latty interviewed Bobby Birt, who voluntarily admitted to all of the attacks. Bobby said, "I shot him (Criswell) four times, and he fell off a little wooden bridge into the creek. I reloaded my pistol and walked down to where he was. I grabbed his long hair in my left hand and put the gun to his head with my other hand. He begged me not to kill him because he would go to hell. I told him I wouldn't and that I hoped he would live so I could do this to him again someday."

Some months later, Latty testified in Bobby Birt's trial and read the confession to the jury. He was convicted and sentenced to twenty years with ten to serve in prison on three counts of aggravated assault. He served about half that time and was paroled. Bobby, along with his brother Ray, had done time, more than a year, in the early seventies after being convicted of aggravated assault. "He fought all the time," Shane said.

But Shane said his Uncle Bob was a different man after he got out of prison the last time. He did one more job with Bill and then quit all of his criminal activity, even though Bill tried to tempt him to help one more time. It happened one day when Bob entered a room in a Barrow County residence and found Bill with about three-hundred thousand dollars—money from a bank robbery—spread out on a bed. Bill looked at his brother and asked if he wished he had not stopped doing jobs with him. No, Bob said, I don't regret it at all.

Bob had become a Christian. He died June 29, 2017.

John Latty also was a different man after narrowly escaping death at the deft gun hand of Billy Sunday Birt. That predawn intrusion dramatically affected his life, the way he viewed the world. Afterward, he said, he always made sure he had a firearm close by.

"I still am startled by unusual sounds during the night," he said. "I have frequently gotten out of bed and patrolled around my house in the dead of night, armed, as always. I have shared the experience with others, including law enforcement officers that

CHAPTER SEVENTEEN

I have had the privilege to train over the years." Latty taught for twelve years in the Georgia Law Enforcement Command College after retiring in 2002 as assistant chief of the Gwinnett County Police Department.

Latty said God provides His own with guardian angels, and "it was obviously His purpose that I not die that night" in 1970. The Latty guardian angel was there for everything that happened, he said. He doesn't attribute his being alive to luck. "I attribute it to the Lord having a plan for my life and teaching me a lesson," he said.

He was and is grateful for life. He really didn't need to be told to be grateful, but one of the investigators told him anyway. "Son," he said after meeting with the GBI agents, "I don't know if you are a believing man or not, but if I were you, I would not lay my head on my pillow tonight before I got down on my knees and talked to the Good Lord. You see, we have connected Billy Sunday Birt to fifty-six murders so far, and you are the only one that he confessed to killing that we have found alive."

John Latty was thought to have been murdered in 1970. But it was only Billy Sunday Birt who thought that.

No one smiling during visit with Bill at Marion.

CHAPTER EIGHTEEN

I'VE ALWAYS BEEN RELUCTANT to talk about my problems. As you know by now, I've had plenty of them. But I'm an extremely private person. I look for opportunities to pray for others and to counsel with them, but my problems are between me and the Lord. I don't want to burden others who no doubt have troubles of their own.

One time, though, several years ago, I opened up to my pastor, Tim Hammond, minister at New Life Apostolic Church in Watkinsville, Georgia, the same church Shane, Jill and their family attend. The preacher and his wife came to see me at the Northeast Georgia Medical Center in Gainesville, where I was about to undergo surgery to remove eighty-five percent of my colon. I told the pastor I had been praying about all of my health issues. I had undergone surgery after surgery, four major operations over five years. I'll tell you about some of them, not to burden you, but because I want to tell the whole story.

I told Pastor Tim that I asked the Lord, "Why me?" And then I caught myself and said, "Why not me? What makes me different from anybody else? Other people are going through stuff. So why not me?"

I think Mr. Hammond was surprised by my words. "Did you hear what she said?" he said he asked his wife later. He couldn't believe I said, "Why not me?"

So, please, as you read further, please don't take this as a *woe is me* story. I don't want anybody to feel sorry for me or to think that I am special and should be exempt from problems. Really,

I don't feel like I've been through too much. I am a survivor. I know what the Lord has done for me. I've seen it in the past, and I see it every day now.

As I said earlier, I became a Christian as a young girl attending the Church of the Nazarene in Winder. Then, when I was about thirty-five—Bill was in prison and couldn't keep me from church—I began attending the Church of God, which was located where the Master's Table catering business stands today. I was baptized again—my first time as a Nazarene in a lake, the second time in a baptistry of the Church of God.

At some point—I don't remember exactly when—I moved over to the Church of the Lord Jesus Christ, which is of the Assemblies of the Lord Jesus Christ. For several years now, I've been attending the Watkinsville church with Shane and Jill. I meet them at their home in Statham, and then we all ride together. It's convenient, and I like that church and the pastor.

Allow me to tell you about the Apostolic church, which emerged from the Pentecostal movement. It is a Christian denomination that adheres to the teachings of the twelve apostles who followed Christ. The church goes back to the 1904–1905 Welsh Revival, which was the largest Christian revival in Wales during the twentieth century, one that triggered revivals in several other countries. Our goal is to follow first-century Christianity in faith, practices, and government.

Our worship is more open and demonstrative than that in mainstream churches. People are free to lift their hands in worship and to say amen, praise the Lord, hallelujah. Pentecostals believe that every Christian should be filled with the Holy Spirit.

We also believe that baptism should be in Jesus's name, while most other churches baptize in the name of the Father, the Son, and the Holy Spirit. Peter said to repent and be baptized in the name of Jesus Christ. So we don't baptize in what some call the *titles*. We baptize in the name of Jesus, basing our belief on Paul's command in Colossians 3:17: "And whatsoever ye do in word or deed, do all in the name of the Lord Jesus."

CHAPTER EIGHTEEN

We in the Apostolic church believe the scriptures. If the Bible says it, we believe it. We're conservative in our beliefs and in our dress. The church teaches that women should dress modestly. People have asked me why I dress the way I do. Well, I dress like I want to. I can't stand being told I have to do something or not do something. I wear long skirts because I want to. I don't cut my hair because I don't want to. I don't wear makeup and jewelry because I don't want to. The way I dress is not a burden. Some people think I dress this way because of the church. I don't. I used to wear jeans around the house, but I didn't wear them in public. I don't wear pants to church out of respect for my Savior. That's His house. I didn't give up wearing pants until I felt like it.

Don't get me wrong. I don't look down on women who wear pants, even to church. That's their business, not mine. Some in our church wear pants. Neither do I look down on people who don't believe in speaking in tongues. Frankly, I myself was skeptical at first about folks falling out in the Spirit and speaking in tongues. But then I told the Lord, if it's real, I want it.

I was actually overtaken by the Holy Spirit one time at the Church of God. It was the best feeling in the world. I felt like I was having an out-of-body experience. It was like I was standing a little way off, listening to myself speak these strange words. I even passed out one time while praying for my sister, Runette, who had been seriously injured in an automobile accident. I was in the hospital chapel, and all of a sudden, I was out cold. It was like I had gone to sleep temporarily. Afterward, I felt drained, but it was a wonderful sensation.

Now, before you assume something, I must tell you I don't believe in drinking stuff, like poison, or handling snakes. The Lord gave me a body, and that body is the temple for Him. I need to take care of it, and it would be wrong for me to damage that body.

But I do fast on occasions. Some people might think that's damaging to the body, but I find it cleansing. It helps me focus on God and what He wants for my life.

I pray all the time, several times a day. If I get something on my mind, I'll walk out into the yard and pray. Sometimes, I sit on the back porch, rain or shine, and pray. God has gotten me through some tough times, and I owe Him my gratitude and my praise.

When I was young, some people called me a prude. I never drank, smoked or cussed. I couldn't then, and I can't now. Something keeps me from all of that. As a teenager, I tried drinking beer one time. Someone said it was good for the kidneys. Well, it wasn't good for anything, if you ask me. It tasted awful.

I don't believe in divorce, but I got one. Norma Jean had graduated from high school, and I was burdened. I was overweight and working several jobs to keep our heads above water. And, as I told you, I was still afraid of Bill—and afraid of people who might seek retribution for something he did to their loved ones.

"You will never be free of me," Bill told me one time, and I believed him.

I was tired of driving for hours to see Bill, me and the kids, to some prison in South Georgia or sometimes in another state. The children got sick and upset every time we went to a prison to visit. Sometimes it took two or three weeks to get them straightened out. They stayed mixed up all the time. So I decided I wasn't going to put them through that anymore. I started visiting Bill less, and if the kids didn't want to go, I didn't make them.

We have a photograph of the whole family gathered around Bill when he was in prison in Marion, Illinois, where he spent four years before being transferred to Reidsville, Georgia. I look at that photo today and want to cry. No one was smiling. No one. Everybody looked haunted-like, depressed. It was too much.

So I filed for divorce in 1986, I believe—I told Bill about it in a letter, and I think he understood—and I actually felt relieved when it was all over.

I made other changes later on. I weighed 348 pounds, and I was tired of carrying all of that weight around. I couldn't do anything without getting out of breath. I was in agony. Dr. Skelton said

CHAPTER EIGHTEEN

I showed signs of heart trouble. That wasn't surprising. So he and two other doctors signed for me to undergo gastric bypass surgery. The operation was successful. In all, I lost two hundred pounds.

I credit Shane and Jill's oldest child, Madison, with saving my life. My mom and I were very close, and she was always helping me do something. We were always together. When she died, the Lord gave me Madison. My job was to pick Madison up at her school bus stop on Friday afternoons, and she would stay with me until Shane or Jill could come to get her. But I weighed so much, I was exhausted doing practically nothing. Madison depended on me. I had to do something. That's when I decided to get the bypass surgery done.

It was hard holding down three, four, five jobs to put food on the table and clothes on our backs. But, finally, with Bill gone, I was my own person. The same was true for Jill when she and Shane were divorced for seven years, seven months and seven days.

"God made me a different person" during that time, Jill said, sitting at my dining room table. "When you're as young as Ruby was with Bill and I was with Shane, you sometimes lose your identity. Instead of being me, it was always Jill and Shane."

A teacher for many years, Jill mentors girls at school, encouraging them to be themselves. She does the same with her daughters. "Be who you are," she tells them, "not who he wants you to be, or who you *think* he wants you to be." Jill said she lost herself in her marriage to Shane. She was close to being thirty-one, divorced, and with a new baby. "It was awful," she said.

And then she said this: "Through it all, the Lord always fills the void. Whatever I was lacking, He fills the void. I had to pray there, especially in the beginning, that God would take away my love for Shane. I couldn't be a good mom and be worried and panicked all the time."

Frankly, I didn't think she and Shane would ever get back together. Others felt the same way. Shane was too far gone, hooked on meth, but Jill had become her own person. Jill said she wasn't sure she even wanted him back. But, eventually, thank goodness, she changed her mind. She and Shane started seeing each other on the sly. She didn't want people to know she was seeing him again. "I needed to find out if I even liked him," she said, "much less loved him." And then, finally, they remarried.

Substance abuse messes up a lot of marriages and relationships. It messed up Shane and Jill's. But, believe it or not, Shane said, "It was worth losing them for that while to have what I've got now." He believes that rock bottom is nothing but the hand of God. He had hit rock bottom.

Bill had also hit rock bottom, but he never changed until after many years of imprisonment. And, even then, I'm not sure how much he had changed. We never had a good life together. We enjoyed good times occasionally, but not a good life together, not a good marriage. When he was home, which was seldom, he was usually in the bed resting. He'd been out doing his dirty work, and he needed to rest.

We never sat down and watched a television program together. When he was running the pool room, sometimes he would come home for lunch and watch *Get Smart* on TV. He liked that show. I enjoyed *The Andy Griffith Show* and *The Waltons*, but I usually watched them without Bill.

The kids and I had some good, close times together after Bill left. In fact, some people called us the Waltons. We would say goodnight to each other, like they did on *The Waltons*, and finally somebody would cut it off with "Goodnight, John Boy. Now go to sleep."

My prayer is to have those good times again—at least one more Christmas and Easter with all the children, grandchildren and great-grandchildren here in my home. Because they live in Wisconsin, I don't get to see Montana and Ann and their families very often. About twenty years ago, Montana was trying to find his way in life, and he found it in Wisconsin. His dream was to be a minister in a prison, and that opportunity presented itself in Wisconsin. A couple from our church moved there and encouraged him and his family to follow. Ann moved there about ten years ago. For them, at the time, Winder was a place of bad memories.

As for me, I never wanted to leave Winder. Jill explained it well: "It's familiar here, and there's something comforting about a familiar place." Winder has been good to us, and, for the most part, the people have been good to us. There have been some who assumed the kids and I were bad people because of Bill's actions, and they had nothing to do with us. But they were in the minority. Frankly, I was afraid that the boys would inherit whatever gene it was that made Bill the way he was, but they didn't. They've had their problems, but, overall, they turned out well. I have been blessed.

People are surprised when they hear that: I have been blessed. But I *have* been blessed. God says in His word that He will never leave us, and He hasn't left me for one minute. I have been blessed with wonderful grandchildren and friends, and I enjoy being with them. As I've said before, my most frequent prayer over the years has been that God would allow me to live until my children were grown and could care for themselves. He did that. God has saved me and mine through a number of miracles.

One night when Shane was a baby, I knew I was dying. I could feel pain and death creeping up from my feet to my head. It was like a warm numbness. So I started praying, again: "Lord, let me live long enough to see my kids all grown." I hugged up to Shane and prayed as hard as I could. The pain left me.

I told you about Montana and his brain tumor's healing at the Ernest Angley revival. And about when the devil came after him, but he couldn't take him. Both of those experiences ended with miracles, I believe.

I've worked hard to buy food and clothing, but sometimes we were down to nothing to eat. And then I'd look into my chest-of-drawers and find money, or just out of the blue, someone would knock on my door, hand me money, and say, "The Lord told me to do this."

About four years ago, I got really ill while visiting Montana and Ann and their families in Wisconsin. It was on Mother's Day, and we were having a cookout before I had to catch my flight back to Georgia. I began to feel worse and worse. Finally, I told Montana I needed to go to the hospital.

Where they live is like Mayberry, so Montana drove me about ten miles up the road to a hospital. From there, I was sent to the Mayo Clinic in Minneapolis. The doctors thought I had cancer; I was bleeding internally. They didn't think I would make it. And then, get this, the doctors, nurses, Montana and Ann gathered around me and said a prayer for me. Turned out, a hernia inside my body had burst and I was hemorrhaging. I almost died. And if I had gotten on that airplane, I would have died, no doubt.

My car was repossessed one time. And then, while we were at the Master's Table, Dr. Skelton and his wife, Nora, heard of my predicament. "Rube," Doc said, "if I give you the keys to this car outside, would it help?" He did that three times. I can't say enough good things about Doc Skelton.

Losing 200 pounds was a miracle in itself. Today, at 140-something pounds, I'm able to work in my garden and work at the Master's Table whenever Lynn Walls calls me.

As I said, it has been one miracle after another. One time, Jill, her four children and I were driving to Wisconsin when the weather started to look bad as we entered Paducah, Kentucky. We decided to stop there and get a motel room for the night. In just a short time, a tornado roared through down the highway where we had been driving.

Twice, when I arrived home from my school bus route, I discovered that someone had broken into my house. One of those times, the security service telephoned and told me that help was on the way. I told the caller that everything was all right; no one was in the house. "Ma'am," the caller said, "your security system

CHAPTER EIGHTEEN

went off and we called your house. And Leonard answered the phone. He did not give the correct security password, so we have help on the way." Later, we found tracks from someone walking outside the house. And I don't have any friend named Leonard.

You might remember my story about people crawling around in the attic of our home—we heard them, and the kids and I left for the night. If we had stayed there, someone might have been hurt or killed.

So, you see, I'm not exaggerating. I am a walking miracle. I survived Billy Sunday Birt, and I survived all the illnesses and threats I have faced over the years.

Yes, indeed, I have been blessed.

CHAPTER NINETEEN

You would think Shane and my other four children would wince every time someone mentioned one of their daddy's many murders. But Shane sat there in that conference room of the White County Sheriff's Office and hardly blinked when Chief Deputy Bob Ingram asked about this killing and that killing, each one included in ATF agent Jim West's report.

"You get used to it," Shane had said earlier. So when Ingram passed around photographs taken after the couple in Wrens, Georgia, were brutally murdered in 1973, Shane was not visibly repulsed. He had seen them many times years ago.

I'm not saying he's been totally unaffected by Bill's criminal activities. My husband's murderous past scarred us all in some way. In fact, Shane told Ingram during their meeting, "Nobody should be burdened like we had to be."

Ingram's theory is that Bill "compartmentalized" his wicked actions. "He put them over here," he said, pointing to the back of his head. "That's how he was able to live with himself."

As Shane has said, one of Bill's many faults was that he couldn't let it go if he perceived he'd been done wrong. He had to get even. And the one who supposedly offended him or made him mad didn't have to be a bad person. Jesus was the greatest man who ever lived, and yet religious leaders of his time viewed him as a threat to their power and way of life. That's apparently the way Bill looked at everybody. If they were a threat to his way of life, they would be gone.

"When Billy Birt told you 'no hard feelings,' watch out," Ingram said. "If he perceived you as having deceived him, it was over."

Through it all—all of Bill's deceptions, his running around, his life of crime—I just depended on God. The Lord got me through it all. Deuteronomy 31:8 says: "And the LORD, He it is that doth go before thee; He will be with thee, He will not fail thee, neither forsake thee: fear not, neither be dismayed." I take that passage for exactly what it says.

I'm not implying I've been a perfect wife, a spotless Christian. I've made some terrible mistakes. My daughter Ann can tell you about one of them:

"We were living on Virginia Avenue, and this woman, a neighbor, cussed at Norma Jean, who must have been about four years old. Whoo wee! Mama cut out across that road, and she grabbed that woman, and they went to fighting. I'd never seen that side of Mama. She was a tiny thing, wore about a size three dress. Well, this woman jumped in her car, and Mama grabbed a tricycle and was beating that car window out with that tricycle. The woman yelled, 'I'm pregnant!' Mama yelled back, 'I'm pregnant, too!' Mama was pregnant with Shane. The woman got out on the other side of the car, and Mama ran around the car to get her. The woman's husband was trying to protect his wife when Daddy pulled up in his Mercury Cyclone. Daddy put a .38 pistol to the husband's head and said, 'Don't touch my wife.' Then he told Mama, 'Now, honey, that's enough. Come on.'"

I told the woman, "You don't cuss my babies." Somebody called the law, but, fortunately, no charges were brought. Bill was arrested on the Loganville bank robbery a short time after that incident.

One time while he was in prison—I don't remember which one, he was in several—Bill asked me to smuggle a hacksaw blade into his cell. Before my next visit, I threaded a thin hacksaw blade through a cloth-covered belt, put the belt around my waist, and went to see Bill. He put his arms around me as though he were hugging me, worked the blade out, and hid it in his cell. As far as I know, he never tried to use it.

CHAPTER NINETEEN

As I told you earlier, I've even felt the urge to get even with somebody. It happened when Bill was on the stand in Cobb County Superior Court testifying about Billy Wayne Davis's part in the Matthews murder case. Bill looked at me, and I silently mouthed, "Take him." Turned out, Davis was apparently innocent. But I didn't know that. I wanted Bill to get even with his former friend for testifying against him in the Loganville bank robbery and the Wrens murders. But the Bible says, "Vengeance is mine; I will repay, saith the Lord." I guess I ignored that scripture.

Yes, you get used to it, as Shane said, but bad memories surely were conjured up, once again, as my youngest son sat listening to a litany of his daddy's horrendous crimes from the past, crimes investigated by Ingram, Jim West, Earl Lee, Ronnie Angel, and numerous other lawmen. Some of the cases mentioned in the West report, Shane knew nothing about. Others didn't happen the way Bill explained them to Shane later. Still other cases were spot-on accurate.

One of the most convoluted cases involved the death of James O. Daws, the grocer who lived in Monroe, Georgia, about fifteen miles from Winder. Daws was married to Ruth Chancey, leader of a gang of thugs and mother of Harold Chancey, the notorious moonshiner. But Daws didn't like being married to Ruth; in fact, he was getting a divorce.

"Mr. Daws told me that Ruth Chancey more or less tricked him into marrying her," West wrote. Here's the story as told by West and Billy Wayne Davis:

Daws was home recovering from injuries suffered in an automobile accident when Ruth Chancey dropped by to check on him. Daws apparently didn't know the woman that well. He had seen her occasionally in his store, but they certainly weren't romantically involved.

The next day, she visited again, and before long, she was there every day, often bearing food. She also took him for rides in her car.

One day, she drove to her son Harold's home in Winder, where she introduced Daws to Harold's wife and another woman. "This is James O. Daws, my husband," she said.

Daws said they'd never even talked about marriage.

After they left the home, Ruth Chancey said, "Well, I guess you and I will have to get married now because Harold is going to think we're married."

Maybe being married to Ruth Chancey wouldn't be a bad thing, Daws apparently decided. After all, she has been very nice and friendly. As a matter of fact, she has been "so kind that butter wouldn't melt in her mouth." So on February 25, 1969, they became a couple—an odd couple.

They had been married only a short time when Ruth said to her husband, "Well, I'll tell you what let's do: Let's put your property here (in Walton County) in my name and then I'll put my house over in Winder in your name."

Daws acted like he didn't hear her.

After a week or so, she offered the same proposal, but this time she was a bit more emphatic. Daws tried to ignore her again, but she wouldn't have it. Her proposal immediately turned into a demand: This is what we're going to do, Daws.

On May 24, 1971, Daws contacted his lawyer, Bill Preston, to talk about a divorce. He didn't feel safe in his own home. One day, his wife pulled a gun on him, and when the phone rang and she backed up to answer it, he ran out the door, jumped in his truck and drove to the sheriff's office. When he and the sheriff arrived back at his house, his wife had left. But she came back later, grabbed her husband's new Florsheim shoes and slammed them into a television set, smashing the picture tube to pieces. She also left with some things that didn't belong to her. It was payback time for Ruth, who had been on the receiving end of beatings from her husband.

It wasn't long before Daws obtained an injunction forbidding Ruth from coming near his house. Not to be outdone,

CHAPTER NINETEEN

Ruth threatened to have her husband killed by her brother, C.W. Royster. That never happened.

Harold Chancey, in the meantime, was hiding out from the law. He had been indicted in a liquor conspiracy case, and James Daws was scheduled to testify against him in federal court in Columbia, South Carolina. West had interviewed Daws two or three times and had taken a signed statement from him saying he would testify in the case.

Actually, Bill was paid twice for the same hit on Daws, Shane said. The money came from a man and a woman—Shane didn't want to say who, because he was not sure—and each person didn't know the other one had paid. First, the woman approached him—but don't say anything, she said—and then the man paid for the same contract—but don't say anything, he said.

Bill was told he could keep all the money he found in Daws's home. Daws had recently filed for bankruptcy, and it was assumed he would have a lot of money hidden in his house.

Bill and Otis Reidling went to Daws's home, cut his telephone lines, and tried to force Daws to tell them where he kept his money. Daws said he had fifteen hundred dollars in a pair of pants hanging in a closet. They got that money. That's all I have, Daws said. They didn't believe him. They forced their victim to crawl into the trunk of Daws's new car and drove him from Monroe, in Walton County, to the Birt home in Statham, in Barrow County. That car, West said, ended up in Lake Lanier.

Using coat hangers, Bill and Reidling tied three concrete blocks around Daws's legs and neck. They took him to the Little Mulberry River, dragged him out of the trunk and onto a bridge.

(There's been some disagreement on where Daws's body was found. The local newspaper, *The Winder News*, said it was in the Thomas River. Jimmy Terrell, former chief investigator for the Barrow County Sheriff's Office, said he accompanied Sheriff John Robert Austin to the very stream where the body was found. He identified it as Rocky Creek. But Bill himself said it was Little

223

Mulberry River—and he put it in writing in a memoir—so that's what we're going with.)

West's report on what happened at the bridge differs with Bill's account. West said his informant, Davis, told him that Bill and Reidling gave Daws one last chance to come up with money. Daws said he was telling the truth; what they found in his pants was all he had. "But if you won't kill me, I'll get more money," Daws told them. They apparently didn't believe him and threw him into the water alive.

Bill, however, told Shane he and Reidling hadn't planned on killing Daws. They just wanted to scare him. But Daws got to struggling frantically to get away and accidentally fell into the water. He wasn't pushed, Bill said.

Daws disappeared on November 22, 1971. Less than a month later, on December 17, 1971, two fisherman found his body after it floated to the surface of the river, cement blocks still attached and his mouth gagged with two ties. An autopsy indicated he had drowned.

Bill's former brother-in-law spotted the cement blocks that had been used and realized they came from his homeplace. He was afraid he would be implicated, although he knew nothing about Daws's death and was never even questioned. It was just a matter of Bill's knowing where he could obtain some blocks, so he "borrowed" a few.

Looking for clues to solve other crimes, divers searched one river in the county—which river is unclear—and found several bank deposit bags, a battered postage machine, and a vending machine for Lance crackers.

"We don't know what else is in there," one officer was quoted in *The Winder News*. "There might be bodies, safes, or who knows what."

Two months earlier, divers had recovered five large safes from the same spot.

When Daws's body was found, Bill and Charlie Reed were in Florida, probably on a hit because Bill never went on vacation.

CHAPTER NINETEEN

Bobby Gene Gaddis and one more man—possibly both of them—telephoned Bill, told him the body had been found and said he should head back home. "No," Bill said, "sounds like y'all need to get down here."

When he did get back to Winder, several men—Bill, and probably Reed and Gaddis, Shane said—were picked up and questioned about the death. They were sitting in a line in Sheriff Howard Austin's office when the sheriff's wife walked in and started looking at photographs of Daws's body. Tears welled up in her eyes.

She showed the photos to Bill and said, "What do you think about that?"

"Don't know who did this," Bill said, "but Jim looks pretty bad here. But whoever took these pictures knows how to use a camera. If you'll give me his name and phone number, I want to get him to do a family portrait for us."

The sheriff's wife thought she was speaking to a man who had a conscience. "Billy Birt," she said, "you're the coldest man I've ever known." And she was telling the truth.

Jim Daws had planned to go to dinner with friends the day he disappeared. He was dressed for the occasion.

CHAPTER TWENTY

Reading the report Jim Earl West prepared, one might wonder if the man was obsessed with tracking down every tiny detail about the ungodly criminal acts of Billy Sunday Birt. And he didn't stop there. He also investigated cases that Bill *might* have been involved in, even if evidence against him was not strong, or was nonexistent.

West apparently looked under every suspicious rock and noted everything he heard about Bill. Much of his information came from Billy Wayne Davis, who was a frequent partner in Bill Birt's crimes.

West, agent with what was then the federal Alcohol, Tobacco and Firearms division, recorded the murder cases in chronological order. Some of them have been covered in previous chapters of this book. Following are others, with most of the details taken from West's report:

On January 10, 1971, Bill is said to have killed a woman he had been dating. (Remember, we are not using names of Bill's girlfriends.) After taking her life, he laid her body in the roadway of Highway 29, just outside of Winder and near the home of U.S. Senator Richard B. Russell. The Georgia Bureau of Investigation, which investigated the death at the time, said the woman was run over by a car and that her right hip and ankle were broken.

Driver of the car was identified as A.B. Bryant, who was traveling east on Highway 29 at about one o'clock on this foggy morning. He reported what happened to authorities. West assumed that Bill killed the woman because he thought she informed his wife about his dating other women. Bill is said to have told Davis he killed "four girls" for that very reason. However, "information to this effect was received but not confirmed," West reported.

At about 7:30 a.m. on May 12, 1971, Dutch Leachman was found murdered in his grocery store and residence in Farmington, an unincorporated community in Oconee County, Georgia. Leachman, West said, "was a bootlegger and large raw materials dealer who dealt with Harold Chancey many years. . . . It was well known by people who knew Dutch Leachman that he wouldn't let anyone in after business hours, except those people he knew very well."

West said he confirmed that Chancey sold liquor to Leachman and was supposed to have delivered a load to him the same night Leachman was murdered. Investigation by the sheriff and GBI revealed the place had been burglarized. Leachman kept money in three different places in the living quarters of his store, West wrote, but only one of those three places had been ransacked.

"During the last seven or more years of whiskey and raw materials traffic with Leachman, Chancey would have known about these three hiding places," the report said. "Billy Birt in his conversations with our informer did not relate the information on this particular killing."

So, obviously, we must conclude that West included in his report murders that Bill may have committed, but he wasn't sure of his theories.

Another murder West believed Bill committed occurred on a rural road near Dacula, Georgia, part of Gwinnett County. Geke Lee, father of Sonny Lee, one of Bill's friends, was standing outside his truck loaded with concrete blocks, when Bill happened along. The two were standing in the road talking, when the truck started rolling. Lee "is supposed to have fallen underneath the truck, and it ran over him," West wrote. "The information we

CHAPTER TWENTY

have is that Billy had some reason to kill Mr. Lee to keep him from telling something he knew."

Shane, however, said he'd always heard it wasn't his daddy who caused Lee's death. It was someone else. Not being one hundred percent sure, he didn't want to say who.

Geke Lee—whose real name was Herschel Junior Lee of Winder—"was supposed to have been taken to his home after the truck ran over him," West said. He walked into his home under his own power and was put to bed. When his children returned home from school at about 4:00 that afternoon, they found their father dead.

On May 20, 1971, at about 10 p.m., an autopsy by Dr. Larry Howard and G.B. Dawson of the State Crime Lab indicated the cause of death was shock and hemorrhage, and secondarily, a crushed pelvis.

In the summer of 1971, a man named Wayne Hall, a security guard at the University of Georgia, was shot in the back of his head and his body thrown into a river. Hall was a relative of Willie Hester, one of Bill's partners. West said a woman Bill was dating confirmed in an interview that she had dated Hall and that Bill was jealous. She said Bill had been paying rent on a house where she lived and "was with her most every night," the report said.

"When Billy Birt dated girls," West wrote, "although he was married and had a family himself, he was very possessive and was the type of person who could not stand to lose or share his girl with another."

On November 4, 1971, Mr. and Mrs. Moss S. Wilbanks, and their daughter and son-in-law, Warren and Doris Wilbanks Whitehead, were murdered inside the Wilbanks home. The informant, no doubt Billy Wayne Davis, said Bill told him what happened:

Bill heard that the Wilbanks had sold some property and "had a lot of money in their house. He went to their house to rob them at about 8 p.m., or a little before. He went in and killed Mr. and Mrs. Wilbanks and was searching the house for their money when someone knocked on the kitchen door."

Bill had locked the door on the inside, hoping the visitors, who happened to be the Whiteheads, would leave. But they persisted, knocking again and again.

"So finally he saw that they weren't going away, so he walked to the back door and opened it," West wrote. "When he opened the door, this man and woman were standing there. The woman said, 'Are my mother and father here?' He said, 'Yeah, they're in here, come on in.' He said he turned and started walking down the hall toward where the mother and father were and when he got to where you turn into the bedroom door where he had killed them, he wheeled around and killed Doris and Warren. He set the house on fire and left."

To start a fire, according to West's report, Bill would cut the top out of a plastic jug, fill it with gasoline or kerosene, light it and leave. The jug would melt down, releasing the fuel, causing the entire structure to burn.

Autopsies showed that none of the four had smoke in their lungs, indicating they were dead when the fire started.

The Wilbanks had sold some land and cattle just before the murders, according to West, and were expected to have a considerable amount of money in their home. They were reluctant to put their money in a bank.

On October 27, 1972, James Edward McCarty and Helen B. McCarty were found dead inside a store, Lucky Dollar, which they operated on Highway 106 just outside of Athens, Georgia.

Bill told the informant that a man who lived in a trailer close to the Lucky Dollar supposedly kept a lot of money hidden in a compartment of a hot-water tank inside his trailer. Bill killed the McCarty couple, the report said, robbed them and set the store on fire. Then he waited for the man to leave his trailer so

CHAPTER TWENTY

that he could also rob him. But the man never came outside, and Bill left the scene.

Shane knows of a murder near Barrow County that was not included in Jim West's report. This one was just a routine hit, the gang would call it, one to be paid for by a man named John who faced drug charges and wanted Bill to eliminate someone expected to testify against him in court. Bill Birt carried out the job and buried the body near the Mulberry River.

"How do I know the guy is dead?" John asked angrily when Bill showed up at his home to collect his fee. Turned out, Bill had to prove it, and he was not happy about it. He went back to the river, dug up the body, cut off the victim's head with an axe stolen from a man's chop block, put the head into a trash bag, and went back to John's house. By then, it was about four o'clock in the morning.

John screamed like a banshee when he looked inside the trash bag. He threw the bag out the door and onto his porch. He told Bill he would meet him at the bank the next morning. Bill got his money that morning, and John got in his car and drove off.

So where is the victim's head?

Shane said his father didn't want to walk nearly two miles down that river bank again, so he put a large rock into the trash bag and tossed it into an old, muddy lake between Winder and Hoschton. The remains of that bodiless head are still out there somewhere, in deep, muddy water.

What was believed to have been the man's skeletal torso, Shane said, was discovered in the 1980s by a crew dredging the Mulberry River, eliminating debris that collects around bridges. The Jackson County Sheriff's Office was notified about the headless skeleton, and "the sheriff came out and gathered the bones. They had a full skeleton, all except for the head," Shane said. "The sheriff told them we'll just make sure it gets a good burial. Nothing else was ever said."

On May 2, 1973, Rose Marie Salzer died in a mobile home fire the "next day after she was seen talking to me," West wrote, referring to himself.

About 8 a.m. the day before the death, West said he met Salzer when he arrived at his office in Athens. Agent Bobby Whittemore was also present. West said he didn't recognize Salzer at first, but then remembered she used to work for the government in the ATF's Jacksonville, Florida office while West was doing some work there.

The woman told West she grew up in Statham but had been living in Winder for some time. She said "a lot of crime (was) going on around there and she wanted to help catch Harold Chancey and some of the group there and Billy Birt." West asked Salzer what she knew about criminal acts around Winder, and "she wrote some things on paper. . . ."

West said he asked her if she realized how dangerous these people were. She said yes, but she wanted to help investigators arrest them.

West said, "Well, I don't think that they would ever let you know anything that they are doing."

Said Salzer, "Well, I've already bought beer from Bush Chancey several times." Chancey, West said, sold beer at his house and also out of Chancey's Place, located on Highway 81, "which we think is a front for Harold (Chancey)."

The day the two met at West's office, Salzer asked the agent if he was headed to Winder, and he said yes. She asked if he would drive in front of her vehicle; she said she was "afraid of someone." She followed West to Winder where the agent visited with Judge Mark Dunahoo in his office. Salzer, in the meantime, "went up there and waited to finish writing out the list of things she knew about this group." Her list included accusations about the Chanceys, saying that "Bush Chancey was selling beer and Billy Birt was selling pills." She also named others who were part of the criminal activity.

Salzer told West she was having her car washed, and she needed a ride home. So West took her home to her trailer.

CHAPTER TWENTY

"The following night," the report said, "her trailer burned and she burned up in it. She had already heard this group talking about me (West), and my name had come up several times, and I cautioned her about saying anything about my name with that group."

West said he made some assumptions: that Salzer had bought a six-pack of beer on "this particular day, and she was drinking some, and I just assume that maybe she made the remark that she was going to help catch them." Or perhaps she said she was going to tell West "a lot of things." Whatever happened, word obviously got back to the criminals that she was cooperating with investigators.

West assumed something else: that Bill Birt set the trailer on fire, "because she had been living there and nothing had happened to her prior to this."

Rose Marie Salzer was thirty-six years old.

So it is obvious that Jim West sometimes would get a little information about a case and then assume that Bill Birt was the perpetrator. He may or may not have been involved. But West was bound and determined to put the man in prison.

That's where Bill Birt eventually ended up, of course, but West couldn't take much credit for Bill's murder convictions—in the deaths of Reid and Lois Fleming in Wrens, Georgia, and the murder of Donald Chancey of Winder.

233

Jimmy Terrell.

CHAPTER TWENTY-ONE

Jimmy Terrell thought he knew how to handle tough guys. He served in the Army's Special Forces—no namby-pamby assignment—worked for the police department at the University of Georgia, and was about to graduate from the Northeast Georgia Police Academy.

But then he took a job as chief investigator for the Barrow County Sheriff's Office. Danny Bennett, then a Barrow County deputy and a classmate at the police academy, had told him about the opening. He applied, interviewed with Sheriff John Robert Austin, and was hired. He started working January 1, 1975.

He was still in the Army Reserve, which he said "made me a little more comfortable doing what I was doing. I thought I was bad as they were. I wasn't, but I thought I was."

After about two weeks on the job, Gerald Thomas, investigator for the district attorney and former Winder police chief, called him to his office and handed him a paper sack. "Here, you'll need this," Thomas said. The sack contained a sawed-off shotgun.

By 1975, Bill Birt and several of his gang were either in prison or dead, but a few associates were left on the streets. There were also some wannabes—men who thought of themselves as part of the pack, even if they weren't. Terrell wrote about his remembrances in 2016: "A lot of braggarts and a lot of fools claimed to belong to the Dixie Mafia, a loose organization of criminals who made their fortunes and their destinies with liquor, fast cars, amphetamines, murder, burglary, and armed robbery."

Some were dangerous, however, and would back up what they claimed. One day, word apparently got out that the new investigator wanted to talk to someone who ran around with the bad crowd. Terrell was looking into an arson case.

The man called Terrell at the county jail, identified himself, described his car, even gave him his tag number. And then he said, "And you're welcome to stop me, but just know that when you do, I'm going to blow your ass up because I've got twelve sticks of dynamite in the car."

Terrell immediately went out and bought a German shepherd puppy named Jason and trained him as an attack dog. Jason went to work with his master every day and rode with him at night. A few times, the dog put the bite on perpetrators, but, fortunately, Terrell never had to fire his shotgun in the line of duty. Still, he carried it for three or four years, especially at night. "There was a lot of night work," he said, "meeting informants, stakeouts, serving warrants." Sometimes others in the department had his back as he met informants in the middle of the night.

On the afternoon of November 19, 2019, James Floyd "Jimmy" Terrell sat in the conference room of First United Methodist Church in Winder, where he and his wife are members, and talked about his years as chief investigator. The quiet church room was perfect for recalling unquiet times.

Besides working with the sheriff's office, Terrell was made available to other law enforcement agencies that needed him. During the day, he investigated cold cases, burglaries, thefts, and other crimes for the sheriff's office. At night sometimes, he worked with the GBI and ATF. Some federal agents were still in town, trying to close out cases and make new ones.

"It was cowboys and Indians that first year," Terrell said.

CHAPTER TWENTY-ONE

Caught in the middle were innocent, peace-loving people still afraid to be seen talking to an investigator, even though most leaders of the gang were gone. "They might look over their shoulder and whisper back to you," Terrell said. But mostly they avoided eye contact with an officer of the law.

One of them was Otis Reidling's father, O.R. Reidling, who was sure that Bill Birt and his band had something to do with his son's disappearance and death. He turned up missing on Sunday, November 4, 1973, and his body was found in a shallow grave by the Mulberry River in April of 1974.

"I would meet him at 1 or 2 o'clock in the morning," sometimes on the Walton County line, sometimes on the other side of Statham, Terrell said. "If I met him on the street, he would look the other way."

Bill Birt had protected Otis Reidling as best he could, but he was irritated that Reidling risked going to prison doing petty crimes, such as stealing tape decks out of cars at the University of Georgia. But, in the end, Bill Birt was with Otis when Billy Wayne Davis shot and killed him.

Terrell admitted to fellow lawmen that he knew little about the so-called Dixie Mafia when he reported to Barrow County. But he learned fast.

"A lot of career criminals in South Georgia and across the Southeast have claimed to be the real Dixie Mafia," Terrell said. "Many left their signature crimes across vast regions in the Southeast to lay claim to their share of the title. None, however, deserved the title any more than the group that worked across North Georgia and into several adjoining states."

One group, he said, worked out of Barrow County; separate packs operated in nearby Jackson and Hall counties; another group claimed the Athens area. "Information was swapped between the various groups like stock traders in New York," Terrell said. "Some of the Dixie Mafia soldiers were feared, or respected, more than others.

"No one, however, had more respect than the Barrow County group." That bunch moved like ghosts in the night, he said, and several major burglaries occurred within a stone's throw of the sheriff's and police departments. A truckload of pants was stolen one night from Superior Garments less than two hundred feet from the county jail.

Criminal activity in the late 1960s and early 1970s—a period of seven or eight years—brought a rush of state and federal agents to Barrow County, sometimes outnumbering local law enforcement officers of all agencies combined, Terrell remembered.

It was a period of stakeouts, telephone taps, and even attempts at ambushes. Two federal agents tried to ambush Bill Birt and Bobby Gene Gaddis in Walton County. They pulled up beside Bill's car and opened fire.

"They shot up Billy's car," Terrell said. "He just swerved off the road, drove into a pasture and kept going." No one was hit.

But among the excitement of cowboys and Indians lurked considerable danger. Terrell received a couple of death threats during his tenure. In one instance, he learned that a man was paid two thousand dollars—a measly fee for a life—to take him out.

The Dixie Mafia had changed with the times and new opportunities. Burglaries turned into armed robberies and murder in Barrow and nearby counties, and moonshine-running turned into drug-running, bringing in more money for the runners and more trouble for the chasers. A trip to Mexico for a load of amphetamines could bring a profit of hundreds of thousands of dollars. Illegal drug-running exploded into a major criminal enterprise.

CHAPTER TWENTY-ONE

But some enterprising criminals believed in diversifying. They even stole gasoline. Several men somehow located a cross-country line near Tallapoosa, Georgia, drilled down into it, and siphoned enough gasoline to fill tanker trucks. "They were selling all over the place," Terrell said.

The FBI asked Terrell to help with the investigation. He obtained a warrant to search the home of Ruth Chancey, Harold Chancey's mother, to look, presumably, for gas receipts. He accompanied agents to her home. "She said, 'They can come in, but you can't, Jimmy.' One of the agents stepped up and said, 'Mrs. Chancey, Jimmy wrote the warrant.'" The agents didn't find anything incriminating.

Ask Jimmy Terrell what the inside of an abandoned well looks like, and he can describe it in full detail. He descended twenty-three of them over a five-year period, looking for bodies. Many of the wells were overgrown; some had caved in after dynamite was set off.

He found body parts of Charles Martin in a well in 1976; he found the body of Willie Hester buried in the same area in 1978; the next year, he and fellow officers discovered the remains of Donald Chancey, thanks to information from Bobby Gene Gaddis.

Why, Terrell said he thought to himself at the time, why would Gaddis turn on his friend, Bill Birt? "I think Billy probably told him to do it with his blessings," Terrell said. "He wouldn't hold it against him. So Bobby Gene gave me a statement about Chancey."

Terrell was correct, Shane said. Gaddis was following Bill's orders in testifying about Chancey's death. Gaddis was hoping for a favor in return—getting paroled—but parole never came. He died in prison.

Investigating crime scenes was Terrell's specialty. In fact, he taught it at two police academies. But finding a body years after it was buried proved challenging. Gaddis wasn't sure of the exact location of Donald Chancey's body. Then he spotted a deer stand that had rotted and fallen from a tree. Gaddis remembered the stand, still useful at the time, in 1972. The ravine was about seventy-five yards away.

Terrell had broken an ankle in a parachute jump, so he watched as others dug at the head of the ravine. Six shovelfuls later, they found a boot, Chancey's boot.

Terrell worked other cold cases. At the direction of Sheriff Austin, he investigated the murders and robbery of J. Marion and Beulah Kilgore, found dead in their Winder home June 20, 1972. Bill Birt and Bobby Gene Gaddis were the suspects, but Terrell believes Billy Wayne Davis was involved, too. It was Davis who told Jim Earl West about the murders. West's report did not mention Gaddis or Davis.

"At the time I read Jim West's report, I believed every word of it," Terrell said. "But I came to realize that West was so gung-ho to get them and make cases," he became skeptical about some of the agent's information. In some cases, he said, Davis probably told investigators what they wanted to hear, and it wasn't always the truth.

"I don't want to say anything disparaging against him (West)," Terrell said. "He had a job to do."

Terrell got to know West and other ATF agents well. He accompanied one of the agents to Louisville, Georgia, to attend the trial of Bill Birt in the murders of Reid and Lois Fleming of nearby Wrens. Gaddis and Charlie Reed would be tried later. Davis turned state's evidence to avoid prosecution—claiming he was waiting in a motor home when the killings occurred—but Gaddis told Terrell that Davis was also there at the Fleming home.

Gaddis said Bill Birt was there, too, but Bill later said he was out burglarizing houses at the time. His claim, however, never came up during his trial.

Terrell said he believed Bill was telling the truth.

"I truly believe that Charlie Reed would do whatever Billy told him to do," Terrell said. "Billy loved safes; he loved to crack

CHAPTER TWENTY-ONE

them.... I believe he (Bill) and Charlie did the burglaries, and Bobby Gene and Billy Wayne did the killings."

But Bill would not claim he was innocent, Terrell said, because he was part of the overall plan. "I believe that if Billy were sitting here, he would tell you that he was rightfully convicted."

Terrell also accompanied ATF agents on liquor raids. He watched them crawl under a house near Oakwood, Georgia, put a bucket under a sink, knock on the door, and wait for the residents to answer.

"I ain't got no liquor in here," they would say, having poured their illegal booze into a sink whose contents exited into the agents' bucket.

"I loved it," Terrell said. "I thought it was big-time. It was better than television."

Because he worked with other law enforcement agencies, Terrell often worked outside Barrow County. "A guy here might hijack a tractor-trailer load of men's dress pants," he said. "A few calls could be made, and the pants might end up in South Carolina, Florida, or Alabama."

A fellow can learn a lot about good law enforcement when he works with good people, and Terrell said he worked with some of the best. "Anything I accomplished," he said, "I accomplished because I had those people on my side working with me or helping me or whatever."

He believes Sheriff John Robert Austin and Sheriff Earl Lee of Douglas County emerged from the same mold. Both were knowledgeable and great to work with. The main difference between the two sheriffs was, "Earl might have been a little calmer. I thought the world of him."

Austin never doubted Terrell when he went to him with a possible case. "If you have the information, work it," the sheriff would tell him. He never said, "Don't waste your time."

But Austin was a bit skittish when he had to ride with Terrell. The chief investigator carried a Combat Commander .45 caliber pistol, and he carried it locked and loaded. If he was wearing it, the sheriff wouldn't get in the car with him; he was afraid it would accidentally go off.

"I'd said, 'John Robert, it can't go off.' But he didn't believe me. I'd have to take it off, put the hammer down, take the magazine out, and put the gun in the trunk."

Like Shane Birt, Terrell never knew Bill Birt outside of prison walls, but he heard stories about him from Austin, Gerald Thomas, and others. And some of the stories showed a different side of the man. They talked about the times Bill gave poor people clothes during the wintertime and money for groceries. And when he heard about a man who drank and gambled all the time and didn't give his wife grocery money, he fixed the problem. As Earl Lee said several times, Bill didn't have a great start in life. Terrell recalled this story from a letter Bill sent to his son Stoney:

Bill was in the third grade, the last grade he completed, and one day he told the teacher, Betty Maddox, he didn't want to go outside during recess. It was wintertime, and Bill didn't have any socks. His feet got cold. The teacher padded his shoes with newspaper and brought him socks a couple of days later. "Billy never forgot that," Terrell said.

Stories of Bill's kindness are not meant to minimize the suffering Georgia's Number One hit man caused so many families. He disrupted many lives. He ended many others. But there was the good side of a bad man, someone careful about whom to trust. He actually trusted some people. "I think Billy trusted me," Terrell said, "and he told Stoney to listen to me."

CHAPTER TWENTY-ONE

Terrell resigned from the sheriff's office after five years and became chief of the Winder Police Department, a position he held for thirteen years. He later took other jobs inside and outside of government.

During part of this time, he and Bill Birt corresponded. Somebody else penned Bill's last letters to Terrell as Parkinson's Disease squeezed Bill's body tighter and tighter. Bill never mentioned his crimes in any of his letters, Terrell said.

Many stories died with the men of the Dixie Mafia. And, as Terrell said, "There are still some bodies here (in Barrow County) that haven't been found."

Millard Farmer.

CHAPTER TWENTY-TWO

MY HUSBAND ALWAYS SAID he deserved all the punishment he received for his crimes. He believed in the death penalty. For his part in the deaths of that nice, church-going couple in Wrens, Georgia, he deserved to die, he told me and our children more than once. He had been sentenced to death after being found guilty in June of 1975.

When petitions to eliminate the death penalty were being circulated while Bill was in prison, he told us, "If you ever sign one of them petitions, don't come back and see me."

And yet, as far as I know, he did nothing to discourage appeals to reduce his death sentence to life imprisonment. He even encouraged filing a writ of habeas corpus in Tattnall County Superior Court. Reidsville prison is located in Tattnall County. And in 1979, following an evidentiary hearing, a state judge threw out Bill's death sentences. He said the jury had not received proper instructions during the sentencing phase of the trial.

Bill said his good friend Sheriff Earl Lee had talked to the judge before the death sentences were overturned, and he credits the sheriff for saving his life. Bill explained the process in a letter to his sons:

Bill was serving twenty-five years in a federal penitentiary in Marion, Illinois, for robbing the bank in Loganville, Georgia. In 1978, Bill thought the state of Georgia "wanted to be the first state to put a man to death under the new death penalty law." So he was returned to Georgia after he had served four years of his twenty-five-year term and was facing execution for his part in the two murders of Jefferson County, Georgia.

"Well, back then," Bill wrote, "when a man on death row got his last date to be electrocuted, the governor of Georgia would give him a ninety-day stay." His date for execution was set while he was still at Marion, "and my lawyers sold me out," he said. The lawyers asked the governor for the ninety days when they should have waited until Bill was transferred back to Georgia. "I had four days left on the ninety days when I got to Reidsville, Georgia," Bill wrote.

Attorney Millard Farmer of Atlanta visited Bill on death row at Reidsville. The state is going to execute you, he told Bill, and recommended that he fire his lawyers and hire him. Bill did just that.

The next day, Bill said, Millard filed a writ of habeas corpus in Tattnall County Superior Court to receive a hearing before a judge in hopes the execution would be set aside. Bill said he was taken before the judge who was to rule on the habeas. But before the judge made his ruling, Douglas County Sheriff Earl Lee, who had become a good friend, visited Bill on death row and asked the name of the judge. "I know him," Lee said, and he left to pay the judge a visit.

"In a couple of hours, my counselor came and told me I had a phone call," Bill wrote. "It was Mr. Lee." The sheriff told him the judge decided to delay his ruling on the habeas for three months. "That really ease my mind," Bill wrote. At the end of the three months, the judge ruled in Bill's favor, overturning the death sentences and ordering a resentencing. "And it don't take a genius to figure out why the judge ruled in my favor," he wrote. "So I really owe Earl Lee my life here on earth."

Millard was to handle the resentencing ordered by the judge.

Millard Farmer became a dear friend. I sometimes made him red velvet cakes, and we hugged each other every time we met.

CHAPTER TWENTY-TWO

I saw Millard not too long ago, actually in late 2018. Shane had telephoned him and said, "We're taking Mama out to the Varsity to eat, and she wants to come see you." Millard lived and worked in Atlanta, where the Varsity, famous for its hamburgers and chili dogs, is located. When I saw him, I grabbed and hugged him. He hugged me back. Anyone who saw us could tell he and I care a great deal for each other. And for good reason. Our relationship was one of mutual admiration.

Millard said he loved people who stand by somebody in trouble. Many people in prison don't have anybody caring for them, so Millard's office always takes them a holiday package at Christmastime. Bill told Millard to give his package to somebody else. He didn't need it. He knew he had people on the outside who cared about him and came to see him.

While Bill said he believed in the death penalty, Millard obviously does not. He is known nationwide as the lawyer to call if you or your loved one is facing the death penalty. He has fought against the death penalty since the 1960s and has represented several defendants *pro bono*—free of charge—simply because he feels strongly that capital punishment is wrong.

"I don't interrogate people when they call and ask for something," he said in a telephone conversation. "If it's something I can deal with, I take the case."

Fortunately, he took Bill's case.

"When I go in to represent somebody and they're on death row and about to be executed," he said, "I don't care if they kissed their mama goodnight or not, you know what I mean. What I look for is who is the human being in terms of the law. What does the law say his problem with them is, and then I start addressing (that). And later on, I learn about something else."

One reason he doesn't interrogate people on death row is because in some cases he has little time to read details of a case before it is heard. He may have a day, sometimes only an hour, to figure out his arguments.

"I care for everybody," he said. "My duty is to heal that person's problem with being executed."

Millard Farmer's name and reputation reached all the way to New Orleans, where a nun, Sister Helen Prejean, was the spiritual advisor for a man on death row. Her story became a best-selling book, *Dead Man Walking*, and a movie in 1995 by the same name.

"I didn't know anything about the law," Sister Helen said in a telephone interview from New Orleans. "Somebody told me, 'Look, there's this Millard Farmer in Atlanta that tries to help death row inmates. Call him.'"

She called him. "So he came in," she said, "and I hit him (with questions) like a fire hose. . . . He was overworked, but he said he would go to any length to try to help people."

Millard and his associate would drive from Atlanta to New Orleans, pick up Sister Helen, then drive to Louisiana State Penitentiary in Saint Francisville, two hours away, to talk to Elmo Patrick Sonnier, who faced the death penalty after being convicted of killing a teenage couple.

"He did everything he could to save this man's life," Sister Helen said. "He was never paid a dime. He did this because he cared about people; he cared about the issues. He was my lawyer hero in *Dead Man Walking*. He would teach me things. . . . I didn't understand how the court system worked. He would explain things to me: how during a trial if the lawyer didn't raise a proper objection, you know, for the record, and it wouldn't be in the transcript. I had no idea how that worked."

You need a lawyer to protect a person's constitutional rights, she said. And Millard went all out. Before Sonnier was executed, Millard approached then-Governor Edwin Edwards during a cocktail party—at some event at the governor's mansion. He slipped into the mansion to try to persuade the governor to give him and Sister Helen more time to present their appeal.

He was not successful. Millard and Sister Helen witnessed Sonnier's execution together. "He held my hand, and we watched

CHAPTER TWENTY-TWO

this man be killed," she said. Later, she got involved in two other death-penalty cases because of Millard Farmer. "I tried to protect myself by saying I wasn't going back," she said. "But here was this man (Millard) going back."

Sister Helen got to know district attorneys prosecuting cases. She took Millard's advice. "He said, 'Sometimes you got to go fishing with them or go duck hunting, you know what I mean.' He always said, 'You know what I mean.'"

She telephoned Millard in September of 2017 to ask him to come to New Orleans to see the premiere of a documentary of the *Dead Man Walking* case. He went. "He has never, never, never, never questioned the money," she said. "He did what he did because he's so committed to it."

Now there's an opera based on *Dead Man Walking*. Said Sister Helen, "You don't have operas about real people who did real things. You know Madam Butterfly—she kicked the bucket. All of them have kicked the bucket. But *Dead Man Walking* is different."

Millard Farmer believed Bill Birt was a different man after spending years in prison. "You talk about being rehabilitated or redeemed or whatever that word is for people who change their life entirely—he is a person who changed his life," Millard said.

So what did he have to say about Bill Birt's case? Did he get a fair trial in Louisville, Georgia? Were Bill's constitutional rights violated? Millard's first complaint was about helicopters flying over the scene of the trial and law officers everywhere on the ground. "What we are saying is, how can anybody receive a fair trial under those conditions? . . . He must be a dangerous killer. That may have been true at one time, but it had nothing to do with what he was being tried on. . . . We were opposed to anybody being treated like Billy was treated, as far as the trial goes."

As I said earlier, I didn't really question why security for the arraignment and trial was so heavy. Law and court officials were afraid one of Bill's buddies would try to swoop in and set him free. But I didn't argue with Millard.

Finally, although Bill's conviction was upheld, his death sentences were vacated and a resentencing hearing was to have been held. That hearing never came about. And in early 1997, Bill was taken off death row. Bobby Gene Gaddis was taken off death row, too, leaving space for other convicts facing execution. We believe Earl Lee had something to do with Bill's being transferred to "general population," where inmates have more freedom.

Not everybody in the region agreed with the decision not to execute Bill.

"Billy Sunday Birt may have been the worst murderer in Georgia history," Rick Malone, district attorney in the Middle Judicial District, was quoted at the time.

Mark Williamson of the Jefferson County Sheriff's Office, who investigated the Fleming murders, described Bill as "mean," adding, "I'd have volunteered to pull the switch on (him)."

I understand how they feel. What Bill did was unspeakable. I am still haunted by what I know of his murderous actions. Bill and his partners murdered two innocent people in Wrens, Georgia, people who deserved to live out their final years in peace. Bill stole that right from them. And he murdered many others.

Millard knew that a lot of people were angry that he would represent people like Bill. I can understand that, too. But here is what Millard Farmer believes: Every life is worth something. Yes, goodness is hard to find in some people. But what is accomplished by taking another life?

As I said, Bill Birt himself said he deserved the death penalty. One day, several years after his imprisonment in 1974, he wrote a letter to the editor of *The Winder News,* estimating how much state and federal governments had to spend just to keep him alive.

When a petition was circulated among death row inmates in Georgia, Bill apparently refused to sign it, because the unsigned petition was turned over to me. Millard Farmer, on the other hand, said he should be allowed to live. He *was* allowed to live—live

CHAPTER TWENTY-TWO

without his children and grandchildren for the rest of his life. A life in prison, Bill said, was worse than death.

By the time Bill got off death row, he and I had been divorced for several years. Whether to divorce him is something my best friend, Lynn Walls, and I prayed about every day for a long time. Even though Bill was in prison at the time, I was still afraid of him. Lynn knew that. If Bill heard that I was seeing another man—whether it was true or not—he might well have ordered a hit on me. A lot of people on the outside were indebted to him for some "favor" he'd done for them, and he could make one phone call and get that favor repaid. I was equally afraid of possible retribution from family members of Bill's many victims. The only way they could hurt Bill was to hurt us.

One day, after we prayed, I told Lynn, "I'll do it." I filed for divorce. I had stayed with Bill during the tough years, but now I had to look out for myself and the children.

Ever since I was seventeen years old, it had been prisons and jail, prisons and jail. And just about every time I went to see Bill in prison, he made a joke out of his running around with other women. His jokes weren't funny to me, and I was tired of hearing them.

Bill Birt was a complicated man. He always looked sharp on the outside. When he was a free man, he kept his hair combed perfectly, and he changed clothes every day, sometimes more than once a day. I never saw him dirty—I mean really dirty. He wore washed, starched and ironed clothes when he was with me, and I did all the washing, starching, and ironing. He was five feet, eleven inches tall, dark-haired and good-looking. He was strong as an ox and well-mannered, most of the time. He always smelled of Hai Karate cologne and Vitalis hair tonic.

But inside that good-smelling head of his was a jungle of confusing thoughts about a lot of things: about right and wrong, about what it means to be a good husband, about getting even with people, about finding gratification in life, about life itself.

Inside that jungle, he apparently could justify doing anything he wanted to do. Everything was about him.

Retired GBI Agent Ronnie Angel said Bill had "a weird sense of justification about him." Unlike some other murderers, he didn't kill people because he enjoyed killing people. He killed them for a reason: to rob them and leave no witnesses behind, because of jealousy over a woman, for getting back at someone who supposedly did him wrong. In his twisted thinking, he could justify every killing.

Murdering somebody is never justified. Bill realized that at the end, I believe. He really was a changed man.

"Blood money won't last," he told Shane during one of his prison visits. You can get a lot of money sometimes after robbing and shooting people, but that's blood money. And blood money always disappears somehow.

I am grateful to a lot of people for helping me and my children survive a tough life. Millard Farmer is one of them. He is one of the people who helped pay for lodging when the kids and I drove to Marion, Illinois, to see Bill.

Millard was a gentleman and a gentle man. I will never forget his kindness to me and my children.

Several months after he was interviewed, on March 20, 2020, Millard Farmer died of a heart attack. He was eighty-five.

Bob Ingram photo of Durham home at Christmastime 2020.

Sheriff Len Hagaman.

Billy Wayne Davis.

CHAPTER TWENTY-THREE

One night in early spring of 2019, Shane Birt and his wife were watching the movie *Bull Durham* on television. It's a 1988 romantic comedy about a veteran baseball player, Crash Davis, played by Kevin Costner, who was hired to mentor a rookie pitcher for the Durham Bulls, a minor-league team in Durham, North Carolina.

Durham, Shane thought to himself as he sat and watched the movie. *Durham . . . that name.*

He was remembering a conversation from more than three decades ago, a conversation with his father, Billy Sunday Birt. And it had nothing to do with baseball or romance or humor.

It was about a murder. Actually, three murders.

"The way the story came about was, Daddy was telling me about a snowstorm," Shane said later. "He almost got trapped . . . ."

Besides "snowstorm," his dad also used the word "Durham" in his conversation. He mentioned "the mountains." And a "four-wheel drive car." And, finally, "Boone."

"I remember like it was yesterday," Shane said. "Daddy said, 'Boone, do you understand? Boone, like in Daniel Boone.'" His father often asked his listeners, "Do you understand?" because of his speech problem.

Actually, Boone, the city, is named for Daniel Boone, one of America's most famous pioneers, the rugged frontiersman who explored the area before this budding nation fought itself loose from British control.

The triple murder happened in North Carolina decades ago, and all these years—from the time he was a teenager until the spring of 2019—Shane thought his father was referring to Durham, North Carolina.

But then, watching the movie, it came to him: His daddy was not talking about the city Durham. He was talking about the last name of the victims: Durham.

The word "Boone" meant nothing to Shane back then. He was sixteen or seventeen years old, old enough to drive—but never to Boone, North Carolina, a city that sits atop the beautiful Appalachian Mountains. Shane had never heard of Boone. He didn't even know it was a city.

So his daddy talked about these murders, and to Shane's surprise, he named the people involved—the names of the killers.

"Why Daddy gave me names of everybody, I don't know," Shane said. "Because it was real, real rare for him to give me everything like that."

Shane had already met with Bob Ingram, chief deputy of the White County Sheriff's Office and former GBI agent who investigated the double murder of the Fleming couple in Wrens, Georgia, at Christmastime in 1973. At that meeting on April 30, 2019, they talked about a report in which ATF agent Jim Earl West described numerous murders Bill Birt was thought to have committed.

Now, with pieces of a decades-old conversation swimming around in his memory, Shane wanted to meet with Ingram again.

So on May 17, 2019, Shane sat down with Ingram again and told him everything he remembered from his father's story of the night a fierce snowstorm in the mountains almost trapped him and his partners. Then, the next day, a Google search brought up a 2012 newspaper article in the *Winston-Salem Journal* that recapped the cold case on the fortieth anniversary of the murders. It presented details of that night that matched Shane's bits and pieces, fitting perfectly, like a jigsaw puzzle.

CHAPTER TWENTY-THREE

Shortly after talking to Shane, Ingram sent a copy of the interview to North Carolina authorities.

Len "L.D." Hagaman Jr. was serving in the Army in 1972 when he read in his hometown newspaper that three people had been brutally murdered inside their home just outside the city limits of Boone, county seat of Watauga.

On the morning of October 22, 2020, Hagaman, sheriff of Watauga County since 2006, sat at a table in his office and recalled from numerous reports what happened the night of February 3, 1972. A 64-quart plastic storage box filled with documents, evidence, and photographs—all dealing with the triple murder—rested on the table.

"I've got another box of stuff, too," the sheriff told author Phil Hudgins.

"It was a big deal (in the local newspaper)," he said, "because, number one, there weren't that many homicides back then, and number two, it was unusual to have a triple homicide."

Shane's father had told him that two men and a woman were killed that night. "If anybody ever said that Daddy said he killed a grandmother or grandfather or a man and his wife, they're lying," Shane said. "He would never say, 'The people I killed was a husband and a wife.' No. He would say a man and woman or two men and a woman."

But two of the Boone victims, Bryce Durham, fifty-one, and Virginia, forty-four, were definitely husband and wife. The third victim was their eighteen-year-old son, Bobby Joe, a freshman at Appalachian State University who was living at home.

The Durhams had moved to Boone about eighteen months earlier. Bryce, a native of nearby Wilkes County, had been in the car loan business and always wanted his own auto dealership. He found it in Boone, where he purchased the Modern Buick-Pontiac dealership.

It snowed heavily in Boone that Thursday night, February 3, 1972. It had started about three o'clock in the afternoon, and by nine o'clock, at least three inches of snow and a thin layer of ice had covered roadways. Temperatures fell as time passed. Winds gusted up to forty miles per hour.

Despite the blizzard and treacherous road conditions, Bryce Durham decided to go ahead and attend a meeting of the local Rotary Club at Appalachian Ski Mountain in Blowing Rock, about seven miles away. Only a handful of Rotarians were there because of the weather, but Durham, a Navy veteran of World War II, was determined, even as the snowstorm intensified, to support a detachment of Green Berets who were to demonstrate their military ski training. The demonstration was canceled because of the snowstorm.

But Rotarians did receive samples of K- or C-Rations, canned combat foods once used in the military, to take home with them.

Durham left Blowing Rock at about 8:15 and drove to the dealership on Boone's East King Street. A fellow Rotarian followed in his car, possibly to offer help if needed.

Virginia Durham was working late on bookkeeping at the dealership, Hagaman said, and the son was to meet her there.

Once he arrived at his business, Bryce, concerned about his family's safety, asked an employee to gas up a four-wheel-drive GMC Jimmy that had just arrived on the lot. The three Durhams then headed home, located on Clyde Townsend Road at the end of a steep hill off North Carolina 105 bypass, about a mile from the sheriff's office downtown. They were spotted motoring up the icy hill at about 9 o'clock.

Once inside their home, Virginia left her boots and Bobby Joe his shoes at the front door; Bryce apparently went to the master bedroom upstairs, where his overcoat was found, and slipped off his rubber overshoes, worn for the snowy weather. The three of them had started eating a snack—apparently including C-Rations—and watching television in their den. On the kitchen table was a partially eaten baked chicken.

CHAPTER TWENTY-THREE

The Durhams' daughter, Ginny Sue Durham Hall, and her husband, Troy Hall, lived in a mobile home about four miles away, behind what is now Walmart. Troy told authorities he had been at Appalachian State University's library studying for hours and arrived home about 10:00 that night. The Halls said they watched the Winter Olympics from Sapporo, Japan, until their television went on the fritz. Then they put a record on their stereo and were listening to music when a phone call came in at about 10:15, according to Troy.

Troy answered. "Is that you, Virginia?" he allegedly said. Virginia Durham was practically whispering, Troy told his wife; he could barely hear her. His mother-in-law said three Blacks were in the house. Troy said he thought at first it might be a practical joke.

"The *n*-words are attacking" Bryce and Bobby Joe in another room, Hagaman said, paraphrasing Hall's message to his wife and cleaning up his racist language. The phone went dead, and Hall said he tried to call back. The line was busy.

Troy and Ginny left their home immediately, and Troy tried to get his car started. It would not crank, he said. They had befriended Cecil Small, a neighbor two trailers down and manager of the mobile home park, called Greenway Village. Small, a private investigator, agreed to drive the couple to the Durham home.

The three arrived at the home, and Small parked at the bottom of the hill, which was slick with ice and snow. Ginny Hall stayed in the car while her husband and Small trudged up the slippery hill to the split-level house.

"The garage door on the house was up just a little bit," Hagaman said. "That's how they (the killers) got inside the house," through the garage, which had a door connecting the den.

"They (Hall and Small) went into the house and saw what was going on. From there, it turned into an investigation."

Asked what the men saw once inside, the sheriff dug through his box of documents and brought out a binder filled with eight-by-ten photographs taken by a free-lancer: photos of the living room, the den, the bedroom, and other rooms ransacked, papers and other objects all over the floors. Drawers had been pulled out and their contents dumped on the floor, spreads pulled from beds, pictures from walls. Snacks were found half-eaten in the den. A telephone cord had been ripped from the wall in the kitchen. The lights were on. The television was on.

Hall and Small said they heard water running in the bathroom, the sheriff said. They went to investigate.

Afterward, they hurried outside and down the hill, but Small's car was stuck in the snow. They walked to a neighbor's house and telephoned the Watauga County Sheriff's Office, whose calls at the time were received by the Boone Police Department. Dispatcher Johnny Tester, son of Police Chief Clyde Tester, answered. It's an emergency, he was told. Send investigators.

Strangely, there was no mention of anyone telephoning the law earlier, after Virginia Durham allegedly whispered her plea for help.

Officers found three fully clothed bodies—those of Baxter Bryce Durham, Virginia Church Durham, and Bobby Joe Durham—crammed together side by side over the lip of a bathtub, their heads bent down in water. Their hands had been bound. Water still flowed from the faucet. The tub was full. The overflow drain kept water from spilling onto the floor. In fact, there was no water at all on the bathroom floor, indicating to investigators that there was little struggle, little chance to struggle, before the three were murdered.

The blizzard roared outside as three people died violently and mercilessly inside. If there were screams, apparently nobody heard them.

A ligature—described as a nylon sash cord—was tied loosely around Bryce's neck. Autopsies showed that he and Bobby Joe had water inside their bodies, indicating they were still alive when their heads were pushed down into the tub of water. They also

CHAPTER TWENTY-THREE

had been strangled. So had been Virginia Durham, but her lungs were dry. All of them had rope burns on their necks. "They obviously used the same ligature for all three deaths," Hagaman said. Bryce had been struck on the head with a blunt instrument; Virginia's nose was bloodied. Blood was found on the shag carpet in the den.

It would have taken three, four, maybe more men to subdue the Durham men, investigators surmised. Bryce Durham weighed about 190 pounds. His son was a strong, athletic teenager—an Eagle Scout—who played football in high school.

Highway patrolmen found the GMC Jimmy stuck in a ditch and abandoned about two miles away on Poplar Grove Road. The car's lights were on, the engine was running, windshield wipers were flapping. The patrolmen got out to make sure nobody was hurt.

"There was silver service (inside a pillow case) in the vehicle," Hagaman said. "They didn't pay that much attention and then moved on to the crime scene" at the Durham home.

One of the first investigators on the scene was the late Wallace Hardwick, an agent with the North Carolina State Bureau of Investigation (SBI). Over time, about two hundred people would walk through the crime scene, looking for something, anything, that would lead to the killers.

"The crime scene was a disaster," Hagaman said. "The receiver for a wall phone was hanging down, but a deputy hung it up.... He thought it was in the way, so he picked it up and put it on the hook." A hole, apparently from a gunshot, was found in the wall near the phone.

Silver plates were thought to be the only things of real value missing, although the victims' wallets apparently had been emptied. "Supposedly," Hagaman said, "there was thirty-five thousand dollars cash—a lot of money back then—but that was just a rumor. We never found that." But a bag containing the dealership's daily receipts lay in plain sight on a dining room chair.

A few weeks after the crime, four men—all white—were arrested, held and questioned. They were finally released for lack of evidence. "It was just jailhouse talk," the sheriff said. Somebody was "trying to get out of something (a crime), trying to make a deal. There wasn't much to that."

Rufus Edmisten, a native of Boone, took special interest in the case and was in a position to do something about it. He had served for ten years on the Washington staff of North Carolina Senator Sam Ervin, eventually becoming deputy chief counsel for the Senate Watergate Committee and serving the original subpoena for President Richard Nixon's Oval Office tapes.

He returned to North Carolina in 1974 and was elected the state's attorney general, and sometime afterward, formed a special squad of agents to investigate the triple murder.

The case was troubling to Edmisten—and everybody else who knew about it or investigated it. But no good leads were ever found, although one agent said he worked on the case for eight months.

The Watauga County Sheriff's Office, the State Bureau of Investigation, and the FBI have run numerous checks for fingerprints. They sent the ligature to an agency that has equipment capable of extracting DNA from objects that had been submerged. "No luck," Hagaman said.

Other fingerprints were found inside the home, but none from the killers, who no doubt were wearing gloves. Most of the prints were from the scores of investigators who combed the crime scene.

The Watauga County Sheriff's Office reopened the case several years ago, and since then, off and on, officers have gone through the boxes of documents and photos, looking for clues. Hagaman started looking into the murders in the 1970s, back when he was a Boone city policeman.

The murder scene had the appearance of a robbery/burglary, but some officers speculated the rummaging was staged. "That was one of the theories," Bob Ingram said, "but I believe they were looking for money."

CHAPTER TWENTY-THREE

After receiving the videoed interview with Shane in May of 2019, North Carolina authorities discussed the case with Ingram on July 10, 2019, and began making plans to visit Georgia. Making the trip in September of that year were Sheriff Hagaman, Chief Investigator Captain Carolynn Johnson, and Larry Wagner and Wade Colvard, both with the State Bureau of Investigation in North Carolina. Wagner has since retired.

Johnson, who described herself as "an obsessive, compulsive notetaker," furnished the dates and outcomes.

On September 30, 2019, the North Carolina team visited Billy Wayne Davis, who at the time was being held in Georgia Central Prison in Macon, Georgia. Davis was one of the men who showed up in Wrens, Georgia, the night of December 22, 1973, planning to rob Reid and Lois Fleming at their home. When they left Wrens, the Flemings were dead, strangled with coat hangers. Davis, who claimed he was not at the Fleming home, turned state's evidence and was not tried in the case.

The same four men involved in the Wrens case also committed the triple murder in Boone: Billy Wayne Davis, Billy Sunday Birt, Bobby Gene Gaddis and Charlie Reed. That's what his father told Shane more than thirty years ago. Bill Birt implicated himself and those other three men in recalling the night they were almost trapped by a snowstorm.

The North Carolina team, however, didn't get much from Davis, Hagaman and Johnson agreed. Davis was more interested in getting out of prison. "All Billy Wayne talked about was he wanted out, he wanted out," the sheriff said—and he wanted to work out a deal. But no deal was on the table.

The next morning, October 1, 2019, the officers met with Stoney Birt in Winder. Stoney may not have known about the Boone killings, and if he did, Johnson said, he didn't reveal anything. "He seemed to idolize his father," she said.

On their third interview, held the afternoon of October 1, they talked to Deborah Westor, whose son at one time had shared a prison cell with Davis. She had talked to Davis by phone, but "she didn't want to ask him anything at the risk of upsetting him," Johnson said. "She knew from her son that Davis was a very dangerous man in prison." If Davis needed something done on the outside, she tried to help.

The interview revealed nothing useful, Johnson said.

A year later, on October 21, 2020—coincidentally the day before the meeting in Boone with Hagaman, Johnson, and Hudgins—Bob Ingram drove three hours to Augusta, Georgia, where Billy Wayne Davis had been transferred. Because of his age—he was seventy-nine—and possible health reasons, he had gone from the prison in Macon to Augusta State Medical Prison. Ingram's goal: to see if Davis would corroborate Shane's account from his father about the Boone murders.

"I'm not surprised that Davis didn't want to talk to the North Carolina authorities," Shane said. "He didn't want to talk to any strangers. A couple of other men went down to talk to Davis about another murder case, and he didn't tell them anything. Davis knew Bob Ingram, and he respected him, even though Ingram is the one who helped send him to prison. Ingram was in a much better position to get Davis to talk."

Ingram, in fact, knew Davis well. He had arranged for him to receive immunity from prosecution in exchange for his returning state's evidence in the Fleming murders. Billy Sunday Birt, Bobby Gene Gaddis and Charlie Reed were found guilty in that case.

CHAPTER TWENTY-THREE

Ingram got to know Davis even better during his trial on ordering a hit on Mack Sibley in 1971. Angered that Davis had testified against him twice—on a bank robbery in Loganville, Georgia, and on the Fleming murders—Birt was easily persuaded to testify in 1976 that Davis ordered the hit on Sibley, who was demanding Davis pay off a gambling debt owed him. Davis was found guilty and sentenced to life in prison.

"Davis is still clever," Ingram said. "He's not as clever as he was, but he's still got it. He has his mental faculties. . . . The only thing he takes (as medicine) is protein." Davis is in charge of the recreational center in the Augusta prison and claims he usually walks three hours a day to stay in shape.

"He may outlive us all," Ingram said.

Recording the interview inside the prison, Ingram began by reminding Davis of what happened in Wrens, Georgia, forty-eight years ago. They talked about Bill Birt.

"Billy Birt was the meanest man I've ever dealt with," Ingram said.

"Me too," Davis said in his deep, gravelly voice.

"I know he would have killed me," Davis said later. Birt also talked about wanting to kill Gaddis at one time because he knew too much, both men agreed.

"You two (Birt and Davis) together were really dangerous," Ingram said.

Davis agreed.

"He (Davis) told me he wasn't as mean as he once was, but he's still mean," Ingram said. "You can see the evil in his eyes. He's been in prison forty-six years, and he's still functioning. . . . He would kill me in a heartbeat if he had an opportunity. I never underestimated these people."

Prompted by his interviewer, Davis began recalling what happened in Wrens at Christmastime in 1973. He talked of other crimes. Twenty-one minutes into the interview, Ingram asked about the Boone case. "The cases (Wrens and Boone) are almost identical," Ingram said. They're like bookends.

In each case, it was Birt, Davis, Gaddis and Reed. In each case, there was no forced entry into the home. In each case, the victims were tied up, tortured and then strangled to death. In each case, the homes were ransacked. In each case, one of the victims was a car dealer. In each case, the driver apparently left three of the men at the house and then drove to a predesignated location. In each case, the killers stole the victims' car to return to their vehicle a mile or two away.

With some prompting, Davis indicated he remembered what happened in Boone. He claimed he was the driver both times—in Wrens and Boone—and did not enter the homes. But then, when shown a photo of Bryce Durham from the Boone case, Davis said he remembered the man's face. How could he remember Durham's face if he stayed in the car?

Davis said he was driving a late-model Chevrolet with a slanted trunk.

"Two-wheel or four-wheel?" Ingram asked.

"Two-wheel," Davis said.

"You were lucky to get out" and back home driving a two-wheel-drive car in deep snow, Ingram said.

"Do you regret what happened to those people?" Ingram asked.

"Oh, Lord, yes," Davis replied.

Twice, Ingram showed Davis photos of the three Durhams, and each time Davis said, almost inaudibly, "What a waste."

Asked how much money he and his partners got in Boone, Davis said "a wad of it," but he didn't know the amount. Authorities, however, have not been able to determine that a large amount of money was taken. The most valuable pieces missing were the family's silver service, they said.

Ingram said when he asked who ordered the hit, "Davis laid it off on Birt, said Birt got the information probably from a family member, but he didn't know who."

Ingram believes, however, that Davis "was the one who got the information."

CHAPTER TWENTY-THREE

Asked about the hereafter, Davis said he had made peace with God, but, Ingram interjected, "You've got some confessing to do."

"Too much," Davis said.

Davis's one desire before he dies is to get out of prison. "My mother would love to see me before I die," he said.

He had been before the parole board several times, but parole was denied each time.

Ingram told Davis he'd be happy to tell the parole board that he cooperated in the interview. "Do you want me to do that?" he asked.

Finally, Davis, a desperate man who had been in prison for more than four decades, said yes, tell the parole board.

"Anything you want to ask me?" Ingram said at the end of the interview.

"Yes," Davis said, "when are we going home?"

On November 16, 2020, Sheriff Hagaman and Captain Johnson drove to Cleveland, Georgia, to meet again with Bob Ingram. Shane joined them at the White County Sheriff's Office. Shane said he told them the same story he told Ingram months earlier, the story of how his father and three other men almost got trapped by a fierce snowstorm in Boone. Shane gave the North Carolina authorities a piece of silver service found in his parents' Barrow County home, silver that Shane thought might have been stolen from the Durhams.

The next day, November 17, Hagaman, Johnson, and Ingram drove to Augusta for another interview with Billy Wayne Davis. Johnson later recalled details of that interview:

Again, Davis remembered the snowstorm. Again, he claimed he was the driver and that he had dropped off the other three men at the Durham home and drove to a predesignated meeting place to await the other three. "What we need to determine," Johnson said, "was whether he indeed put them out and stayed in the car or if he was part of it." Davis, a used car dealer, said he usually furnished the car on the gang's criminal activities out of town.

Sheriff Hagaman asked Davis:

Have you ever been to Boone? Davis said yes, several times.

Do you remember seeing a church that's visible from the Durhams' home? Davis said yes.

That was an important question, Ingram said. "That put him at the scene of the crime."

As he said in the prison interview with Ingram on October 21, 2020, Davis said the men did get some money, but he didn't know how much. "Davis said he thought Birt took a bigger chunk (of the money) for himself," Johnson said. "Davis didn't know how much, so Birt didn't have to split it even."

But Shane said his father told him there was little of value to steal in the home. "He told me he would have killed the one who set this up" if he could have returned to Boone, Shane said. But heat from authorities was too high in town following the murders. He couldn't risk being arrested or shot.

Davis told authorities the crime was "set up, but he couldn't remember who set it up," Johnson said. In the first interview with Ingram alone, Davis said he thought a family member set it up.

Johnson said Davis "also didn't remember if it was just to kill them or to get money," but that money was important in "any job."

A number of theories about why the Durhams were killed emerged and disappeared over the years. One was that the group of Green Berets training in the area was involved, judging from the type of knots used on the ropes. That theory was bogus. An SBI agent theorized that Bryce Durham had information about illegal odometer rollbacks and was killed to keep him quiet. Nothing there.

The late Ward Carroll, Watauga County sheriff at the time of the murders, told newspaper reporters it could have been a grudge killing.

CHAPTER TWENTY-THREE

After the Boone Area Crime Stoppers offered a forty thousand dollars reward to whoever provided information leading to the arrest of the killer or killers, some investigators thought solving the case was close. Surely someone would come through with good information. No one did.

A woman supposedly was seen driving a car that looked like the Durhams' near the crime scene shortly after the murders. Nothing turned up.

Back in Boone following the November 17, 2020, interview with Davis, Johnson joined with SBI Agent Wade Colvard and visited Ginny, the Durhams' daughter, to see if she recognized the piece of silver service Shane had given her to check out. Ginny and her husband, Troy Hall, divorced in 1976. Ginny remarried and moved with her husband to Washington state. But the couple eventually moved back to North Carolina, this time to Mt. Airy, and Johnson and Colvard visited Ginny there.

Ginny, who had retired from teaching school, told Johnson the silver service did not match hers, but her parents often received silver in awards and contests connected with their car business. "So there would have been different silver patterns coming and going," Johnson quoted Ginny.

North Carolina authorities had met earlier with Bill Durham, the victim Bryce's brother, "to help us with details like family dynamics," Johnson said. For example, what did the Durham couple think about Troy Hall? Turned out, as the officers suspected, the family didn't like him and didn't want Ginny to marry him.

"The family wasn't a big fan of Troy," Johnson said. "At one point, she (Ginny) thought things were better between them (Troy and the Durham family). They gradually put up with each other."

Troy Hall was a brilliant man, Sheriff Hagaman said. He skipped grades in elementary school, a classmate told the sheriff,

269

and completed school early. He attended law school, passed the bar exam and became a lawyer. He was sharp.

But he was a suspect.

Officers in North Carolina and Georgia—in fact, several who worked on the Durham case—agreed Troy's story was suspicious. Did he order the crime? Remember, he had told his wife and authorities about a phone call he received from Virginia Durham, his mother-in-law, at about 10:15 on the night of the murders. Her voice was barely audible. Three Black men are attacking Bryce and Bobby Joe, she had said in almost a whisper, according to Troy.

Now we know none of the murderers were Black.

Did Troy actually receive a phone call that night?

If he did, Sheriff Hagaman said, it was probably a message that "it's done." The call would not have come from his mother-in-law, he indicated.

No killers are going to let someone make a phone call, Ingram said. The first thing they do upon entering a house is disable the phones.

Wade Carroll told the *Winston-Salem Journal* in 1982 that he did not believe the phone call ever happened.

Even if Virginia Durham did get a chance to make a call, why not telephone the sheriff's office or any law enforcement agency? Why call Troy and Ginny, who lived several miles away? If Troy did receive a call from Virginia, did he not think of telephoning law enforcement rather than driving almost-impassable, icy roads to the Durham home?

Many questions have hung in the air, unanswered, since 1972.

"I think from day one, he (Troy) has been involved, whether directly or indirectly, I don't know," Hagaman said.

After Ginny and Troy were divorced, Troy moved to Gwinnett County, Georgia, next door to Barrow County, and started a construction company. And, according to Ginny, he used part of the money received from the Durhams' life insurance policy to finance it. Ginny said she was entitled to a fair share of between

CHAPTER TWENTY-THREE

fifty thousand and fifty-five thousand dollars from the insurance, but she received very little. "Troy took charge of the money from the family. She said she barely had enough money for college fees (at Appalachian State)," the captain said.

"She was mad," Johnson said, "because he took most of her portion of it. He used some of the money to fix up his sister's house."

After Troy started his construction business, Ginny said, he defaulted on a loan. "And so at that point, she gained access to the money, and that's how she was able to pay off her school," Johnson said.

The late Carroll Gardner, a lawyer in Surry County, confirmed to the SBI that Ginny Sue and Troy received all the proceeds from the Durham estate, which included the sale of the Durhams' automobile dealership. That information came from retired SBI agent Larry Wagner, Sheriff Hagaman said.

Settled in Georgia, Troy started a training program for people arrested for driving under the influence, and "worked for Gwinnett County's DA's office for a while," Hagaman said, "but when the DA found out Troy was on somebody's radar screen, he basically cut him loose."

Law officers from different agencies have interviewed Ginny off and on for years. They would show up at the school where she was teaching, at her home, or wherever. Sheriff Hagaman said he had harassed her so much over the years, she refuses to talk to him.

But Johnson said she thought Ginny was innocent. "After talking with her," she said, "I don't feel like she had any part with Troy. . . . I think she was absolutely scared of Troy."

By the way, Bob Ingram said he would keep his promise to Davis to write a letter to the parole board about his cooperation, furnishing information in the Durham case. He would also tell the board that Davis admitted to being involved in a triple murder in 1972.

On August 3, 2021, Len Hagaman and Carolynn Johnson drove to Georgia in separate cars to meet one more time with Davis, still imprisoned in Augusta. Bob Ingram joined them. North Carolina authorities had hoped to present a lineup of several photographs, including one of Troy Hall, but a suitable photo of Hall had not been located. They wanted to see if Davis would recognize Hall, nearly fifty years following the murders. Ingram said he believed it was Davis who set up the hit.

On this trip, however, Davis provided no new information about the killings. In fact, he attempted to walk back his earlier confession, Ingram said, saying he was not there on the night of February 3, 1972. He was his old self again: defiant, surly, uncooperative.

Another confession or not, the cat was already out of the bag. Davis had confessed during two separate interviews.

"I have no doubt Davis was there that night," along with Bill Birt, Charlie Reed, and Bobby Gene Gaddis, Ingram said. Questioned by Hagaman, Davis even remembered the church and its steeple visible from the Durham house.

About two and a half months after the Durham murders, on April 22, 1972, Bill Birt visited the photo studio of Pierson Stell in Winder to pose for portraits, according to information in Myles Godfrey's book, *Barrow County: Photographs from the Stell-Kilgore Collection*. Bill liked being photographed. He always did.

Over the years, the Durham case birthed numerous podcasts, detective magazine and newspaper articles, and even books. Rufus Edmisten, one of North Carolina's most colorful storytellers, wrote of the case in his memoir, *That's Rufus*, which featured stories of Tar Heel politics and his public life. He told this story:

One day, after being elected state attorney general, he received a call from Collie Durham of Wilkesboro, mother of Bryce Durham.

CHAPTER TWENTY-THREE

"Mr. Edmisten," she said, "I know you're a good man. I wonder if you would help us try to find out who did this? I just want to know the answer before I die."

Edmisten routinely flew to Wilkesboro on his way to Boone, and the parents—Coy and Collie Crabb Durham—sometimes would meet him at the airport to hear the latest about the case.

"I learned that the investigation had turned up nothing substantial and hence had kind of fizzled out," Edmisten wrote in his memoir. "I created a new squad (in 1982) just for this case and authorized resources for the SBI to work on the case. I had strategy sessions with the sheriff, met with the chief of police, and assigned SBI Agent Charlie Whitfield to help with the case."

Edmisten said he spent more time on the Durham case than any other.

As long and hard as he and others worked with local and state authorities, the renewed investigation turned up nothing concrete. Even a psychic detective was brought in at one point, Hagaman said, but the murders remained a mystery.

"I truly regret that I was not able to fulfill Mrs. Coy Durham's dying wish and solve this mystery," Edmisten wrote. "To this day, the people of Boone remember the Durham murders."

Tim Bullard, who took photos at the crime scene, wrote two books, one of which dealt solely with the murders. It is titled *The Durham Murders*, a detailed account of what happened that terrible night during a fierce snowstorm in Boone. The book is not an easy, pleasant read. It often uses medical terminology, even in explaining what happens to a person being strangled.

Bullard's other book is titled *Haunted Watauga County*—about so-called spirits of Watauga County people long passed, including the Durhams in their home.

The oddest side story came from Sheriff Hagaman, who suggested a Google search on the name Cecil Small, manager of the mobile home park who drove Troy and Ginny Hall to the Durhams' home the night of the murders.

The Internet search revealed that Small, now deceased, claimed to have offered a ride to a neatly dressed man with a poorly concealed rifle with scope after Small lost his way in front of the Book Depository in Dallas, Texas, on November 22, 1963, the day President John Kennedy was assassinated.

The man's name, Small insisted, was Lee Harvey Oswald, the suspected assassin.

Apparently, the FBI did not take Small's story seriously, because his name could not be found in documents concerning the Kennedy assassination.

So now the long, sad story of the Durham murders—once thought to be an eternal mystery—has just about come to an end, fifty years, as of February 3, 2022, after it began during a howling snowstorm.

But at least one more interview was needed. Troy Hall, the "person of interest," as North Carolina authorities called him, should be questioned again, now that officers had new information. But Troy was hard to find, Captain Johnson said. He apparently had changed his name, had started using his first name. He went from Troy Hall to Justin Hall—Justin T. Hall.

That's how his obituary was listed by a funeral home in Duluth, Georgia, discovered by North Carolina authorities in early 2021.

Justin T. Hall passed away on December 19, 2019, at the age of 68, the obituary said.

He died from natural causes.

"Justin was born on November 8, 1951, in North Wilkesboro, North Carolina, to Robert and Carrie Waddell Hall," the obituary said. "He received his law degree and practiced law for over 30 years...."

CHAPTER TWENTY-THREE

Bryce, Virginia, and Bobby Joe Durham had been described as quiet, reserved, hardworking people who thought they had found a bright future in Watauga County, North Carolina, a pretty, normally peaceful, pristine setting in the Appalachian Mountains.

Bryce and Virginia were building their business at the Modern Buick-Pontiac dealership. Bobby Joe, a freshman at Appalachian State University, was determined to finish college in three years.

But, on the snow-ravaged night of February 3, 1972, evil crept under a garage door, made its way into their home and annihilated all their hopes and dreams.

All for perhaps a fistful of dollars and a few pieces of silver.

In the spring of 2021, Sheriff Len Hagaman and Captain Carolynn Johnson were planning their third trip to Georgia to interview Billy Wayne Davis. But on April 28, 2021, two of the department's deputies — Logan Fox and Chris Ward — were fatally shot while making a welfare check in a Watauga County home. The shooter, Alton Barnes, also killed his mother, Michelle Annette Ligon, and stepfather, George Wyatt Ligon. The Georgia trip understandably was put on hold until August 3rd.

"My world has been turned upside-down," Johnson said in an email. 'These two deputies, Hagaman said at a memorial service, were heroes,' and he promised to be there for their families in the years to come.

Shane and Robert Polite.

CHAPTER TWENTY-FOUR

Sometimes Bill seemed to have a short memory, or perhaps or he was just trying to convince himself that he was a reasonably good guy before he went to prison. In one letter to me from prison, he portrayed himself as pure as the driven snow.

He began the letter, dated January 11, 1999, by complaining about the doctors not giving him medicine for pain in his mouth, his left foot, his neck, his back, and his right leg. And then he wrote:

> "... I don't know what wrong with my neck can't turn my head but four ways and my head got where it feel real funny in side all the time. Like I'm going crazy. But I know I got plenty of sense left for I go around talking to my self all the times and I keep having bad dreams about dead folks and I really don't know why. I can't remember of ever doing any thing wrong to any one. And as far as I can remember I was always good to you and the kids and I can't recall of ever cheating on you. And I don't think I ever stole anything from anybody. If I have it sure slip my mind, (that) is if I ever had a mind. Sometimes I feel like there just a big hole up there in my head or what I got left of a head.

"I went to the doctor last week and asked him for a few dope pills but he wouldn't give them to me he said that was what was wrong with me. I have had to many damn dope pills already. Right now my head is busted. Big Dummy has been sitting in this cell for the last five hours reading his Bible to me. He was reading so loud. Now I think I am going deaf for I can't hear nothing out of my right ear and the left one is real weak. But other than that I'm doing okay. My toes still work good. Thank God for that."

Bill also said he thought he was going blind in his left eye. "I got where I can't see nothing out of it. . . ." Bill did not have a left eye. He lost that eye when a fellow inmate stabbed him at the prison in Alto, Georgia. His left eye was artificial.

He ended the letter this way:

"It's getting late and I got to go to bed. But I probably want sleep awink got where I cant sleep at night. I don't remember the last time I got 12 hours of sleep in one night. I dont know what wrong. I used to sleep good every night when I was home with you. All but when you kept me awaked or one of the kids peed all over me. But for the last 25 years I have been having trouble sleeping. Well good night pretty girl. If I have a bad dream tonight I hope you [are] in it. Love always from old true blue. Bill."

I received a bunch of letters from Bill—there's not much to do in prison, you know—but there's one in my stack that baffled me. For one thing, the letter is written in small, neat, cursive words. Bill usually printed. When he did write cursively, however, he wrote in fairly large letters. Obviously, Bill dictated the letter to someone. The other odd thing is that the letter was written to support the re-election of a sheriff, John Robert Austin. This letter was dated Monday, July 21, 1990:

> "Dear John,
>
> "I saw in the paper that you are running for re-election for sheriff. I sure hope you get re-elected because you sure was nice to me and my family while I was up there for court.
>
> "John, if you think it would help you get re-elected, I will come back at the August term of court and plead guilty to Willie Hester. I don't see now it can hurt me anymore, and it would just get another murder off the books for you. There's no body involved but me and Otis, and you know it can't hurt him now, because the boy is in Heaven—where I'm going to be one of these days. Ha Ha.
>
> Well, John, I thought this may help you in getting re-elected. So if you think it would, get the show on the road.
>
> Billy S. Birt

In an undated letter, he said he wanted to make a tablecloth for me, but first he needed the measurements of our table:

> "Montana and Ann promised me four month ago they would snake in your house and measure your table and get the shape of it and mail them to me. But they never did. You know [how] kids are. They forget everything.... I can make any color but blue."

One letter Bill left behind was from the Department of Health, Education, and Welfare department of the Social Security Administration. It informed Bill he was to have a hearing September 12, 1979, on his application to receive disability insurance benefits. Six months earlier, on April 3, 1979, he received a letter from the Georgia Legal Services Programs saying the agency was working on his disability case.

Bill was in Georgia State Prison in Reidsville, Georgia, when his hearing was scheduled.

I don't know whether or not he received the benefits.

Bill was upset when Shane and Jill were divorced. They're back together now, of course, and both of them are godly people. But there for a while, we all were worried about them. Here's some of what Bill said in a letter postmarked January 23, 1991:

> "I have been worried about Shane and Jill, Ruby Nell. They came to see me yesterday. I felt so sorry for both of them. They are two beautiful kids it look like God just made them for each other. They have the world at their feet and just don't know it. Old Satan is doing everything in his power to break them up. He hate to see young kids with a happy marriage because Satan know if he can break up a young couple marriage he has almost got them.
>
> "And I told them that in our talk yesterday Ruby Nell. It's been real funny. They were lock in with me and couldn't get away. I made Montana and Lisa leave. So I just had them to my self. Jill road down with Lisa and Shane came with Montana. [Shane said it was actually Stoney and Norma Jean who took them separately to the prison.] But they had to ride back together. Both of them were mad when they got here. But they left laughing and holeing hands. That made me feel real good. Just maybe it will work out for them and we

CHAPTER TWENTY-FOUR

will end up with some beautiful grandbabies from them two. I can't wait to hold one of their baby in my arms. They promised me they would tried it for one week bact together.

"I made Shane promised me that he would take Jill with him over to Ruth (Chancey) house and move his furniture bact to his house. Today I also made him promised that if him and Jill didn't make it, that he would never move back in one of Ruth houses. And I believe he will keep his word to me. And I also made him promised that he would give up his pool rome job. He don't need two jobs. He has a good job with Rider truck co. make all the money him and Jill need.

"Ruby Nell, if I didn't do nothing else by getting them to come to visits me, I did get him out of Ruth house, and that ment more than anything, for as long as he live over there, him and Jill didn't have a chance of happiness. She has got Shane fool in some way. But befor I let Shane live over there, I will have that house burned and destroyed and I don't believed God would hold it against me. And if he does, well, I will just have to pay for it on Judgement Day.

"I feel really bad for even feeling that way now. But I know what going to happened to him if I can't get him to move out of her house. I don't care where he live if Jill and him can't make a go of their marriage. Just as long as it not over there."

Bill ended his letter with his usual signoff ("Love always from Billy") but then he added a lengthy P.S.:

"Ruby Nell, you remember back when we were just kids like Shane and Jill before we had any kids. One day we were laying in bed and we made a deal with each other about any time I asked you to kiss me, you had to do it. And any time you asked me to kiss you, no matter where we were, or how mad we were at each other, we had to do it. Well, Shane and Jill has got to do that. They give me their word. But both of them give God their word too.

"Jill said, 'Bill, Shane will get me in church and make me kissed him.' I said you thinks God would care if you kiss your husband in his church. He gave you two to each other. God would loved to see all holding hands and steal a kiss in his house. But old Satan sure would hate to see all do it. I couldn't help but laugh at both of them. I sure hope they make it for both of them are real good people, and they look so beautiful together."

After Shane visited his dad by himself one Sunday, Bill wrote his son a six-page letter on legal-size paper. Shane and Jill were still living apart, and Shane was still taking meth. In fact, during one visit with Shane—it could have been this particular visit; the date is not on the letter—Bill didn't recognize his son because he had lost so much weight. "He didn't know me until I got real close to him," Shane recalled later. Bill wrote, in part:

"Hello, my boy,

"Hope you made it back home alright. Shane you don't know how glad I was to see and talk with you. Wish we could have had a little more time to spend together. Sure did hate to see you walk out that door.

CHAPTER TWENTY-FOUR

"Son I've been thinking about you every since you left and it got me worried sick. And there nothing I can do about it. But pray. And ask God to give you the strength and will power to help you see what is happened. Son you are followed right in my footsteps. Did you know I was your age 32 before I took my first pill. I will never forget it. Me and Harold (Chancey) took a load of moonshine to Atlanta to a black night club. Well after we unloaded the man at own the club told Harold that he had some new kind of pills he wanting us to try. At that times nither one of us had every took any kind of dope. The pills was call RJS, Black Beautys. He sold Harold one hundred of them. I took two and Harold took two. Son I would give anything in my power tonight if I hadnt been with Harold that night and I bet Harold has wish a million times in his last 35 years that he wasnt there either. Because that bottle of new pills as the man called them cause me and Harold both to lose our home and family in the end, as I recall the man charged him 50 dollars for the bottle. Didnt know it then. But it sure was expensive stuff. Cost me my family and 30 years in prison and still got life to go. Cost Harold 18 years in prison and him family. You and Bobby Chancey and the rest of our kids grew up without a daddy because of dope. Now I'm not blameing pills for what I did. I blame my self for not having wisdom enough to see what they were doing to me. And my whore tried to tell me how the dope

> was changing me. But I didn't want to listen. The dope had me believing that I was having to much fun. Sunday you reminding me so much of my self when I was your age.... But Shane if you don't come to your senses and get some help it will be to late for you to get your family back.... Shane did you know I was 34 year old before I killed anybody and I was 35 before I robbed my first bank...."

Bill was a little confused about his age. If Bill killed as many people as law officers estimate—the most popular number is "over fifty"—then he couldn't have been thirty-four when he committed his first murder. He went to prison for the last time when he was almost thirty-seven years old. That was in 1974. Bill wrote to Shane:

> "Harold Chancey was one of the best man that I have ever knew. He would help a man in any way he could. Has a heart as big as a mountain, do anything for a friend or anybody else. But Harold was like me. After we started takin pills we didnt know how to handle them. And it that way with everybody. Nobody on earth can handle dope for very long it will get the best of a man every time...."

> "Shane I love you so much. I guess you noticed from our table to the door I hugged and kissed you six times I just wanted to hold you in my arms so I could protect you. Sure wish I could kept you down here with me.... Shane when you walked out of the visiting room today I had this strange feeling

CHAPTER TWENTY-FOUR

that I would never see you again. And I wanting so bad to walk out that door with you so I could have took care of you. Son remember telling me that all the family had turned again you and didnt want you around them. No Shane you are wrong, the family love you just as much as they ever did.... Shane your mama raised you all by her self after I got lock up and you were her lifesaver with the heavy load I left on her with five kids to raise all by her self. She might have lost her mind if it hadnt had been for you for her to love on and to take her mind off all the sorry thing I did. She worked her self to death for all kids and brought all up in a good Christian home believing in God and loving each other and going to church. And now she got to watch helpless while this devil stuff destroyed the one she has love the most. Son she has loved you for 33 years, yes while you were in her stomach.... Son I prayed to God every night before I closed my eyes for him to help you and Jill to get back together.... I asked everyone in our church tonight to be praying for you.... Son it going to be tough. But just remember who died on the cross and dont be ashame to asked him for help. Take care my boy. I'll be praying for you. Love for ever, from Daddy."

Shane has said many times that the daddy he knew and the daddy his siblings knew were two different people. Shane never knew his father on drugs. He never knew him as a criminal, as a murderer. He knew him as a prison inmate sober as a judge. He knew him as a father who warned him not to ever take anything that didn't belong to him. He knew him as a father who preached against drugs, a father who wanted his son to treat his wife like a queen, a father who eventually prayed and read the Bible.

Shane also knew Bill as someone with feelings for others. He wrote me sometime after my mother, Nellie Lee, died. The letter was dated February 18, 1996:

> "Well, Pretty Woman.
>
> "I guess you (are) having it pretty rough about now. I should have done wrote but I wanting to wait til you got over the shock of looseing the best friend you had on this earth. And I know right now is worse time for you because it take about a month to get over the shock. Then you will start to missing her real bad. And it want be easy for a long time. But my wonderful mother-in-law left us some good (memories) of her. So do like I do. When you get to feeling real bad and blue, just set down and think about all the fun we had with her and Mack. Back when we were kids and how good both of them were to us. Most men hate their mother-in-law, but most men didnt have a mother-in-law like Nellie Lee. She was more like a mother to me than a mother-in-law and I probably loved her just as much as you and the rest of her kids did. She was just a beautiful person and I'm going to miss her. . . .

CHAPTER TWENTY-FOUR

> "But I do hope to meet her again and your daddy to. I want to tell them how sorry I am for something I done to them while we were down here on this crazy earth. But your daddy burned my car while we were dateing but I don't blame him now. Mack didnt burned my car to be mean. He burned it to keep me from killing you in the junk. I never could keep brake on that car. Everytime I came over to pick you up your daddy would go to my car and check my brake. Then he would say, Nellie let them drive your car tonight. So I really cant blame him for burning the junk. If you had been my daughter I would have burned the junk and kicked my little butt for having you in the junk with no brake...."

Bill apparently was well-thought-of—and was better behaved—inside every prison he called home. Even the guards respected him, Ann said. She talked about the time she and her son, Diamond, visited Bill at Smith State Prison in Glennville, Georgia. It wasn't visitors' day, but the two of them were allowed entrance. They found Bill sitting in the infirmary, awaiting his turn with a dentist. What a nice surprise, he said.

Well, Bill forgot about the dentist, and the three of them sat on a bed and talked for about two hours.

When Bill got back to his cell, one of his fellow inmates asked if he knew the governor.

Actually, Shane said his daddy, unlike a lot of prisoners, was usually courteous to guards and other prison personnel and "never got written up" for misbehaving. "These inmates today," he told Shane in his later years, "they're not worth killing."

Another resident of Winder, Robert Polite, got to know Bill when he was incarcerated at Ware State Prison in Waycross, Georgia. His cell was three down from Bill's in the infirmary.

"At the time, he (Bill) wasn't sick sick," Polite said. "He still knowed everybody, and he still liked them Little Debbie Cakes and noodle soup. . . . He would ask me, 'You got soup to eat later on?' I would say I didn't. And he said, 'Yes, you do,' and he would give me some soup and Debbie Cakes, and that's a meal."

Polite said he and Bill didn't talk much about Winder, but "it was a privilege to meet him because he was a home boy." He said he'd heard stories about Bill's crimes, "but I never judged no one." Polite, forty-eight years old in early 2020, served twenty-five months for aggravated assault.

"I stabbed a dude that reneged on a deal we negotiated," he said. "I slapped him, and he was younger than me, and I got tired. He wanted to keep fighting. They broke us up. But I could tell he wanted to get back at me, which I don't blame him, because when I was young I could go all day. I pulled a knife just to scare him, but he ran up on me, and I couldn't fight no more. I had to stick him."

Bill always shared *The Winder News* with him, Polite said, so he could keep up with goings-on back home. "Sometimes he would come out of his cell; sometimes he wouldn't. But he was real good to me.

"Other prisoners knew that back in the day he was rough. Back in the day, he would kill you."

Shane said he "never had a friend that I fought more with, but thought more of than Robert Polite." They grew up together.

Polite, now a free man and working, suffers from kidney failure and undergoes dialysis three days a week.

CHAPTER TWENTY-FOUR

"I thank God every morning when I wake up," he said.

The last three decades of his life, Bill Birt also prayed to God regularly. And he had much to pray about.

Doc Skelton.

CHAPTER TWENTY-FIVE

THE FIRST TIME BILL BIRT EVER PRAYED, he wasn't praying for himself. He was praying for the "kid," he called him, in the cell next to his at the Georgia Diagnostic and Classification Prison in Jackson, Georgia. The inmate's name was Jerome Bowden.

In one of his letters, Bill said he told God that he probably wouldn't recognize his voice because he'd never talked to Him before. "I deserve everything I get," he had written. And then he prayed, "God, there's no way that kid should go to that death chamber. He is innocent." He was writing as he prayed.

Bill later described the inmate to our son Montana. He said the man had the intelligence Montana had at five years old. He didn't recognize right from wrong. But his last stay of execution lasted twenty-four hours. And then they took him. A guard came back and told Bill his friend was gone.

"Lord," Bill prayed, "watch out for him because he's a great kid."

Believe it or not, Billy Sunday Birt—the infamous murderer named after the famous evangelist Billy Sunday—became one who prayed regularly to God. His voice no doubt became familiar to the Almighty, eventually. The last three times Shane visited his dad at Smith State Prison, Bill wanted to pray. They prayed as soon as Shane arrived in the visitors' area, and they prayed again before he left.

Bill led the prayers. "Each time," Shane said, "he started his prayer by thanking God for his family: how we turned out, about me and my family getting back together. He thanked God for

Mama taking us to see him in prison and for his life with Mama. He always ended up with Stoney and Mama."

Each time, Shane said, he prayed for reconciliation of Stoney with me—his mother—and the rest of the family. He prayed for me. He prayed for Stoney. He prayed that we would find a resolution to our differences, whatever they were. Frankly, I don't know what turned Stoney against me, but something did. If I wronged him in some way, I need to apologize. But I need to know what I'm apologizing for. I love Stoney. I love my whole family. They are the good that came out of the bad.

Bill not only prayed regularly, he read the Bible all the way through. Maybe twenty times, he said.

The first time he read the Bible was to prove Dr. Skelton wrong. My good friend Dr. C.B. Skelton of Winder was a godly man who had written Bill a letter, telling him that no man, even the worst sinner, is beyond God's reach. All who repent of their sins and profess Jesus Christ as their savior can be saved.

At the time, Bill was on death row, sentenced to die for his part in murdering the aging couple in Wrens, Georgia. I had told Doc all about Bill and his evil ways when I first went to work for his daughter, Lynn Walls, at the Master's Table Restaurant, which would eventually become a food-catering business.

"The Lord impressed me, 'You ought to write him a letter,'" Doc said, recalling his conversation with me. So he wrote him a letter, and I took it to Bill in prison. Bill read the letter, kind of laughed, crumpled it up and threw it in a garbage can. I went back and told Doc what had happened.

"Well, I did my part. I wrote him a letter," Doc said he told himself. "That's what God told me to do."

But Doc couldn't let it go. God *wouldn't* let it go, either. Doc said he "kept being bugged by the fact that God was saying: 'You didn't let me dictate the letter.'" Doc said he was a little stiff-necked. "Well, I did my part. I wrote him a letter."

CHAPTER TWENTY-FIVE

About a year went by, but the Holy Spirit wouldn't let go of Doc's conscience. So my friend sat down and wrote Bill another letter. "OK," he said nicely to God, "dictate." When the Good Lord dictates, a person listens. Doc doesn't remember his exact words, but he does recall the essence of his second letter. It went something like this:

> "To Billy Sunday Birt, who said he'd done more than the Good Lord can ever forgive. You are not talking about the God I serve. The God I serve can forgive anything. Take, for example, the Old Testament. Scripture says David killed tens of thousands, and we know that at least one of those was so he could take another man's wife for his own."

He was referring to the passage in the book of Samuel: David, the commanding officer, sent Uriah, the Hittite, to the front lines of war, hoping he would be killed, leaving behind his beautiful wife, Bathsheba, whom David wanted for his own. David may have sent a squad—perhaps a platoon of men—with Uriah, and all of them were probably killed. Doc said he thought of the part about the platoon of men after he had written the letter. Doc continued his letter:

> "So David would be a mass murderer. And yet, in the New Testament, David is referred to as a man after God's own heart. And look at Paul, the man who became an apostle of Jesus. He had Christians killed. He was one of the approving bystanders as Stephen was stoned to death. Stephen, who really understood the implications of the gospel, was the first Christian to die for his belief. And Paul watched. Yet Paul, then known as

> Saul of Tarsus, became Christianity's greatest missionary and wrote almost half of the New Testament.
>
> Let the past be the past, Paul said. The difference is confession and repentance."

I took Doc's letter to Bill. This time, he read it, folded it, and put it in the pocket of his prison pants. Later, on October 7, 1986, Bill got out his pen and paper and wrote Doc a note. Here's what he said:

> Dear Dr. Skelton.
>
> Thanks for taking the time to write me.
>
> That was the most beautiful letter, and you made so much sense. You wrote it so such a fool like myself can understand what you mean. I will always keep the letter.
>
> Thank you very much.
>
> From: Billy Sunday Birt.
>
> P.S.: Dr. Skelton: I do appreciate everything you done for Ruby Nell and the kids.

Soon after reading Doc Skelton's second letter, Bill picked up the Bible and started reading. And reading. And reading. He couldn't believe that God could forgive a man like him. Surely Doc is wrong. God cannot—*does* not—forgive mass murderers. In the end, however, the Bible proved Doc right. God can forgive even the vilest offender, even a murderer. No one is beyond redemption through Christ, not even Billy Sunday Birt. The Bible proves it.

CHAPTER TWENTY-FIVE

Doc Skelton had planted the seed.

About six years later, on September 6, 1992, Billy Sunday Birt, the mass murderer, was baptized as a believer in Christ. The man who took him to a church in Winder, Georgia, to be baptized is the same man who told him God's plan of salvation.

He was a Georgia sheriff. Bill was supposed to have killed him. He had a hit on the man. For some reason, however, he let him live.

Why did he not kill him? Who stopped Bill Birt from fulfilling his contract, probably for the first time ever?

We believe it was God.

Dr. Charles Bryant Skelton—Doc to most people, but Red to others—died June 4, 2021. Doc was a Bible teacher, local missionary, Gideon speaker, singer and autoharp player, poet, physician, author, humorist, mentor, World War II veteran, community leader, family man, philosopher, optimist, and one of the most generous people we've ever met. Shane Birt, a eulogist at the funeral, along with Michael DeLoach Sr., described his mentor as the North Star that guided our ships. Doc Skelton was ninety-four.

Sheriff Tim Pounds.

Earl Lee, left, and Bill enjoy a moment following the baptism.

CHAPTER TWENTY-SIX

E ARL D. LEE WAS THE SHERIFF who led Billy Sunday Birt to Christ. He died in 1998. But if Bill had gone through with his contract, he would have died in 1973, Lee's first year as sheriff of Douglas County, Georgia. For some reason, Bill did not shoot the man Billy Wayne Davis paid him to kill.

Davis wanted Lee dead, authorities said, because the sheriff was on his tail for ordering a hit on a man named Charles Mack Sibley, a gambler in Lithia Springs, Georgia, who demanded money Davis owed him from poker games. Bill Birt killed Sibley, and Davis gave him four thousand dollars and a car for his service.

Bill had planned on shooting Lee before the sheriff entered a Douglasville church on a Sunday night in 1973. But the first time Bill was there on a street beside the church, holding a double-barrel, 12-gauge shotgun, ready to take him out, Lee was not at church. Tim Pounds, current sheriff of Douglas County, said he was told that Bill had gone to the wrong church. But Shane said his daddy always checked out ahead of time where he was supposed to be for a hit. He was at the right church, he said; the sheriff just wasn't there that Sunday.

The next Sunday night, everything went as Bill expected. Charlie Reed, driving for Bill, had parked two or three cars behind the sheriff's car on a side street. Both men were wearing wigs and dark glasses. The plan was for Bill to get out of his car—actually it was a stolen car—with his shotgun loaded with slugs under his coat, and walk slowly toward the sheriff, while Reed pulled a couple of car lengths in front of the sheriff's car. Bill was to walk by Sheriff Lee, take him out, and then get in his car and leave.

After the church service ended, about 9:30, the sheriff walked out to his car with his wife, another woman, and four small children.

Bill didn't have to get out of his car, it turned out. Where Reed had parked was perfect. Bill could lie down in the back seat and lay his gun barrel in the car window. The sheriff "walked right where I wanted him to, had a bead right on him," Bill said in a letter to Stoney. "But I couldn't pull the trigger. Something stopped me." Reed, slumped down in the front seat, was peeping out of the front window. He said, "You going to shoot?" Bill said, "No, I'm not. I can't kill the man in front of his wife and kids. We laid there (in the car) and watched Mr. Lee drive off."

On the way back to Statham, where both men lived, Reed asked if Bill planned to kill the sheriff later. "I told him no, we were going to give the folks their money back," Bill said in his letter.

The next day, Bill encouraged Davis and others to forget about eliminating Sheriff Lee. Killing him is "going to put more heat on us than we can stand," Bill said.

We in the Birt family believe that God changed Bill's plans. It was no accident that the sheriff's family—and perhaps someone else's children—were walking beside him that night. The hit man who always fulfilled his contract could not, this one time, pull the trigger.

If he had pulled the trigger, Bill would not have known the forgiveness offered through Jesus Christ. Earl Lee was the one who witnessed to him face-to-face.

If he had pulled the trigger, my children would not have received extra presents at Christmastime. Earl Lee played Santa Claus to the Birt children year after year.

If he had pulled the trigger, I wouldn't have gotten a brand new sewing machine. Earl Lee bought that sewing machine and delivered it to me one year. I still have it.

CHAPTER TWENTY-SIX

If he had pulled the trigger, Bill would not have been baptized in our church, the Church of the Lord Jesus Christ, in Winder in 1992.

Let me say it again: The real reason Bill Birt didn't pull the trigger that Sunday night, we firmly believe, was God. God had plans for Earl Lee, and they involved Bill Birt. Nineteen years after that night, Bill and Earl Lee would go to church together, to *our* church in Winder. Everything was working out just as God planned.

"By the time Dad got arrested (in 1974)," Shane told Sheriff Pounds during an interview in Douglasville, "God already had people in place to take care of my mama and her family. He (God) started off with Sheriff Lee. . . . We got people like Earl Lee, Doc Skelton, Dr. Etheridge. Those people were put in place. The only true hero out of this is my mom. . . . But without Earl Lee we wouldn't have made it.

"I've always said that if Daddy could have met Sheriff Lee in his younger years, he'd never have turned out like he did. Sheriff Lee said my daddy was one of the smartest people he ever knew, and with a better start in life, he could have been anything he wanted to be."

Shane added: "There's nobody on this earth that me and my mama appreciate more than Earl Lee and his family. . . . Can you imagine the faith it took for Sheriff Lee to make friends with the man who was supposed to kill him? It's similar to the faith of Ananias." (Ananias of the New Testament learned in a vision that Saul of Tarsus, the notorious persecutor of Christians, had been converted. And, although frightened and hesitant, he welcomed and baptized Saul, who later became Paul, and, through God, healed him of his temporary blindness.)

Who knows why Earl Lee, a tough-as-nails sheriff, and Bill Birt, a cold-blooded murderer, became friends. But they did. Perhaps the sheriff felt he owed Bill for sparing his life. Perhaps Earl Lee saw something in Bill Birt that no one else saw. More than likely, Bill found a law enforcement officer he actually trusted. And the trust apparently was mutual. They actually respected each other.

"They became left-and-right buddies," Pounds said. "I've never seen a relationship like that—a convict and a sheriff. They got close, really close." Lee did things for Bill that a sheriff normally wouldn't do for a criminal. A law officer doesn't take chances with a man like Bill Birt, but Sheriff Lee and Bob Ingram trusted Bill not to try anything foolish, like try to escape, when they took the handcuffs and leg irons off their prisoner before walking into a restaurant for a meal. They were on their way to Douglasville from Marion, Illinois, where Bill was in prison, so that he could testify against Davis, charged with ordering the Sibley hit. Davis was convicted in that trial and sentenced to life.

The sheriff trusted Bill when he accompanied him to a Douglasville studio to be photographed with his family. Bill was all duded up in a suit and tie for the occasion.

Lee trusted Bill when he took him to the Winder church—unshackled—to be baptized. But, just in case, he told Bill before the service, "Birt, if you give me a reason, I'm going to shoot you dead cold." And he would have done it.

The uncommon trust between the two men extended to their conversations, usually held behind closed doors, Pounds said. Bill apparently trusted Sheriff Lee to listen without condemning him as he painted a sordid picture of murders, explosions, robberies, burglaries. In fact, Earl Lee may have been the only person who knew everything Bill did, every crime he committed, during his years-long reign of terror, mostly in Barrow and surrounding counties. ATF agent Jim West compiled a list of possible Bill Birt murders mostly from an informant, but we believe Lee heard the truth from the man himself.

"Earl said Billy was a hardcore criminal that didn't mind killing," Sheriff Pounds said. "But somewhere toward the end of this, he was remorseful for doing that. . . . Billy didn't count the Black folks he killed. I heard he killed fifty-six, not counting Black people. . . . Billy shot one Black man over a nickel. He shortchanged him a nickel, and Billy shot him. Earl told me that."

CHAPTER TWENTY-SIX

And yet, do you remember the name Jerome Bowden, the Jackson, Georgia, prison inmate on death row in the cell next to Bill's, the "kid" Bill prayed for because he was facing execution? He was Black. He didn't know right from wrong, Bill said. Bowden was convicted of murdering a fifty-five-year-old Georgia woman and severely wounding her mother during a robbery. The mother later died.

Bowden's IQ at the time was measured at fifty-nine. The State Board of Pardons and Paroles requested another test shortly before the execution—about ten years later—and the IQ score was sixty-five. He could not count to ten, one report said.

Bowden signed a confession, although he denied taking part in the murder. When his attorney asked him if he read the statement before signing it, he said, "I tried." In a rambling explanation, Bowden said he was told he probably wouldn't be executed if he confessed.

Here are Bowden's last words before being electrocuted:

"I am Jerome Bowden, and I would just like to state that my execution is about to be carried out. And I would like to thank the people at this institution for taking such good care of me in the way that they did. And I hope that by my execution being carried out that it may bring some light to this thing that is wrong. And I would like to have a final prayer with [the] Chaplain if that is possible. Thank you very much."

Jerome Bowden was thirty-four years old.

The execution on June 24, 1986, drew widespread attention and protests, and in 1988, the Georgia legislature passed a law—the first of its kind in the nation—forbidding execution of those found guilty but "mentally retarded," the term the state used to describe people with intellectual disabilities. At the same time, however, the Georgia legislature imposed the beyond-a-reasonable-doubt burden of proof that the inmate is mentally incompetent. Apparently, however, there's not been a single finding of intellectual disability at trial in a case involving intentional murder in Georgia.

Bill Birt was one of the most racially prejudiced human beings who ever lived, Shane said, and yet he came to know, love, and pray for a Black man facing execution. "Lord," Bill prayed, "watch out for him because he's a great kid." Stoney said his father also came to the defense of a Black man threatened by two brothers while incarcerated in Reidsville. Later, the man said in a newspaper article that Bill saved his life.

Color of skin apparently didn't influence Earl Lee one way or the other. Pounds, an African American, worked under Lee for seventeen years, rising from deputy to lieutenant during that time.

"He treated me like a son and showed me right from wrong," Pounds said. "I'd go to him and ask why people call me nigger. He said it's culture. He explained it in a nice way. 'That's the way some folks are,' he said. 'But don't let that bother you. You are one of God's creations.'"

Lee retired as sheriff the last day of 1992, and Pounds continued to advance in the department, eventually to division commander. He resigned in 2016 to run for sheriff and was elected over five other candidates.

"Earl was long gone before I ran for sheriff," he said, "but folks knew that I trained under Earl. And that helped me tremendously."

Pounds said there'll never be another sheriff like Earl Lee. "You can't police the way Earl did it. You can't do that today. Like he had a man charged with murder, but he'd let him go home on weekends. He always came back like Earl told him, but he let him go home to take care of his family. He was a good Christian man, but he was tough as nails."

Lee was a master at getting suspects to confess, Pounds said. He didn't physically force anyone to confess. He just talked. And talked. It might take him four or five hours of talking. He'd keep bringing suspects cigarettes and coffee and something to eat, and the inmate would still be in there talking—until he confessed.

CHAPTER TWENTY-SIX

"I learned really and truly how to fight crime from Earl," Pounds said. "And the extent you have to go to get the answers. You don't do a little short sweep and say, 'OK, then.' You continue on with that investigation until you feel like it is done."

A good law officer, Pounds said Lee told him, "will do as much trying to prove that they didn't do it as he would trying to prove that they did do it. That way, it will balance itself out. I do that to this day. That's the kind of stuff I learned from him." And Lee always knew when somebody was lying to him. "I wish I knew how he knew, but he did know," Pounds said.

Earl Lee must have known Bill wasn't lying when he told him he "wouldn't try anything" when he took him to be baptized at the Church of the Lord Jesus Christ in Winder on September 6, 1992, a day before Labor Day. But he warned him just in case: If you make one wrong move, I'll kill you.

How Bill ended up at our church for his baptism is a story in itself. The three of us, the sheriff, Bill and I, discussed the baptism in Lee's office in Douglasville. (Bill said in a letter that Stoney and son Stone were also there.)

The kids and I had talked about getting Bill baptized, but Sheriff Lee didn't know that. The sheriff had gone to Jackson, Georgia, and brought Bill to Douglasville for something—I don't know what—but, as far as we knew, it wasn't to talk about Bill's baptism. The sheriff brought up that subject, it seemed, out of the blue. So with Bill and me on the sofa and Sheriff Lee at his desk, Earl Lee began thinking. He closed his eyes and leaned back in his chair. Then he started talking.

His first idea was to baptize Bill in his cow pond in Douglas County. And then he said, "I'll take you to my pool. I'll take you anywhere you want to go, but they (Bill's family) have the right that you come to their church, where they prayed for you, and be baptized. Give me your word, and I'll take you to be baptized."

Bill didn't think it was possible for him to be baptized in a church. "I've never been to church a day in my life," he said.

303

"Maybe not your church, but your family's church," the sheriff said. That's where you should go, he said, but the pool and the cow pond are open, too. The sheriff also suggested his church.

Getting baptized was not an easy decision for Bill. His route to redemption had been long and curvy, and he had doubts. There are no dead ends for God's salvation, but Bill was having second thoughts even a couple of months before the baptism was celebrated.

In a letter to me postmarked August 4, 1992, Bill wrote from prison in Jackson:

> "Ruby Nell, I was going to get you to call Mr. Lee and stop him from comeing after me. But it might be for the best. It will make the kids feel better. . . . I need to talk to you in the bathroom by our selfs. Then I will run everything down to you. Then you can help me make up my mind if I am doing the right thing (or) not. . . . But now I think Montana will be the best man for the job if I go through with it.
>
> "But I (won't) say nothing to Mr. Lee or nobody until we talked it over and you don't say nothing to nobody. . . . But listen don't forget the potatoe and biscuit the first time you and Stoney come, and meat and biscuit. You don't have to bring many, 4 for me and 2 for him. I dont want to work you to hard. . . . Well, I will close for now. It time for the mail man. Ruby Nell, be sure dont say nothing to nobody about what I told you not even Mr. Lee. Good night, sweet dreams, love all ways. From Bill."

CHAPTER TWENTY-SIX

When Bill wrote that "Montana will be the best man for the job," he was referring to the person who would baptize him. Today, Montana is a Pentecostal minister in Wisconsin, where he holds worship services in prisons. But at the time of the baptism, he was twenty-five years old and living in Barrow County. He's a good man; he was certainly the "best man for the job," as Bill said.

Our church that Sunday night was filled mostly with family members. (In a letter to Stoney, though, Bill said the church was full.) I had encouraged some of my folks to attend, but I didn't tell them why. So they didn't expect to see Bill walking through that back door, unshackled, ready to step into the waters of the baptistry. If they had known, they might have been a little uneasy.

Carol Chancey, wife of Donald Chancey, one of Bill's murder victims, was sitting about three rows from the back. Ann Birt saw her get up and leave sometime during the service.

Dr. C.B. Skelton and his wife, Penny, were there. Doc, you'll remember, is the one who wrote two letters, both planting the seed of God's love in Bill's heart. In his second letter, Doc told Bill, again, that no one, not even a murderer, is beyond God's reach. Bill started reading every night from an old, ragged Bible that Lisa, Montana's wife, had given him. He read it first to prove Doc wrong: God couldn't save a man like him. But, according to the scriptures, Doc was right: No one, the Bible says, is beyond God's love and saving grace. So, for the first time in his life, Bill started to believe his salvation was possible.

About six years after receiving that letter, Bill actually made a profession of faith. Sheriff Earl Lee—along with, I believe, our son Montana—brought him to that profession.

I had known Dr. Skelton for more than thirty-five years, ever since I started going to the Master's Table restaurant to eat. Later, I became an employee. He is a godly man, and I love him for who he is.

Something special filled the inside of that little church on the night of Bill's baptism. I believe it was the Holy Ghost.

Before the baptism took place, Brother Tommy Baker, pastor of the Church of the Lord Jesus Christ, said a few words of introduction. "I don't know anything about this man," he said, "but I can see by the tears in this place that no doubt this is a glorious, special occasion. There is nothing out of reach for God. There is a God that we serve that is the Authority of all authorities.

"All I got to say is hold him down good, Montana. Baptize him deep."

Stoney, dressed sharply in a suit and tie, introduced Montana, attired in a plaid shirt with a tie tucked inside to keep it out of the water. Bill was wearing dark pants and a white shirt with the initials I.D.—Inmate in Detention—on the back in large print. Standing behind the baptistry, Montana began speaking, his voice filled with emotion. "Have you ever dreamed a dream, prayed a prayer you never ever figured would come true?"

He had dreamed that dream, he had prayed that prayer: "Lord, before You come back, let me baptize my father." The Lord answered his prayer. He said yes.

There was a glow around Montana after he finished speaking. Many of us in the congregation were crying happy tears.

"Dunk him good," someone heard Sheriff Lee say.

Montana held tightly onto the new convert, who was sitting on a bench, chest-high in the water, and placed a handkerchief over his mouth and nose. Suddenly, Bill pulled out something from his shirt pocket and held it against his chest. We found out later that it was a photograph of his mother, who told Bill many times that he would reap what he sowed.

Then Montana leaned over and lowered his daddy backward into the water, covering his whole body and fulfilling an ordinance instituted by Jesus Christ. "I baptize you in the name of our Lord Jesus Christ," he said. As I said, Pentecostals hold that a believer should be baptized only in the name of Jesus.

Montana pulled his daddy upright, stood up straight, reared back and raised his hands in praise as Bill sat staring ahead for

CHAPTER TWENTY-SIX

a few seconds, obviously taking in what had just happened. A man who killed people for money was granted salvation free of charge.

The baptizer and the baptized hugged each other, and Bill spoke briefly to his sons after he stood up in the water. But songs of Pentecostal praise mixed with shouts of joy covered his words. I couldn't hear what he said. He stepped out of the baptistry, changed into dry clothes, and walked from the front toward the congregation.

Brother Baker asked Bill if he would say a few words to the congregation. Much to my surprise—Bill never liked to talk in front of strangers because of his speech problem—my former husband stood at the front of the sanctuary and thanked Jesus Christ for saving him, the church for having him, Earl Lee for bringing him, and Doc Skelton for writing that letter telling him salvation was possible.

Remembering the event later, Bill wrote in a memoir dated March 18, 2008:

> "...Anybody who know me will tell you it would take a pure miracle to get me to walk out in front of a whole church full of people and give my testimony for I always figure if God had wanted me to get up and talked and give testimony in front of people he would have made me to talk real plain. I couldnt wait to get them wet clothes off and get out there and tell the folks about Jesus and give my testimony."

Afterward, little children—his grandchildren—ran up to him, their arms opened wide, inviting a hug. They were not disappointed.

And then, instead of coming down to his seat on the front left bench, Bill walked down the middle aisle toward the door.

Sheriff Lee was sitting in a choir seat on the left side facing the pulpit. At first, he must have thought Bill was headed for the door, because Penny Skelton said she saw him reach quickly for his sidearm. But Bill was only walking back to speak to Doc Skelton, who was seated with Penny on the left side, about middle way back.

Bill leaned over, shook Doc's hand, and thanked him for the letter assuring him that even he, a killer, was not beyond redemption.

"I want you to know I've read it every day," Bill told Doc, "sometimes two and three times a day since then."

Doc thanked him and wished him well.

"Was he a changed man?" Doc asked later in an interview. "Everybody thought he was. All I did was show him that he could be forgiven."

Following the service, on the church steps outside, Sheriff Lee assured everyone that he and Bill weren't *using* the church for anything, certainly not to lessen Bill's prison term. We "didn't want anything except the salvation of his soul," the sheriff said.

"I don't want nothing," Bill said after the sheriff spoke. "I'm not going to get out anyway."

We celebrated that day with food and fellowship in the church's gymnasium. I had cooked turkey and dressing for the occasion, and other people brought other food and drinks. We all gathered to eat, to fellowship, and to offer praises to the Lord: Billy Sunday Birt was now one of God's children.

Bill greeted friends and strangers alike. He had never been to church—everybody knew that—but he seemed to feel at home in our little Church of the Lord Jesus Christ.

Outside in the parking lot after the meal, the whistle of a freight train sounded in the distance as people gathered around the opened hood of Shane's 1969 Camaro, admiring the engine.

Bill hugged the grandkids one more time, I handed Sheriff Lee a cake I had made, and then they were off, headed back to

CHAPTER TWENTY-SIX

the jail in Douglasville. But, first, with darkness settled in, they detoured out of their way and stopped by the cemetery of White Plains Baptist Church in Jackson County for Bill to place flowers on the graves of his mother, Eunice, and stepfather, Pete Phillips. "He was a fine man," Bill said of his stepfather, standing beside his grave, still unshackled.

Surely Bill again remembered his mother's words: "You reap what you sow." Her son knew she was right, but sometimes he couldn't help himself.

We all believe that on this night, September 6, 1992, Bill allowed Somebody else to help him, the Authority of authorities who can forgive the most horrific of sins. It had been a good day, a day Montana and the rest of us thought would never happen. It happened. "For with God," Luke 1:37 says, "nothing shall be impossible."

We tried to keep Bill's presence in Winder quiet; we didn't want the news media there making a big deal out of the baptismal service. But word apparently got out, and a reporter from one of the television stations in Atlanta showed up at Sheriff Lee's office a day or two later with a cameraman. She heard that a convicted murderer was brought to a church without any restraints to be baptized.

The Atlanta Journal-Constitution received the same report, and Bill and Sheriff Lee were in the news for a few days. "A Killer, a Sheriff, a Ride to Church," the headline on an *AJC* story read on September 12, 1992, six days after the baptism. "Proper Restraints Not Used in Trip," the article's title continued.

As expected, not everyone was happy about the occasion. "We were appalled," said Andy Bowen, who at the time was a spokesman for the Department of Corrections. "And the more we thought about it, we were outraged that Sheriff Lee would take a death row inmate out of a secure situation, such as a jail, into an unsecured situation, such as a church, without proper restraints."

However, the newspaper said Douglas County District Attorney David McDade "didn't balk when the sheriff approached him for help in securing a court order to check Birt out of prison and into the county jail (in Douglasville). The sheriff told the prosecutor he wanted to interview Birt about an unsolved murder, Mr. McDade said."

Sheriff Lee may very well have interviewed Bill about an unsolved murder, but he also got him baptized.

"Folks here in the courthouse are not too pleased as to what happened," said Judge David Emerson, who signed the court order that instructed the Department of Corrections to release Birt to the sheriff's custody. "Both Mr. McDade and Judge Emerson said they had no idea of the sheriff's evangelical plans," the newspaper reported.

The Department of Corrections, following a "strongly worded request from state Sen. Wayne Garner of Carrollton," the newspaper said, "dispatched a van to Douglasville Friday afternoon (September 11) to retrieve Birt from the jail and return him to the Georgia Diagnostic and Classification Center at Jackson."

If Sheriff Lee was worried about being reprimanded for bringing Bill to our church, unshackled, to be baptized, he never mentioned it to us Birts. Sometimes, retired GBI agent Ronnie Angel said, you would think Earl Lee was the sheriff of Georgia.

All we can say is we're thankful that the sheriff witnessed to Bill, brought him through the Holy Spirit to the saving grace of Jesus Christ, and then transported him to Winder for his baptism. Nothing bad was going to happen, because first, Bill trusted Sheriff Lee, and second, he knew his friend would kill him if he made a wrong move.

Besides, nobody in the church complained about his daddy's being there that Sunday night, Montana told a newspaper reporter. And I told that same reporter: "It was a miracle for our family. It's a result of twenty years of prayer by his family. It's the first time in our life that the whole family has been together."

CHAPTER TWENTY-SIX

Montana said it best with one short sentence: "The Lord has his way of working things out."

Billy Sunday Birt was now one of God's redeemed children, we believed. He was remorseful, especially, Shane said, after the double murder in Wrens, Georgia. He regretted his past criminal life. When we were living in Statham, Bill woke up one night talking about "something floating over him." He said he could see the image of a hand, a hand reaching out to him. It was peaceful. He said he thought if he had reached up and taken the hand—perhaps it was the hand of God—everything would have been all right. But he didn't reach up.

When he was in prison, he told about the nights everybody he had killed came to the foot of his bed. He was terrified.

When Shane and his wife, Jill, were having problems with their marriage, Shane asked Bill, "Daddy, can you imagine how stupid I was to throw everything away like that?" And Bill said, "Son, if I don't know, don't nobody know."

So here was this man who lay down at night with regrets, who ruined the lives of countless families by killing their loved ones, by burning their homes, by robbing them of their possessions, a man who wanted to be like his pawpaw, Pink Hegwood, who helped raise him and the rest of the Birt family after Bill's father died. And now Billy Sunday Birt, once the deadliest man in Georgia, asked God for forgiveness.

And, we believe, God forgave him.

It would not have happened, this forgiveness, if it hadn't been for Earl D. Lee. We in the Birt family will never forget him.

Neither, apparently, will the people of Douglas County. Voters there elected Lee to four four-year terms before he retired. In 1973, he was named Douglas County Citizen of the Year. On October 12, 2012, the street leading to the new Douglas County Jail was officially named Earl D. Lee Boulevard. On October 5, 2018, Sheriff Lee's daughters—Lynn, Susan, and Cathy—along with other family members gathered to celebrate his life on the twentieth anniversary of his death. They, along with Sheriff Pounds and about twenty other people from the audience, shared remembrances of the man they called "a Douglas County icon and legend."

We thank God that Bill Birt—dubbed in newspapers as "the deadliest man in Georgia"—did not carry out his contract in Douglas County that Sunday night in 1973. And we're also thankful to Ronnie Angel. Had it not been for his quick action, Sheriff Lee probably would not have lived to serve beyond 1974.

On December 18, 1974, Agent Angel and Sheriff Lee were transporting an American spree killer named Paul John Knowles to find a murder weapon he used to kill two of his victims. Knowles had been tied to eighteen deaths, although he claimed to have killed thirty-five people.

On the way to Henry County, Georgia, Knowles, riding in the back seat, used a paperclip to free himself from handcuffs. Then, according to authorities, he "grabbed Lee's handgun, discharging it through the holster in the process and while Lee was struggling with Knowles and attempting the keep control of the vehicle, Angel fired three shots into Knowles's chest, killing him instantly."

Angel investigated some of the GBI's most infamous cases, including the Alday family murders in Seminole County, Georgia, the assassination in Jackson County of solicitor general Floyd Hoard, and, of course, some of Bill's victims. He will talk about those cases, but, to this day, he does not speak publicly about killing Knowles.

Paul John Knowles, by the way, was known for his good looks and his smooth and charismatic nature. To some women who met him, he was a "cross between Robert Redford and Ryan O'Neal," one report said. To others, he was just a cold-blooded killer who looked out only for himself. Sounds familiar, doesn't it?

But Knowles and Bill were different in other ways. Knowles wanted his crimes known. He longed for infamy. Bill, on the

CHAPTER TWENTY-SIX

other hand, never talked about his crimes to anyone he didn't know, and seldom to those he knew well. And Knowles didn't need a reason to kill someone. Bill always had a reason, flimsy though it might be.

Here were two men, both murderers. Both were self-centered. But Billy Sunday Birt was a different man at the end of his life. Thanks to Montana, our son, to Doc Skelton and Sheriff Earl Lee, Bill Birt discovered that the Heavenly Father loved him more than he could ever pretend to love himself.

Mugshot of Bill.

CHAPTER TWENTY-SEVEN

In a series of letters, Billy Sunday Birt wrote what he called his testimony to his wife, children, and grandchildren. The letters were sent to his prison pastor and Sunday school teacher at the Georgia State Prison in Reidsville, Georgia. The pastor, a man Bill called Brother Rick, recorded the testimony onto a cassette tape. Bill didn't like his voice because of his speech problem. Brother Rick included several gospel songs as Bill requested. The stabbing incident Bill referred to occurred at the Lee Arrendale State Prison in Alto, Georgia. At the time of this recording, in December of 1999, there were seven Birt grandchildren. Today, there are eleven grandchildren, and sixteen great-grandchildren.

"Kids, Brother Rick is my pastor and also my Sunday school teacher. And he also is my good friend. God really has blessed us here at Reidsville prison when he sent Brother Rick to us, and we all thank God for him. Kids, Brother Rick has a beautiful voice, much more beautiful than mine. My voice sounds like a chipmunk. So that is why I asked Brother Rick to put my words on tape, and we can have tapes recorded in prison.

"I am writing these letters myself, and I will mail them to Brother Rick. Kids, Brother Rick has wrote some of the most beautiful songs I have ever heard. But you probably won't get to hear none of them, because he won't share them. He just sings in the church. But I hope there's room on this tape for him to sing a few for all of you. There's one song that when he sings it, I feel like he wrote my life, all but the part where he says abused and battered. Lord knows, I never was abused growing up at home. I had one of the best moms and dads God ever put on this earth. Pete was one of the best Christian men that I have ever known. If I had just listened to him and Mom, I would be home with you tonight. But both of them are in heaven now and I will meet them again someday."

Brother Rick sings a song. Then Bill's testimony.

Kids, I'm going to tell you a story and you can call it my testimony. But I'm telling you this story just the way I remember it. There is not a lie in this story. Kids, I know for a fact there is a burning hell for your daddy almost went there.

Kids, on October third, 1983, around 7:30 p.m., I was sitting on the floor in this man's cell, playing poker with him, and this kid came up behind me and stabbed me thirteen times: ten times in the back, two times in my chest, one time in my left eye. Kids, I saw the knife later on. This was a long knife. Without God's help there, there is no way I could be sitting here telling you all this story tonight. I should have been dead before they got me out of the prison door. They rushed me to Hall County Hospital. I stayed there fourteen days—or that was what I was told. Kids, for the first eight days, I was unconscious, in a coma. Mr. A.C. Thomas was the warden, and he's a very nice man. He let your mama sit in my room the whole time I was in Hall County Hospital. I remember after I came out of the coma, every time I opened my eyes, Ruby Nell was just sitting right beside my bed.

Kids, during the eight days I was in a coma, every person that I had ever killed came to the foot of my bed. Not just one time, but a lot of times. Sometimes there would be five or six together. Sometimes there would be just one. Sometimes there would be three or four together. And this went on for a long time, I think for the whole eight days I was in the coma. Kids, I had done forgot about some of these people, couldn't

CHAPTER TWENTY-SEVEN

even tell you what their faces looked like if I had met them on the street. But, kids, tonight, I remember every one of them people's faces.

Kids, I hate to say this, but out of all the folks who came to the foot of my bed, didn't but four of them make it to heaven. Them four always came together, and they had this beautiful glow on their faces. I could just see the love shining on their faces. And, kids, these four people held their hands out to me, like they were begging me to come to them. And, kids, I wanted to go to them so bad, but I couldn't.

And, kids, all the other folks who came to the foot of my bed, they were laughing at me, and they held their hands out begging me to come to them. But, kids, these folks were in hell, for I could see the torment in their faces. And I kept twisting my head, no, no, I didn't want to go to them. I was scared to death to go with them. But, kids, one of these persons kept coming to the foot of my bed by hisself, and he didn't want me to come there. He kept motioning with his hand for me to go back. But he was the only one that didn't want me to come there. But I will never forget as long as I live of seeing the pain and torment in these persons' faces. And, kids, tonight, if I could swap places with them to get him out of that place, [I would,] even though I am scared to death of hell.

Kids, during the eight days I was in that coma, I didn't have any dope shot in me, for when you are in a coma, you don't have pain. So there was no need for any dope. So what I'm about to tell you now has nothing to do with dope. Kids, during the eight days, a few times I came out of the coma, and your mama would be sitting there holding my hand. Then I would go back into the coma. Kids, during the eight days, and this happened many a time, I would look down at my feet, and my feet and legs from the knees down would be on fire. There would be blue flames shooting up from my feet, and it was like no heat I had ever felt before. Even in the coma, I knew your mama was sitting by my bed, and sometimes I would open my eyes and she would be holding my hand. And I remember begging her to wash my feet in cold water.

I kept telling her, "Honey, my feet are burning up. Pour some cold water on them." Kids, just ask your mama if I didn't beg her to wash my feet. Kids, in these days and times, I don't believe nobody has died and come back to life. But I believe God has let some folks get real close to death. Now, I don't know why God didn't just turn loose of me that night and let me go on into hell, for my legs and feet were already in hell. And it would have been so easy for him to let me go right on into hell. I don't know why, but he had his reasons. And tonight and every day, I thank God for not turning me loose. For, kids, if God had let me go that night back in '83, your daddy would have busted hell wide open. But, thank God, he held onto me. And sometimes I wonder why, after all the evil work I did for the devil.

Kids, on September 25th, 1996, I was moved off death row after being there for over twenty-one years. I was sent to Georgia State Prison here at Reidsville, Georgia. After I got here, I was kept on lockdown for over two years. I got to go to a little yard one hour a day.

One day, I was walking on the yard and I heard somebody knocking on the window. When I looked up, it was the kid who had stabbed me in Alto more than thirteen years ago. He called me over to the window, and he said, "Mr. Birt, I want to apologize to you and tell you how sorry I am for what I did. I had no reason for doing it."

I said, "Son, you probably won't understand this, but you done me a big favor that night, and I have forgiven you a long time ago, back in '92." The kid looked at me like he thought I was crazy. The kid had been on lockdown for the last sixteen years. And you know something, kids, maybe Daddy was crazy back then or I never would have done all the evil things I did for the devil.

CHAPTER TWENTY-SEVEN

But you know something else, kids, Daddy is not crazy today. I have plenty of sense. I have accepted Jesus Christ for my personal savior. And, kids, when Jesus died on the cross at Calvary two thousand years ago, he took all of my sins and all of the terrible things that I have ever done upon Himself, and he washed my slate clean. All I had to do was to believe in him and ask him to forgive me of my sins. And, thank God, he did forgive me. And now, I will see all of you again someday. And, kids, even though Jesus has forgiven me, there's not a night that goes by, before I close my eyes at night, I don't think of the one who came to the foot of my bed. And it is still a big burden on my heart. I ask all of my kids to remember your daddy in your prayers, and I ask all of my grandkids to remember their Pawpaw in their prayers.

Song by Brother Rick.
And then the next letter.

To my wife, Ruby Nell:

Honey, tonight I want to thank you for all you have done for me over the last 25 years. I want to thank you for becoming my wife and giving me five beautiful kids and seven beautiful grandkids. And I want to thank you for bringing the kids to visit me before they all got grown. No matter what prison I was in and no matter how far it was, you made sure I got to see my kids regularly. And you just don't know how much that meant to me, and I want to thank you for not bringing another man in over my kids, and I want to thank you for the good years before I got locked up. We got married when we were just kids. You liked one month being thirteen, and I was sixteen. I could have searched the world over, and I couldn't have found a better wife than you. If I had had any sense, I could be there with you today to enjoy our grandkids together.

When I look at our grandkids, I can see you in every one of them. And I want to apologize for all the hurt and pain I put you through.

Lord, girl, you deserve a lot better man than me. You should have married a king, as good a person as you are. God has never put another woman on this earth that was a better wife and mother than you. I know you won't believe this, but I have never loved no other woman but you. Baby, the rest of them were just whores, something the devil gave me.

Listen, Pretty Woman, I don't know what God has planned for us after we leave this world, but when we get up there, maybe we could ask God to be together again with our kids and grandbabies. I just got a feeling we will know each other up there, and God will let us be together again, that is, if you will take me back. I promise you this: I will be true blue to you. No more running around. Just think, Darling, how beautiful heaven must be, where we will meet all of our loved ones again. I can't wait to see my dear old mother-in-law again and Mama and Pete and Mike and everyone. Darling, God bless you, and thank you again for everything. From Bill.

New letter following songs by Brother Rick.

To the kids and grandkids: Stoney, Ann, Montana, Norma Jean, Shane: Boy, there's not enough room on this tape to tell you how much I love you. And, kids, I'm so sad for not being there with all of you while you were growing up into fine young men and women. I lost so much, and you all did, too. And it was all my fault. I got nobody to blame but myself and the devil. But I want you all to know one thing: Your mama did a beautiful job bringing you all up, and I'm so proud of all five of you. God couldn't have given a man a better bunch of kids.

And I want to thank all of you for sticking by me the way you have and for bringing my grandbabies to see me. I don't have a favorite kid. I love you all the same, and I have a special place in my heart for each of you. But me and Stoney were always so close. While he was growing up, from the time he was a baby, he

CHAPTER TWENTY-SEVEN

went everywhere with me. I'm ashamed to say this, but I even took him with me when I used to haul moonshine. His mama would have had a fit if she knew that back then. So there will always be a closeness between me and Stoney. There will always be a closeness between me and all of you. And tonight, I thank God for giving me and your mama five beautiful kids, and I love you all very much. But I'm going to tell all of you kids something: You should get down on your knees every night and thank God for your mama. What if you hadn't had her when I got locked up? There's not another man in prison that's had his family stick by him the way my family has me. And there's not words to say how much I appreciate and love all of you for staying with me. I just wish I could have had had the chance to make it up to all of you someday. . . . Diamond, Chastity, Cody Bug, Stone, Madison, Smiley, Little Bibbie, I don't have room on this tape to tell all how much you mean to me. All you grandkids have been the joy of my life for the past thirteen years. You have brought your old Pawpaw so much joy, and there's not a day go by that I don't thank God for giving me seven beautiful grandbabies.

New letter following song.

To Montana: Montana, I should have told you this a long time ago, but sometimes it is hard for a man to say what's really in his heart. And you know I never was much for talking. But tonight, time 11 p.m., date September the 19th, 1999, I got a confession I want to make to you, and I really don't know where to start. So I will start back in 1965, the day you were born. Son, the first time I saw you, I knew you had a special gift from God, and your mama knew it, too. And I think the whole family did. Now we didn't love you any more than we loved the rest of the kids, but there was just something special about you. And back then, I couldn't understand why. But today, I do understand why God gave you to me and your mama. Son, I believe now that God was just looking out for me, for he was looking ahead in my life, and he knew what I was fixing to become.

Montana, if you hadn't been born, I would have busted hell wide open, for there is no other person but you that could have got me back to Jesus. And you probably didn't even know what you did. Son, you remember after you joined the church, you used to come to see me on death row. Well, all you wanted to talk about was Jesus, and I didn't want to hear it. But on a Saturday before Easter Sunday, in 1992, you brought Chastity and Cody Bug to see me. Chastity was six; Cody Bug was four.

I had them in my lap playing with them, and you said, "Daddy, if you were to die today, you would never see your grandkids again."

And I asked you, "What are you talking about?"

And you said, "Daddy, you ain't been saved, and you ain't been baptized. And these two kids are going to heaven, and, Daddy, if you die right now, you are going to hell."

Son, you don't know this, but just them few words changed my life, for I went back to my cell and I couldn't get my mind off what you said about not ever seeing my grandkids again. And, Son, that was the first night I had ever got down on my knees beside my bed and prayed and asked God to forgive me. But God didn't forgive me that night or the next night or the next. Son, it was a long, hard road back to Him. And I thought there for a time He wouldn't ever take me back.

Son, you don't know how many nights I pleaded and begged to Jesus to take me back. I used to lay in my bed and hold my hands up to him for hours at a time, till my arms gave out. But Jesus wouldn't take my hand. Son, this went on for months, but He never would take hold of my hand. And, Son, the last night I held up my hands for over three hours or more. But He didn't take my hands.

CHAPTER TWENTY-SEVEN

So I just told Jesus, "I know You're not going to take me back, and I can't blame you, not after all the things I did for the devil." So I told Jesus I wouldn't be holding my hands up anymore, for I knew it was no use. And I went to sleep crying about my grandkids.

Montana, you remember the beautiful Bible you and Lisa sent me in 1989 that I didn't want. Well, it was lying on my top shelf, and around 3 o'clock in the morning, it fell off the shelf and woke me up. I turned on the light, and I saw your Bible laying there on the floor. I got up to put your Bible back on the shelf, and, Son, the second my hand touched your Bible, I knew Jesus had took me away from the devil. My old feelings had come back, the ones I had before I started killing people.

Son, I felt so good standing there in that cell on death row at 3 o'clock in the morning. From that moment on, I couldn't wait to be baptized. And you know the rest of the story. Montana, I owe you a debt I can never repay. Jesus worked through you and my grandkids and saved me from going to hell. And I thank God for sending you to us, and I thank God for all of my kids and grandkids. I thank God for Ruby Nell, for without her, I wouldn't have my kids and my beautiful grandbabies. But, most of all tonight, I thank God for taking me back and giving me another chance to be with my family again.

The tape ended with Brother Rick singing more songs. The last one was titled "The Anchor Holds."

After hearing of Bill's conversion, Bob Ingram said this: "I don't doubt the fact that he changed in prison. He had forty-something years to change. I'm sure he did. I'm sure he knows the Lord and knows how to pray. He had to live with what he did, and you can't erase that. You can't ignore that. There are consequences, and he had to experience those consequences. I hope he was what he said he was at the end. . . . He had to relive this (life of crime) in prison and see these people's faces and what he did to them."

Ruby makes visitor welcome at her home.

CHAPTER TWENTY-EIGHT

I HEARD BILL'S TESTIMONY FOR THE FIRST TIME on June 20, 2018. Shane had brought the tape recording, and we sat there at my dining room table and listened to what my husband had to say about his spiritual life, about his conversion to Christianity.

Some of what he said brought tears to my eyes. But I understood it all, and I guess he told it like it was, from his perspective at least. Of course, he could say nothing that would justify any of his criminal acts. And he seemed to brush off his seeing other women just as he had always done. In fact, he didn't sound repentant at all about his many love affairs, but God didn't make me a judge.

What he said, though, may have proved he was two different people. He could be kind, and he could be a killer. To this day, I don't understand how someone could take the life of another person. As I said before, Bill wouldn't have hurt a lightning bug, but he could have shot or strangled a human being without blinking an eye.

Was Bill schizophrenic? I don't know enough about mental illnesses to answer that question fully. But I do know he was two different people in one body. And it wasn't just his personality that changed when he was upset—his appearance changed, too. I talked earlier about his eyes, about how they were sky blue when he was in a good mood and green as grass when he was mad about something. His complexion also changed. When he was happy, his face was natural-looking and tanned. When he was angry, he was white as snow. You could see the color drain from his face when he got upset. You could see the hardness take over his very being. You certainly couldn't talk to him when he was that way.

Bill talks in his testimony about being stabbed thirteen times while he was an inmate at the state prison in Alto, Georgia, in October of 1983, and about later meeting the man who stabbed him. As he said, he almost died; he was in surgery for about seventeen hours at the hospital in Gainesville; he was in a coma for eight days and remained in the hospital for about a month. Moreover, he lost his left eye in that stabbing and had to get a glass eye to replace it.

Eventually, he was taken to Augusta, Georgia, to get a false eye put in, and, because he had been hard-shackled the whole way down there, he was angry. His good eye was green. So, naturally, the doctors matched that eye. His glass eye was also green. That meant that when Bill was in a good mood, he had one blue eye—his good eye—and one green eye—his glass eye. But when his eyes matched and they were both green, he was angry about something.

About 2007, Shane drove down to Waycross, Georgia, to see his father, who at the time was an inmate at Ware State Prison. This was right after one of Bill's girlfriends had bought a car from a used car dealer. Bill came to hate used car dealers because that's what Billy Wayne Davis was. Davis had testified for the prosecution in the Walton County, Georgia, bank robbery case. Shane said he and his daddy sat and talked for about an hour, and finally, Shane asked, "Daddy, what do you think about the deal she (his girlfriend) got on her car?"

Shane said Bill's complexion and one good eye changed in just a few seconds. He turned white as a ghost, and his eyes suddenly were the same color: green.

"I'll tell you what I'd do," Bill told Shane. "I'd wait three or four months, and that used car dealer would wake up with me sitting in his bedroom. And I'd show him what I'd think."

CHAPTER TWENTY-EIGHT

This conversation happened a long time after Bill accepted Christ as his savior. So was he a Christian?

Here's what Shane believes: "I think, yes, he was a Christian. But my way of thinking is, nobody is perfect. Every Christian does as well as he can and fights every temptation that comes his way. For some Christians, temptations are stronger than for others. Every Christian has a struggle. For a young person, it might be pornography. My daddy's struggle was not in telling the truth. He was brutally honest most of the time. My dad's biggest struggle was his urge to get even. He never forgot anything, especially any wrong done against him or his folks."

For example, Bill never forgot about a man who came to my house to ask me a question about something. I don't remember what the question was. I answered him, and he said I was lying and that I was "just like the rest of them." I told Bill what he said, because I told Bill everything. From then on, Bill lived for the time when he could walk up and kill that man. Two things denied him that pleasure: Bill was in prison, and the man died of a heart attack.

One time, when we were living on Highway 29, about a mile from Statham, I was driving home from buying groceries in Winder and had a flat tire in front of Wade Grizzle's package store. I was walking to the service station to call somebody to come fix the flat. The station wasn't far away, but it was full of cars getting gas. So I parked in the package store's lot.

I was walking toward the station when somebody ran out of the package store and yelled at me. "You can't park here!" he screamed. "You might as well move on. We don't cotton to your kind. We know who you are." I asked nicely if I could leave the car there and have Bill pick it up later. He said no.

I had my children in the car with me, so we hobbled home, about a mile away, with that bad tire. That very night, Bill dynamited that package store. Fortunately, the place was closed at the time. Grizzle, by the way, said later it wasn't him who told me

I couldn't park in the lot. It was one of his employees. Whatever the case, the package store disappeared.

Another time, Bill argued over a girlfriend with his brother Ray, who was good with his fists, possibly the best fist fighter in the county. But Bill was better with a gun. When they faced each other to settle their case, Bill shot his brother six times, causing eleven bullet holes. Ray, who never landed one punch, lived to fight again.

At least one time in Georgia, though, Bill ended up the victim in a shootout. He was hospitalized with a leg wound and was supposed to have stayed overnight. But he climbed out a hospital window and went home.

Bill's uncontrollable urge to get even actually went back to his boyhood. After his father, Claude Birt, died—Bill was nine years old at the time—the man who owned the farm the family sharecropped claimed that Claude had borrowed money from him right before he died. So he took all of the cotton the family had harvested, along with a hog and baby pigs. Bill's widowed mother was left with nothing. When he became a teenager, Bill wanted to get even with the man—he never forgot his mother's being wronged—but the man had already died.

I didn't know the full extent of Bill's many crimes until after he was arrested the last time, in 1974. Even then, I didn't know everything he did. I told you about some incidents, but I want to tell you again because they have haunted me ever since.

I told you about the night I saw and heard something outside our home. I was asleep in bed when I heard someone banging on our front door. Bill was out, as usual. I went to the door. No one was there. I got back in bed and looked out a window. There was Bill's car parked outside. I saw a streak of fire at the car and heard what must've been a gunshot. Not long after that, Bill walked

CHAPTER TWENTY-EIGHT

into the house. I fixed his breakfast later that morning. I always wondered if the person who knocked frantically on our door was trying to get help.

One day, I was standing on our back porch when a woman came to see Bill. She wanted to hire him to kill her husband for five thousand dollars. I heard nearly everything they said to each other. I assume Bill took the job.

Three times, Bill brought me *gifts* from his mistresses. The first time, he tried to blame me. I was the one with the sexually transmitted disease, he said. He knew that wasn't true, but it was his way of telling me I needed to see a doctor.

You would think I'd be free of Bill's other women when he was at home asleep. But sometimes he talked in his sleep. One night, he carried on a conversation with one of his mistresses, and he was sound asleep.

Other times, I told you before, he had nightmares. One night, while we were living in Statham, he sat up in bed and said he felt like something was floating over him, and he could see the image of a hand. Everything around the hand was peaceful. If he had reached up and taken the hand, he said, everything would've been all good. But he didn't take the hand. For once, he actually sounded remorseful.

I'm retelling you some of these horrible things for a reason. Think about it. How could someone with such a sinful, sordid life—a leader of the so-called Dixie Mafia, no less—get the same chance at heaven as people who worshiped God and served other people all of their lives? How could this be?

Yet, the Bible teaches us that everyone can be saved if he or she repents and accepts Jesus as savior. Look again at the Apostle Paul. I can't stop thinking about Paul's murderous past. He murdered countless Christians, thinking that was what God wanted him to do. But once Saul, who became Paul, met Jesus Christ on the road to Damascus, he vowed to leave all of his terrible acts behind him and work exclusively for the gospel of Christ.

Look at King David. He committed adultery, fathered a child out of wedlock, and caused the murder of at least one man, and no doubt many others, when he sent his paramour's husband to the front lines of war and sure death. And yet God said David was a man after his own heart.

So was Bill Birt a Christian at the end of his life? Was he sincere in his professed belief in Jesus Christ? I listened intently to his tape-recorded testimony, and I prayed, "Lord, let it be so. Lord, was Bill Birt a believer?" I believe he was a believer.

Only one thing is certain: We won't know the answer in this life.

CHAPTER TWENTY-NINE

Bill Birt had never apologized to me in a serious way. I told you that. He would halfway apologize and then make a joke about running around with other women. I was the only one who mattered to him, he said, sometimes laughing after he said it. It wasn't funny.

But starting in 2016, he was telephoning around apologizing to everybody: to the children, to me, maybe to others. He talked a lot about getting the family together again, not that he could be there with us, but it was important to him that the rest of us gather and enjoy being a family again.

Bill said I was the only important woman in his life, but that obviously was not true. One night, he telephoned me with a request. One of his girlfriends had died, and she had no cemetery plot. Bill wanted me to agree that she could be buried in our plot at White Plains Baptist Church, where Billy Jr. and Bill's mother and stepfather were interred. Bill said he really didn't need to ask about that, because the plot belonged to him. Actually, I paid for that burial site, not him, but he was claiming it anyway.

As a matter of fact, he proposed his "request" as a stipulation: You may be buried beside me, he said, if I agreed for this other woman to be buried there, too. "She was a good woman," he said.

As crazy as it sounds, Bill wanted his grave to be flanked by two women—his girlfriend on one side, me on the other side.

"I'll have to think about that," I said.

It didn't take me long to think about it. We talked again, and I told him no—no way would I be buried there. My grandchildren would see those two graves, and they'd want to know who that other woman was. Grandmother here, and over here her competition. How would that look? My name is on the tombstone, but my body won't be there.

I told him it was okay for the woman to be buried beside him, but not me. To be honest, she was a big help to me and my children. She actually moved down to Waycross, Georgia—bought a house there—to be close to Bill, an inmate at Ware State Prison. She visited Bill often, relieving the kids and me of traveling about 245 miles south to see him. She was good to our children, and I was grateful to her.

This woman didn't start visiting Bill in prison regularly until she found out that Bill and I had divorced. Obviously, she had been in his life a long time, but I didn't know anything about that. Her parents had operated a little store close to our home soon after Bill and I married, and sometimes Bill would go over there and play poker. I didn't know until later who she was and that her folks ran that store.

So is it possible that she and Bill were merely good friends, not lovers? Let me put it this way: Bill had an affair with practically every woman he met. Even good friends of mine, and—get this—even some kinfolks. I found out about one of those close relatives from my mother-in-law. Bill couldn't believe his own mother would squeal on him. But his parents loved me, and they thought I should know what was going on. Bill's stepfather considered me his daughter-in-law, too. He was such a nice man.

The last time we talked by phone, Bill apologized to me again. He said he was sorry for all the hell he put me through, for all the other women who stepped between us. I told him that was water over the dam. I had forgiven him and all those women many years before.

CHAPTER TWENTY-NINE

April 6, 2017, was a Thursday, eight days from Good Friday. It was late in the evening, somewhere around 11:45, when Billy Sunday Birt, lying in bed in the prison infirmary, grabbed hold of the metal triangle above his head—the trapeze bar infirm prisoners use to move in bed. He had ripped off a strip of his bed sheet, tied one end of the strip around the bar, and the other end around his neck. Holding onto the bar, he slowly leaned back. And with that one simple movement, Bill Birt took the life of one more human being.

He was pronounced dead at 1:44 the next morning, April 7. He was about four months away from being eighty years old.

Bill had been in the infirmary of Ware State Prison for about two years, I'm guessing. He had developed Parkinson's Disease, and the only way he could move around was in a wheelchair. He had to ask someone to write his letters for him.

Both Shane and sister Ann said they knew their daddy would never go to the electric chair, although he'd been sentenced to die. He'd always planned to take care of matters himself. He told Shane he would take an ink pen, take the plastic out of it, sharpen it to use like a syringe. He'd stick it in a vein and bleed out. But, crippled by Parkinson's, he chose something different.

My ex-husband was a proud man, a physically strong man, someone who could scale buildings like Superman, walk across a cable over Tallulah Gorge like the Great Wallenda, outrun the cops and anybody else who challenged him. And he ended up in a wheelchair. Helpless.

His worst fear was that he would live a long life in prison away from his children, grandchildren and great-grandchildren. He always said he preferred death over the separation and isolation that came with prison. But he did live a long life away from all of us: forty-three years and three days away from us. Obviously, he didn't want to make it any longer.

Atha M. Lucas, coroner in Ware County, signed off on Bill's death certificate.

"Did he really kill all those people they said he killed?" Ms. Lucas asked when she was contacted by phone. "They told me at the time that he did, and I said this man? He looks like somebody's papa."

He was, of course, somebody's papa, but a very different papa.

Bill had regrets at the end of his life. Over and over, he told about the visions he experienced when people he had killed appeared at the foot of his bed. He was a broken man. He told Shane about killing a man and leaving the body in a hole where a tree had blown over. He didn't take time to bury the body, just threw a little dirt over the depression. But years later, he lay in his prison bed and envisioned this man crawling out from his crude burial site and coming after his killer.

Gangster Al Capone, historians say, was haunted in prison by a ghost named Jimmy Clark, a rival believed to have been one of Capone's victims. Bill Birt was haunted by dozens.

Bill's Parkinson's added to his bad memories. The disease caused his hands to shake, reminding him of a man he murdered near Juarez, Texas, many years ago. Bill was sent there to eliminate this man, who ran a stash house for Bill and Harold Chancey—a place to hide Chancey's moonshine and Bill's illegal pills from Mexico. The man was suspected of stealing, and maybe he deserved to die, Bill thought. But the man's hands were shaking uncontrollably; he was terrified. Bill didn't want to kill him, but he went through with it. He had a contract.

His mother had told him many times, "You will reap what you sow, seven-fold, good or bad, and before you leave this earth, you will pay for everything you've done, and then your life will be judged."

The good news is, Bill had accepted Christ as his savior. This one-time leader of the notorious Dixie Mafia, a murderer of dozens, confessed his sins, and he was baptized.

But then he killed one more person. Himself.

I asked my pastor about suicide. What does the Bible say about suicide? He said he couldn't find anything in the scriptures

CHAPTER TWENTY-NINE

saying specifically that a person is damned if he kills himself. I felt better then.

I also felt better when I received a check from an insurance company. I had paid on a life insurance policy on Bill for forty-five years, and a lot of companies don't pay if the insured person dies of suicide. But this one paid off, thank goodness. On the death certificate under "Describe How Injury Occurred," the words "Hanged Self" were typed in. I really didn't believe he did that to himself until I saw it in writing. But Bill was determined to get his way, one more time.

I got the original death certificate from the funeral home in Hoschton, a wide place in the road northeast of Winder. Someone there didn't want to give it to me, but then I threatened not to sign over the insurance check, and I got it immediately. All the funeral home did was prepare the body. Stoney buried his daddy, and the lot was paid for, so the funeral expense was reasonable: two thousand dollars in insurance money. I never found out why, but I was told the life insurance policy on me had been surrendered.

Visitation for Bill's funeral took place Monday, April 10, 2017, at the funeral home, and the funeral was held the following day at White Plains Baptist Church. Montana and Brother Ralph Black spoke. Montana read some of the notes Bill wrote to himself in the margins of his Bible. Neither speaker mentioned anything about Bill's sordid past. What was the point of that? And they certainly couldn't say his was a life well-lived. But he was a believer at the end of his life.

Gangster Al Capone once said that "this American system of ours . . . gives each and every one of us a great opportunity if we only seize it with both hands and make the most of it."

Sheriff Earl Lee said Bill Birt could have been anything he wanted to be if he had gotten a better start in life. He was one of the smartest men he ever met, he said.

Bill certainly was smart, but he was a smart criminal. He used his intelligence for all the wrong reasons. He was guilty of many horrible, criminal acts, but, at the end, he was a believer in Jesus Christ, and he was not condemned. Romans 8:1 says: "There is therefore now no condemnation to them which are in Christ Jesus, who walk not after the flesh, but after the Spirit."

Did I still love him? Yes, I guess I will always love him. After all, we grew up together.

All spiffed up in a suit, Bill had this photo made in Douglasville.

CHAPTER THIRTY

On March 18, 2008, Bill Birt completed a fifty-seven-page "story," a brief memoir from a bottomless pit of memories.

The hand-printed piece covers various subjects in Bill's life—and not always in chronological order. But he had much to say sitting there in Smith State Prison in Glennville, Georgia, recording his thoughts as they emerged.

> "This story is not true word for word for I couldn't remember all the words that was spokeing back then," he wrote on the opening page, which featured copied photos of him and Earl D. Lee. "But I recalls most of them and I had to use words to tell the story. But I kept to the truth as much as possible. The people are real and the things I told about them is true."

This chapter is presented as if Bill were being interviewed by a newspaper reporter. The questions were made up, but the words belong to Bill, although some sentences and punctuations were altered slightly for clarity. As Shane requested, misspellings and grammar errors generally were not corrected. If Bill happened to be interviewed and gave written answers, here's how it might go:

You said you began to pray regularly to God after Montana came in 1989 to visit you with his children, Chastity and Cody Bug. Montana urged you to accept Christ so that you would see your grandchildren again after you died. Can you tell me about that?

> So I got to where I would talk to God every night after I went to bed. I would prayed and I asked him to forgive me. But I was trying to make deals with God. I was really wanted to be baptized, and I would tell God if he would let me be baptized I would do this or I would do that. And I would start living better and I would start going to church. They held one a week there on death row.
>
> Some nights after I thought everyone had gone to sleep I would get on my knees beside my bed and pray. . . . My prayers just wasn't getting through and I really didn't know what God wanted me to do. I knew what I really needing was a Bible. But I had been locked up for fifteen years and never picked up a Bible and I didn't own a Bible and hadn't read one before I was locked up. So I really didn't know nothing about God words. I thought about borrowing one of the men Bibles but to ashamed to and didn't want to be made fun of. So I stopped talking to God at night and I stopped trying to pray for I know it wasn't doing any good and I really thought God had given up on me for all the bad things I had did and for all the folks I had hurt and killed.

CHAPTER THIRTY

So when did you get a Bible to read?

> One night late I was laying on my bed, couldn't sleep. So I deciding to get up and clean out my locker of old books and junk.... When I removed the books in front, there in the back was a Bible. I had forgot about it. Sometime before this, my daughter-in-law Lisa (Montana's wife) had sent me her old Bible her grandma had gave her for Christmas when she was 12 years old.

You said that when a book was mailed to someone on death row, an approval form from the warden or someone higher up must accompany the book. This Bible from Lisa had no such form, and the mail man would not give it to you at first. But then he called you back as you walked toward your cell. "I'm going to give you this Bible," he yelled, but you really didn't want it, did you?

> I was ashamed to carried it back through the cellblock where all the men could see it.... Well, I took the Bible and before I got back to the cellblock, I put the Bible under my shirt to hide it from the other men. And when I got in my cell I hid the Bible behind all the other books in my locker. And just forgot about it. And now here I was with a Bible and didn't have to ask the other men to borrow one. So I laid back down on my bed and started from the front and read the Bible til daybreak. I didn't read the Bible in daytime. But just as soon as they locked everyone down I would get my Bible down and read it. Took me just four weeks to read

> my Bible from front to the back and during the four weeks I got to talking and praying to God again. But after reading my Bible there was a big difference this time when talked and praying to him. I wasn't trying to make deal with God. When I would asked him for something I would always say before I asked him if it's your will God. And I never asked him to set me free and I never asked him to get me off death row.

You prayed for three things: for God to take care of your family, for him to find a way for you to be baptized—obviously this was before you were baptized—and for God to help you get rid of the terrible dreams and nightmares about people you had murdered over the years. You said some of them were in hell. Could you get any sleep after seeing faces of people you killed?

> I could see the torment in their face and when I would wake up I knew I had put them there and I never could go back to sleep. And I would asked God to give me peace of mind. I prayed for that a lot for it bad being locked up in a cell and can't sleep. All during these months I was reading my Bible a lot of nights, I would just stop. I would reach my hand up for an hour or more begging God to take it. I would hold it up to him til I just gave out, my arm would get so tired. . . . Not a night would pass by I didn't hold up my hand to him.

CHAPTER THIRTY

You ended up in prison after being convicted, along with Bobby Gene Gaddis, of robbing a bank in Loganville, Georgia. Billy Wayne Davis turned state's evidence and got a better deal on his sentence. Tell me what happened at the bank.

> The police pulled up where me and Billy Wayne was coming out the door of the bank. Before they could get out of the car Bobby Gaddis loaded the same double-barrel shotgun I was going to kill Sheriff Lee with in the window and pull both triggers and blowed the windows out of the police car. Some of the shots hit Billy Cody (local policeman) by the time me and Billy Wayne was in the car. But we had to pass right by the police car with me and Billy Cody shooting at each other as we went by. I looked around and Davis was laying down in the back seat. I should have shot him right then.

Davis ratted on you about the Loganville robbery. But why did he decide to turn state's evidence in the double murder Jefferson County, Georgia?

> The last thing I told Bobby was to keep his mouth shut, we would be out in 8 or 9 years. He told me not to worried about him saying anything. Well I thought that was the end of it for Billy Davis would have got out within 3 years. So I thought he would keep his mouth shut on all the other stuff. But in 1975 me and Bobby won an appeal, got our whole (bank robbery) case overturned. Billy Wayne

> got scared we was going to get out. So he told about a double murder in Jefferson County and he got immunity to testified against me and Bobby and Charles Reed.... I can say this, the law used the hell out of him (Davis). Had him tell murder after murder. Took them up in Barrow County and showed them where a lot of body was buried. But he always told them he never was with me when I killed these people.... I guess he thought the law was stupid.

And Sheriff Lee somehow found out about a hit being put out on him. How did he know?

> I dont know how he found out.... Back in 1972 (actually it was 1973, Lee's first year as sheriff), with five (or) six people knowing about it, it hard to keep a secret. But Mr. Lee never could prove it. But he knew about it. Well, in 1975 Billy Wayne was held in Earl Lee jail. So to make points with Lee, he told Mr. Lee about the hit (that) had been put on him. But he told Mr. Lee that it was Harold Chancey who had put the hit on him. (Actually it was Davis.) When a man start snitches for the law there no stoping him but kill the bastard.

Davis obviously ratted on you a lot and even told a federal agent, Jim West, about fifty or sixty murders Davis said you committed. But you got back at him when you confessed to the Matthews murders, which you said involved Davis. Seven men had been in prison for some

CHAPTER THIRTY

time, convicted of those May 1971 killings. How did you feel after the men were released?

> Well, it took around six month but all 7 of the men walked out of Reidsville Prison free. And I really felt good about doing that. No matter how cold-hearted you are you hate to see a man in prison for a crime you did. But if I hadn't got them death sentences (on the Jefferson County murders), all 7 of these men would have spent most of their life in prison. So on that my consciences is clear tonight.

You said Earl Lee never asked you to snitch, but the FBI surely did. Tell me about that.

> I asked them how could I help them. Well it came down to they wanted me to snitch on five people they had been after for a long time. Lee Gilstrap out of Gainesville, Harold and Ruth Chancey from Winder, Reese Spencer from Athens and C.W. Royster from Winder. They said here the deal. If you will help us we can't get you out of prison right now. But we can get your death sentence cut to a life sentence and all 4 of your life sentences will be run into one.... They wanted me to tell them I had killed people for these folks, then I would have to testify in court on all of them. The main one they wanted was the Jim Daws murder. His body found in the Little Mulberry River weighted down with cement blocks.... I would have to lie on

347

> these folks because I aint never worked for none of them (except for hauling moonshine for Chancey), have never asked me to killed for anybody (or) do anything else for them.

Sheriff Lee obviously knew the FBI agents were wasting their time trying to get you to snitch. He knew you wouldn't tell them anything, right?

> I think right there was one of the reason that Sheriff Lee came to respect me so much and I had a lot of respect for him as a man and a sheriff. One thing he wouldn't do was lie to you. If he told you something you could bet he would do it. If he gave his word to you it was like money in the bank. Most folks didn't know this but Earl Lee was a good Christian man. He had a lot of faith in God and he was a good family man.

Something humorous happened when you were in Earl Lee's jail. Tell me about that.

> In 1976 I stayed in Douglas County jail I guess around four months. Well there was an old man by the name of Buddy Bell, kin to Earl in some way. But was in a wheelchair, had been for a long time. Buddy Bell was the best Christian man I believe I have ever mets. Couldn't help but like him.... Well back then I didn't talk to religion folks. If a Christian person came to my cell and started preaching to me I would run them off.... He visited me almost everyday. But we never talked about religion and I got to like old

CHAPTER THIRTY

Buddy Bell real good. . . .

Well one day Sheriff Lee was gone out of town when the deputy push Buddy to my cell. He told the deputy to open my cell door and push him in my cell. . . . The deputy open my cell door and push Buddy in with me. Buddy had a sack in his lap when the deputy locked the door and left. (Buddy handed) me the sack and said here I brought you 2 foot long hotdogs and a Coke.

Well I took the sack and set it on my bed and told him I would eat them later. He said no eat them now while they are hot. So I sat down on my bed and ate the hotdogs. When I got through eating I said thank for the hotdogs Buddy, they are good. He said Billy them hotdogs wasn't free. I thought he ment for me to pay for them so I reach for my money. But Buddy said Billy I don't want your money. I said what you want Buddy. He looked me straight in the eye and said Billy I want you to pray with me. I almost said no. But I looked at him sitting there in that wheelchair with that beautiful smile on his face. So I thought what to heck, what harm can it do. So I said OK Buddy I will pray with you. I bowed my head and closed my eyes sitting on the bed. But Buddy said Billy get down here in front of me so I can hold your hands. So I squatting down on my heels. Buddy said what wrong with your knees. Are they sore. I said no Buddy my knees ain't sore. He said well get on them then. Well to humor him I got on my knees, Buddy took my hands and I bet he prayed for a good 20 minutes. He prayed for me and all of my family and all of the men in jail. I wasn't praying. I was just listen to him. But I was thinking all the time he was praying, damn Birt how cheap can you get. This man has got you on your knees for 2 foot long hotdogs. Old Buddy Bell died a long time ago but he became a good friend of mine.

Let's talk about how your baptism came about after Earl Lee brought you to Douglas County the last week in August of 1992.

I was still on death row in Jackson prison. Through the years Sheriff Lee had check me off of death row and took me back to his jail just so my family could spend a little time with me for I had five small kids and he knew how much I love my wife and kids. Plus I think he did it to repay me for what happened in 72 (actually '73, when Bill decided not to kill Lee outside his church). . . .

When he got me to the jail he took me in his office and told me to call Ruby Nell and Stoney and let them know I was there. I asked him didnt Ruby Nell asked him to come get me. He said no she didn't even know I was there, that he just came and got me on his own. I said Mr. Lee before I got back to death row I like to ask a favor of you. Mr. Lee said you want to be baptized dont you Billy. I said yes but how did you know. Did

CHAPTER THIRTY

> Ruby Nell tell you. He said no, nobody told me.... Well on Saturday morning Ruby Nell, Stoney and Stone came. They were sitting in Mr. Lee office when I got there. After I got hugs and kisses I sit down and told them about I was going to let Montana baptized me in Mr. Lee pool...

Finally, though, they convinced you to be baptized in Montana's church, as they called it, the Church of the Lord Jesus Christ. But you didn't want a whole lot of people there on the Sunday night of the next weekend, when the baptism was to be celebrated. How did you feel when you walked in that day and the church was full?

> There was but five cars park in front of the church. So I thought they were my family cars for I didn't know behind the church was a big parking lot. The best I remember the church had two big glass doors but you couldn't see through them into the church. Well I opened them doors and got the shocked of my life. That church was full of people and all of them was standing up singing. I wanted to run. I saw Ruby Nell and the rest of my family sitting almost at the back. I walked over and said Honey what is all these people doing here. She said Bill it Sunday night. They are having church. I forgot they hold church here on Sunday night. I didn't say this but I thinking it. Girl, this is a fine fix you got me into.

What do you remember about the baptism itself?

> I dont remember how long he (Montana) talked (before the baptism) but what I do remember was sitting there looking at all of them people and how scared I was. If the folks could have seen down in that water they would have saw my knees knocked together. I dont think I had ever been so scared in my whole life. I remember thinking while Montana was talking, Hurry up son. Get this over with, so I can get out of here. I was intending when Montana was through baptizing me to go straight to Sheriff Lee and tell him to get me out of there for I had done asked Ruby Nell when I first came in, these folks dont expect me to give no testimony do they. Ruby Nell said no Bill, they dont expected you to give no testimony.... I remember Montana saying turn sideway Daddy and I remember how good it felt. When he put his hands on my head right then all my fears left me. I wasn't scared anymore and when he put me under that water the best feeling came over me, a feeling like I never had before and I know Jesus had finally took my hand after all them nights laying on my bed on death row holding my hand up to God begging him to take it.

How did you feel when you stepped out of the baptistry?

> Well what happened in that water change my life for ever and anybody who know me will tell you it would take a pure miracle to get

CHAPTER THIRTY

me to walk out in front of a whole church full of people and give my testimony for I always figure if God had wanted me to get up and talked and give testimony in front of people he would have made me to talk real plain. I couldnt wait to get them wet clothes off and get out there and tell the folks about Jesus and give my testimony. I even told them about the man that brought me there, Sheriff Earl Lee I was hired to killed him 20 years before. But something stoped me and now here he was 20 years later bringing me off of death row back to my son church for him to baptized me.

But while I was giving my testimony something happened that made me feel about one inch tall. There was a lady sitting out there with three (or) four small kids. The last time I saw this lady she was sitting at the DA table in the Barrow County Courthouse in 1980 while I was on trial for her husband (Donald Chancey) murder. Now I dont even know why her husband was killed. I had nothing against him. Just a hit job. But I knew these small kids with her was this man grandkids and because of me he would never get to hold them (or) be with them on this earth. And I had four of my grandkids right there in church with me. I wanted to go down there and hug her neck and tell her how sorry I was but I guess I was afraid. Sure wish I had that moment to live over. I would like to ask her to forgive me. But now I cant. A couple of month ago God called her home to be with her husband.

353

What else happened that night?

> I don't remember just how long I talked but while I was giving my testimony I remember seeing Dr. C.B. Skelton sitting out in the back of the church. I just had to talk to him and give him a hug for he and his daughter Lynn have been so nice to Ruby Nell and the kids since I had been locked up. Helped them in so many ways plus around 1989 Dr. Skelton had took the time to sat down and write me a beautiful letter about the Bible and King David. About the time Lisa sent me her Bible, I did my best to proved Dr. Skelton was wrong about what he wrote me in his letter, but after reading Lisa Bible I found out that every word Doc had wrote me was the truth. And his letter was a big turning point in my life and for this I will always be indebted to Dr. C.B. Skelton and his daughter Lynn. . . .

You enjoyed a good meal after the service. What do you remember about that?

> I do know they had a good dinner fix but I cant remember what I ate. I was like in a daze from being around all them good people and having all of my family with me at one time and from just being baptized and for having Jesus in my life for the first time.

You missed your mother's funeral, but you got to visit her and Pete Phillips' graves. What do you remember about that?

CHAPTER THIRTY

Someone put a beautiful flower pot in my hand and Ruby Nell said Bill they are for your mother grave and I didnt even know I was going to visiting mom grave. I will for ever love her for that. I know she had to be the one to asked Sheriff Lee to take me by to see mom grave and that ment the world to me. I will for ever be in her debted. I don't know what time it was when we left the church. Must have been around 11 (or) 12 oclock. All I remember I got a lot of hugged and kisses before I got in the sheriff car with the two deputies to leave so many people I didnt even know came up and huged my neck. I cant remember another time in my whole life of feeling so good and being at peace with everybody and the world.

Tell me about your experience at the cemetery.

We drove to White Plains Church in Jackson County where mom and Pete and all the rest of my family is buried. Mom and Pete grave is right by the highway. Pete bought that lot so he could hear cars go by is what he told me. Well Mr. Lee and the deputies park in the church yard with their headlights on shinning on mom and Pete grave which was around 2 hundred feet away. I asked Sheriff Lee could I go down to mom grave by myself. He said yes. I still didn't have any handcuff (or) shackles on. So they stood in front of the cars while I went to mom grave. I put flowers on mom grave and I think might be wrong about this but I recalled getting some flowers off of someone grave and put them on Pete grave.... I told mom, mom your prayers wasnt in vain for tonight at a little church in Winder, Ga. my son and your grandson baptized me and Jesus took me back from the devil.

How did you feel when you got back to jail?

I was put back in a cell but I didnt get any sleep the rest of the night. Laid awake and thought about what all had happened in the last few hours. I felt like I was on a high. But it wasnt no dope high. It was a high like I never been on before and I felt at peace.

I understand a lot of inmates were not happy with the special treatment you received, getting out of prison to be baptized.

Well, with me going back to my son church to be baptized and the news media getting ahold of it and keeping it on TV for a week (or) more. All the men went to hollered and writing folks in high places saying yall let Billy Birt go back to his son church to be baptize and we cant be baptized. Well it took a month but one day I was standing up front to get my mail, here come 4 guards down the hall carried a real big tub. When they passed by me one of them said see Birt what you and Earl Lee done, putting all this extra work on us. The tub was made to baptized the men on death row and with in the next couple weeks I bet it was over 30 men

CHAPTER THIRTY

> baptized in that tub and no telling how many since I left death row. They still use it.

After that kid stabbed you at the prison in Alto, Georgia, and you recovered, able to walk again, you wanted to kill the stabber. What were your feelings about that incident?

> I use to lay in my bed at night for the next eight years and think about all the ways I was going to kill (him), and some days hate and revenge is what keep a man going in prison. I knew that for suree before 1992 I had passed away many an hour thinking about Billy Wayne Davis, with nothing but pure hate.

But then, after you accepted Christ and were baptized, did you forget about getting revenge against the kid?

> So I told the kid not to worry about it. We all make mistakes and I had forgave him a long time ago.

You talk about how much you love all of your children—you called them "the five most wonderful kids"—but you believe Montana was born for a special reason. Is that right?

> When God sent me and Ruby Nell Montana, I honest believe now that he was looking out for me for God knew my whole life millions of years in advance. He knew what I was going to become and if God hadnt sent Montana to us without a doubt in my mind I would have busted hell wide open when I died.... But God has made me understand. If you

> asked him and really mean it in your heart he will forgive you of your sins. But you can be baptized and saved a thousand times but a person has still got to reap what you sow here on earth.

Stoney was your forever sidekick, wasn't he?

> The one person I owe more to than anybody is my son Stonewall. Lord that kid has been my rock. I dont know of another father and son who has been born as close as we have been from the day God gave him to me and Ruby Nell. There has been a bond between us, from day one that nobody could break. That kid worship me all of his life and I felt the same about him. . . .

What do you have to say about Ruby Nell?

> I will never understand why God has blessed me so much after all the everythings I did for the devil. But he has blessed me more than any one I know these pasts 53 years when he gave me Ruby Nell Lee for my wife one of the best woman that ever been on the earth. And I feel so ashame for the way I did her. And I hope her and God will forgive me.

Shane tells about Gideons and his father at church.

Ruby all dressed up for a special luncheon.

CHAPTER THIRTY-ONE
By Phil Hudgins

For many years, Shane Birt had thought about something he should do. It was the right thing to do, but it was going to be hard. Really hard. On Thursday, October 31, 2019, he got up the nerve to follow through.

I accompanied him on his mission to ride down to Wrens, Georgia and meet with Hugh Fleming. He wanted to look the man in the eye and say, "I'm sorry."

Mr. Fleming is the son of Reid and Lois Fleming, who were found dead—strangled with coat hangers—in their Wrens home two days before Christmas in 1973. Billy Sunday Birt was one of the men convicted of the murders.

Shane's idea was to meet first with the sheriff, Gary Hutchins, at his office in Louisville, the seat of Jefferson County, about fifteen miles from Wrens. He said it didn't seem right to introduce himself cold to Mr. Fleming.

The sheriff was attending a funeral, so we decided to wait until he returned. We figured that the man who had been sheriff since 1993 surely would know Mr. Fleming, a prominent citizen of the county and retired executive of First State Bank. Turned out, he knew him well.

In his retirement, Mr. Fleming has become an excellent woodworker. A collection of his beautiful hand-turned wooden bowls are pictured on his website. "Each bowl is crafted with care and is a unique piece of art," the website says.

We sat in the lobby and waited for the sheriff. Shane was nervous. "My heart's going like this," he said, moving his fingers rapidly back and forth, "and I have a knot in my stomach."

Sheriff Hutchins returned to his office about 3 o'clock. He called us in.

Shane introduced himself at the lobby door, but his last name probably didn't register with the sheriff. Then, inside the office, Shane took a seat and said immediately, "My name is Shane Birt, and Billy Sunday Birt was my dad."

The sheriff's posture seemed to stiffen a bit. His facial expression betrayed his unspoken question: "What does this man want from me?"

That name, Billy Sunday Birt, no doubt is engraved in the memories of many older people in Jefferson County. Every law enforcement officer around there has heard the name. They may not remember or have heard everything that happened. After all, at that time, it all went back forty-eight years, to December 23, 1973.

But Hugh Fleming unfortunately remembers everything. He experienced it, every gory detail. He is the one who found his mother and father on that grim Sunday morning. He went to their home after they didn't show up for Sunday school and church. Reid Fleming taught Sunday school, and he almost never missed. Something must be wrong, the son thought to himself.

Turned out, something was unthinkably wrong.

And then, nearly a half-century later, Billy Shenandoah "Shane" Birt was in Mr. Fleming's home county to apologize. He could not right such a horrible wrong, but at least he could say, "I'm really sorry." And if Mr. Fleming was willing, he could pray with him.

Sheriff Hutchins seemed reluctant at first. How do you telephone someone, eighty-four years old, and say that the son of a man convicted of murdering your parents wants to meet you? "We don't want information," Shane assured the sheriff. "I just want to apologize."

Finally, after one long half-minute, Sheriff Hutchins said, "I guess I can call him and see what he says."

Shane and I walked back to the lobby and waited, again.

The knot in Shane's stomach had not gone away.

CHAPTER THIRTY-ONE BY PHIL HUDGINS

When he called us back in, we could see the answer on the sheriff's face before he said a word.

Mr. Fleming appreciated the gesture, the sheriff said, but he didn't feel like talking. His brother had died a mere two days earlier, and he was still mourning the loss. Adding to his grief, being reminded of the horrific scene that December morning in 1973, would have been too much for him.

We understood.

"At least Mr. Fleming knows we reached out to him," Shane said later. "I wanted to do this a long time ago." And there are other Billy Birt victims who deserve an apology, for whatever it's worth.

The sheriff took Shane's business card in case Mr. Fleming changed his mind.

"From Christian to Christian," the sheriff said softly to Shane, "thank you."

Twenty years ago, a great-niece of Reid and Lois Fleming turned in a research paper for a course in criminal justice at Augusta State University in Augusta, Georgia. The course was titled "Violence and the South."

"I knew immediately what I would write about," she stated in her paper. She chose a fellow student to work with her.

Their goal was to "examine contemporary and historical work about violence shaped by the socio-cultural and historical context of the South, including racial violence homicide, violence against women, violence in the criminal justice system, and any other types of violence that we may decide to explore as individuals and as a class."

Students were assigned to read certain books. One of them was *Culture of Honor: The Psychology of Violence in the South*. According to the authors, Richard E. Nisbett and Dov Coven, "the South has long been thought to be more violent than the North, and we believe that some distinctive aspects of the South are key to this violence."

The students gleaned this from the book:

"If resources are abundant or are not subject to theft, then a reputation for toughness has little value. But if resources are in scarce or unpredictable supply, and if they are sufficiently portable that theft is a predictable route to bounty, then toughness has great economic value. . . . The South was a low-population frontier region until well into the nineteenth century. In such regions the state often has little power to command compliance with the law, and citizens have to create their own system of order. The means for doing this is the rule of retaliation: If you cross me, I will punish you."

That could have been Bill Birt's life motto: If you cross me, I will punish you.

The students concentrated on two of the four men believed involved in the Fleming murders: Billy Sunday Birt and Bobby Gene Gaddis. They wrote, "How did a combination of the Southern culture of honor, history of involvement with moonshining, poverty, lack of education, and association with other criminals lead them down a path of violence?"

They interviewed Joel Robinson, then-sheriff of Barrow County, who noted that as the production and transport of illegal liquor gave way to the drug culture, the economics of moonshining felt a squeeze. That's what happened to Bill Birt, who moved gradually from hauling moonshine for Harold Chancey to robbery and running illegal drugs from Mexico.

They interviewed Horace Waters, a GBI agent who worked on the Fleming case. He died in 2013.

According to the research paper, Waters told the students he "kept vigil in a trailer behind Sheriff Earl Lee's office in Douglasville, Georgia, while keeping Birt and his group under surveillance. Up until then, the men had managed to elude law enforcement officers by covering up any evidence that would connect them to their involvement in numerous unsolved cases."

CHAPTER THIRTY-ONE   BY PHIL HUDGINS

Waters said he "knew that sooner or later the group would become careless enough to leave evidence uncovered or confess to their connection to many of these unsolved crimes. Seven days a week, twenty four hours a day, pressure was placed upon Birt and his cohorts to break their resistance."

The students wrote, "At last the strain became too great for one of Birt's closest friends. The friend called Birt to say that he could no longer eat or sleep, and could no longer withstand the pressure. He decided to turn himself over to police to get everything off his chest. Birt confessed to his friend that he, too, was experiencing those feelings and agreed to go along with him to surrender."

"We found the man's body just a few days later," Waters reported, according to the research paper.

Bob Ingram, who at the time was still an agent with the Georgia Bureau of Investigation, told the students, as he had told Shane: "Billy Sunday Birt is not as well known as Theodore Bundy or Jeffrey Dahmer; however, he is responsible for many more homicides."

Fortunately, the tradition of violence "appears to have been broken in Birt's family," Sheriff Robinson said.

"Mrs. Birt worked hard to overcome the negative effects of her husband's crimes," he said.

Everybody who knows Ruby Nell Birt would agree with the former sheriff: "She went on to raise her five children to become productive citizens and business owners in the community."

Therefore, the students concluded that Edwin H. Sutherland's "differential association theory" seems to be right on target: Criminal behavior is learned, not inherited.

The research paper ends with this: "Birt's reputation among law enforcement, even though it was of criminal nature, placed him on a high status level as the number one murderer in the state of Georgia. He gained respect in the moonshine industry, as well, and was feared by all."

Having worked for the Gainesville, Georgia, newspaper, *The Times*, for many years, I had heard of Billy Sunday Birt when Shane talked to me in May of 2018 about writing this book. My brother, Ken Hudgins, knew more about him; from 1972 to 1980 he was publisher of *The Winder News*, which reported on Bill Birt's criminal activities.

Ken remembers that the office for the Winder Woman's Club was near the newspaper office and that Ruth Chancey, who was active in the club, visited him several times asking that the newspaper lighten up on covering Billy Birt. "He's a good boy," she told him.

I never met Ruth Chancey or her kin; I never met Billy Birt or any of his colleagues; I didn't know any of the victims. So to tell this story, I have depended on the memories and documents from Birt family members, mostly Shane and his mother. I gleaned information from court reports, from former and current law enforcers and their files, newspaper reports, Ruby's letters, friends and associates of the Birt family, and, with permission from the author, Bill's letters from Stoney Birt's second book, *Rock Solid: In His Own Words*. Stoney's first book was titled *Rock Solid: The True Story of Georgia's Dixie Mafia*. Both were published in 2017, after his father's death. I also quoted Stoney from two podcasts: one produced by *CSI Atlanta*, the other from *Imperative Entertainment*. [Episodes quoted from are listed in Acknowledgments.]

Stoney, who spent most of his boyhood days with his dad, received letters regularly from Bill. And he learned a lot hanging around with his daddy and the gang. In his first book, Stoney wrote, "I was probably the only kid in the 1st grade that could tell you the odds of pulling an inside straight in a game of seven-card stud with three players. And I know I'm the only kid who was able to drive a muscle car to school in the seventh grade at twelve years old."

CHAPTER THIRTY-ONE   BY PHIL HUDGINS

In describing Bill's baptism, I relied mostly on videotapes from that Sunday night. But for the more personal information—and, in some cases, to clear up facts—I turned mainly to Ruby Birt and her youngest offspring, Shane.

I wasn't surprised by Ruby Birt's ability to recall events, even events decades-old. She became an adult while still a child and began storing away grownup memories, the best and worst as vivid as yesterday's. Talking to Bob Ingram one day, she remembered that the silver service that may have been taken from the Bryce and Virginia Durham residence showed up in her Barrow County home in 1972 or '73. The Durhams, along with their son, were murdered in 1972 in Boone, North Carolina.

I have been surprised, however, about how much Shane remembers, even though he saw his father out from behind bars only twice—when Bill was baptized in 1992, and when the family posed for family portraits at a Douglasville studio. He heard stories from his dad, sometimes in bits and pieces, and he remembered.

Listening to Holly Dunn singing "Daddy's Hands," he could envision his own daddy's hands, hands he marveled at as a little boy, really big hands. As a teenager, he looked at those same hands and asked himself how and why they killed dozens of people. But Shane's son, Jackson, knows his grandfather's hands simply as praying hands. No killings involved.

Of course, memories fail and sometimes differ: What one sibling remembers about his or her father might not match with Shane's recollection. But I have come to trust what Shane says. If Shane was wrong about some fact, the mistake was of the head, not the heart. Shane and I have ridden around Georgia together, and even to Asheville, North Carolina, and we've had a lot of time to talk. I even attended one of his Saturday morning Gideons meetings in Winder and a Gideons presentation one Sunday at Mt. Calvary Baptist Church near Flowery Branch, Georgia.

When Shane would say, "Now what I want to say about that is this right here"—an introduction he used often—I knew to listen. He had something important to say. He has definite convictions about right and wrong, but I got the feeling he was sometimes conflicted about revealing everything about his father's criminal activities. It's natural to want to respect and even revere one's father, so all of the Birt children, including Shane, prefer to remember the good things their dad did. Love and loyalty can be blinding, and forgetting the bad can be a blessing. But Shane wanted to remember it all—good and bad. He wanted this book to tell the truth, as far as it can be told, so neither he nor his mother held back, that I know of. In at least one instance, they withheld the name of a Billy Birt accomplice in a killing because "he had never been implicated in any crime," Shane said. The man is deceased.

In the end, both Shane and Ruby approved everything in this book. And Shane wanted to make one thing clear: "What I told you came from Daddy," he said. "Information about what happened came from him. I didn't make anything up."

Ruby telephoned me at home on Sunday, April 19, 2020, to say she had finished reading the manuscript, all but one chapter, at that time yet to be written. "I couldn't put it down," she said. "It was so true . . . I cried a lot." (Other stories have been added since that April conversation.)

I asked her what she'd been doing besides reading the book. Like most of us during that time, she was forced to stay indoors by the Covid pandemic that was torturing the world.

"Well," she said, "I've been making masks. They need them at the (Winder) hospital. And I made one for you and your wife.

"Next, I'm going to make some gowns. The hospital needs them, too."

CHAPTER THIRTY-ONE   BY PHIL HUDGINS

I should have known Ruby would use her time in captivity wisely. Her hands know nothing about idleness.

My wife and I received our face masks, along with two for our daughters, a few days after my conversation with Ruby. They were perfectly sewn.

"Have you ever heard of someone laying hands on a sewing machine, praying for it to sew right?" Ruby asked when I telephoned her to thank her for the face masks. Her machine had been acting up, not sewing the way it should.

"No, I don't think I've heard of anyone doing that," I said.

"Well, I did. And it worked."

Ruby in garden.

CHAPTER THIRTY-TWO
By Phil Hudgins

It was the fourteenth time Ruby Nell Birt and I had gotten together to talk, a dozen of those times at her modest home near the Barrow-Gwinnett county line in north Georgia. It was a beautiful, sunny day, and Ruby had returned just days earlier from a vacation with Shane and his family on the Georgia coast. She appeared relaxed and happy.

Ruby knew nothing about vacations when she and Bill were together. The one vacation she recalls with her husband lasted one day and one night in Miami, Florida. Bill was on a "job," she found out later.

"I want you to see my garden before you leave," she said at the end of our conversation. We walked to the backyard, and there in the middle of a freshly mown lawn were stately rows of zucchini squash, yellow squash, okra, tomatoes, peppers, and cantaloupe.

It was a small garden—about twenty feet long and nine feet wide—but it was big enough for someone who can't eat vegetables. Ruby had eighty percent of her small intestine removed about six years ago, and her body doesn't digest vegetables as well as it should. She cooks collards occasionally, but she eats only the soup—the potlikker. She can't even enjoy cornbread with her potlikker.

"You grow these vegetables just to give away, don't you?" I asked her during our next meeting after she insisted that I take some of her bounty home with me.

Yes, that's right, she nodded, but she finds pleasure in the planting, the hoeing, the harvesting for others. "I just love having a garden," she said.

Seeing the neatness of the patch, no weeds between the rows, I remembered her story about Bill's plowing up her garden after he found her hoeing in broad daylight as men, full of lust as Bill imagined, drove by on the highway and possibly looked her way. But I didn't say anything. She seemed joyous as she stood for photographs, and I didn't want to say anything negative.

I reminded her of the first time we met. It was at the Master's Table restaurant, a catering business in downtown Winder, where she works when the owner, and her best friend, Lynn Walls, calls to say she needs help. I didn't ask any questions on that first day, and she didn't offer any answers. She looked at me as though I were an abstract painting she was trying to figure out. She said very little.

"I try to size people up to see if they're real," she said later. "I don't have time for people who are not real. I don't want to be rude about it. I just don't have time for it."

The second time we met, this occasion at her home, sitting at her dining room table, she talked openly about everything I wanted to know. I guess she found me real.

It didn't take long to figure out that Ruby Birt is as real, and honest, as they come. Not to mention generous. Every time I visited, she placed homemade candy, Starbucks Frappuccino and a bottle of water in front of me. I sometimes left with a coconut cake—her specialty—or chocolate-covered peanuts, or brownies, or peanut brittle. Or vegetables. And it's not because I'm special. Wherever she goes—to the drug store, to the doctor, to the car service center—she takes biscuits or pieces of cake or candy. Maybe collards for her doctor. She gets great service wherever she goes.

As generous as she is, Ruby Birt takes no credit for her giving to others; the Bible says she should love, serve, and give, and she does just that.

She does not dwell on her past problems. She had a life to live, kids to raise, jobs to do—*many* jobs to do. But, busy as she was, she took time to listen to the problems of others and offer advice, if it was requested. She made friends easily and earned a reputation in town of someone who would work hard and do her part in whatever task was before her.

She stuck by her friends. She was a pen pal to Harold Chancey, who was in prison with Bill at one time. The Birt family was living on Chancey's land then, and she figured she owed him her friendship.

She was always busy looking after her children and tending to their needs, sometimes trying to attend, in one day, three different ball games at the park and rec field.

Through it all, even on the cloudiest days, she usually managed to find some light. Not that she was without worry, not that she was always quick to forgive and forget, although she did forgive, eventually. She persevered. She worked. She survived. And she finally got the Christian home she had always prayed for—still not a perfect home, but a home, we hope, easing toward reconciliation and mutual love and respect.

Ruby's generosity extended not just outside the home, but also inside the prisons. When she visited Bill, she got around the rules forbidding goodies from the outside by wrapping up biscuits or pieces of cake and taping them to her legs or stuffing them inside her bra. "I would be well-endowed," she said, and laughed. At the prison in Alto, Georgia, she always left the woman at the front desk a treat. "The woman turned her back so she wouldn't see me leave something," she said.

Her daughter Ann apparently learned her mama's deception very well. When her daddy was being held in the prison in Jackson, Georgia, she bought a hot chicken biscuit and stuffed it in her bosom for smuggling. By the time she presented the biscuit to Bill, a blister from the hot aluminum-foil wrap had formed in a rather delicate place.

Ann smuggled a peach the same way. "I got this big ol' peach and put it right between them," she said, "and you couldn't tell it because it evened it out."

Said her daddy that day, "Baby, I haven't had a peach in twenty years."

In 1986, Ann made her daddy even happier. She became a mother, and he became a grandfather.

"When Stoney went down and told Daddy about the birth of Diamond," Ann said, "he jumped up and down hollering, 'I'm a grandpa, I'm a grandpa, it's a boy, it's a boy!' He believed he would never have a grandchild because of his past."

"Daddy's going to kill me," Ann thought to herself. "I ain't even married. And he didn't want me to have an abortion. And I would never do that."

"You don't want to marry the guy?" her daddy asked when Ann showed up at his prison with her three-week-old baby. "Do you love him?"

The answer to both questions was no.

"Then he'll be a Birt," her daddy said of his first grandchild. "And I'll be his daddy"—the daddy of Diamond Sunday Birt.

Ann had flown to Georgia from Wisconsin to see her folks and to meet with me. And I found out after a few minutes that if you don't want to know, don't ask her. Sometimes I didn't have to ask. She is blunt and to the point, and she doesn't hold back when she has something to say. She was dressed comfortably in overalls and a T-shirt, reminiscent of her school days.

With Ann, it seemed, most anything her father wanted was all right with her, not that she approved of his illegal activities. But he had such a charm about him, she said, and she was easily charmed. "We didn't see that [bad] side of Dad, even when it was made public. And we didn't see things as others saw them.

CHAPTER THIRTY-TWO   BY PHIL HUDGINS

A lot of the public didn't see it that way. We all seen what Dad wanted us to see, and we accepted it. We had a good life. He merely wasn't there for Mom like he should have been. Mom was a mild-mannered woman. There is no malice in Mom. . . . My mother is the closest thing to a lady there'll ever be. She don't cuss. She don't smoke. She don't drink. She's never been to bars. Nothing."

Her mama could be manipulated, Ann indicated, but her daddy usually got his way—with just about everybody. He persuaded his sister Jody to marry Don "Booger" Cooper, because he was an only child and he'd take care of her. During her marriage to Cooper, Jody enjoyed fun times with Ann, who moved in with her aunt after leaving home at about fourteen. One of their pastimes was firing one of Bill's pistols—one without serial numbers, of course—out into a pasture where Jody and Don lived.

"Don would say, 'Honey, put the gun up.'"

Ann and Jody were regulars at dances at the local American Legion, and they were always ready for a boat ride on Lake Lanier, even if the hour was late.

After hearing several of Ann's stories, Ruby turned to me and said, pointing to her head, "You see this white hair?"

Ann adored her father—he was a perfect daddy when he was in prison, she said—but he had actually embarrassed her at times when he was a free man. She recalled the day he rode a Harley-Davidson motorcycle to school and made three of his kids—Stoney, Ann, and Montana—crawl on the back for a ride while other kids stood and watched. He swapped sawed-off shotguns with one of his buddies "right there at the school," Ann said. "Our normal was everybody else's bizarre."

But as the others said, her daddy was good to many people, often generous with his stolen money. "He took groceries and furniture to women being beaten, with their husbands sitting there," Ann said. "But they didn't dare cross him. . . . If you crossed him, they didn't come no more cold-hearted."

Ruby and Shane always described Bill as two people in one. Stoney said his daddy had a switch inside his brain, a switch that changed him from a giver to a taker. Ann said he "didn't need a switch. It was just there. It came natural if you crossed him. You could see it in his eyes."

In late July of 2021, Ann traveled again to Barrow County, and both of us were eager to continue our conversation. We visited at Shane and Jill's Statham home on a hot, humid morning. This time, she had dressed up for the occasion. I found her out in the yard fiddling with an electric fan, her ankle-length, white duster flowing in the breeze. We walked inside and settled in the den to talk.

Ann missed her big family, she said, and now practically everybody is gone: her daddy, most of her uncles, her grandparents. But her memories are still strong. Her daddy was in prison most of her life, "but at least we had him," she said.

She longs for the time the family lived on Chicken Lyle Road. "I would give all my tomorrows to go back yesterday and stay right there," she said. "We didn't know then what we had." What they had were Sunday dinners with the whole family gathered: grannies and papas and even great-grandparents.

"I wouldn't care where I was dropped in as long as it's 20 years or more (ago)," Ann said. It would be good "to be stuck in the prison visiting room with my daddy laughing and talking truth, and watching him eat. It was a true sight to behold—and Mama's cooking, Lord have mercy!"

Life was not as good when the Birts lived in Statham. Ann remembers when the law brought in a a bulldozer to dig up everything in their yard, even a pet cemetery. She remembers watching as agents destroyed numerous pallets of empty, plastic milk jugs that sat on a sea of pea gravel. "It looked like snow in our yard," she said. It was strange because it's not illegal to own a bunch of milk jugs, even pallets of them.

She remembers being rousted from bed in the middle of the night while the law searched the house for something, she didn't know what.

She recalls the day her daddy slipped into the house, one of his arms covered in a purple horse medicine applied by a veterinarian to treat a gun wound. He was running from the law, but he obviously thought it urgent to come home briefly and teach Ruby and Stoney how to shoot a pistol. "He let Mama shoot the windows out in the house," she said. "Daddy said, 'Don't be home tomorrow,' and we wasn't. We got home (the next day) and the windows were fixed."

But, to Ann, life in the Birt home wasn't really bad for a long time. "We didn't know," she said. "We didn't know about Daddy's killings until it hit the news. I was eleven at the time. But when it hit, it hit."

Through it all, her mother wanted the best for the whole family. "We had the best clothes, we had the best whatnot, but she worked hard for it. She would not settle for the mediocre. . . . She made Daddy's clothes like Porter Wagoner's on the Grand Ole Opry. His pants and shirts had gold and all in them. He had shirts in every color: black and brown and blue and white. Every shirt there was like that."

Her daddy liked to dress up. He'd leave the house looking like a million bucks and smelling like Hai Karate, his favorite cologne.

Ann knows that smells trigger memories and emotions, so she paid eighty dollars on eBay for a bottle of Hai Karate, and "when I miss him real bad, I'll open that bottle and take a whiff," she said. The smell conjures up the good times, times, for example, when she earned a penny for every gray hair she plucked from her daddy's head.

As you no doubt surmised, Ann Birt doesn't put on airs—"I'm going to be who I'm going to be," she said—and she is not impressed by people who do put on airs. There's no good reason to make yourself look good, she said, adding another one of her favorite sayings: "One word said about you is better than ten words said by you.... If you have to toot your own horn, something ain't right."

She can't change the past. She lives with it and treasures the good times.

Shane spoke up from his den couch: "The thing about Daddy was, it didn't matter if he was in prison or out of prison, when you sat down and talked to him, when you got done, you felt like everything was going to be okay. He had confidence."

"He had insight," Ann added.

One reason for Ann's 2021 visit to Georgia was to give her time to get her head straight, she said. Her house in Wisconsin had burned—no one was home at the time—and she needed to decide her next step: whether to stay up north or move back to Georgia. She had lived in California several years, then Wisconsin, where brother Montana conducts a prison ministry. But Barrow County is where the memories were born. And it's good to reminisce sometimes.

Carrying a bucketful of vegetables, I was headed to my truck, Ruby walking beside me, when she thought of something to tell me: "Oh, I found out who got shot that night I saw fire come from a gun in a car parked outside our house. It was Willie Hester."

"How do you know that?" I asked.

She gave me the name of the person who told her, but later on, requested the name not be revealed. The person wanted to remain anonymous.

"So when you heard someone knocking on your door before you saw the gunfire, was that Willie Hester?" I asked her.

"Yes," she said. "Bill apparently got Willie back to the car (after Willie knocked on the door) and shot him and then put him in the trunk. Bill came in the house and got something and then left. I never mentioned to him about what I saw."

CHAPTER THIRTY-TWO   BY PHIL HUDGINS

Ruby is usually calm and matter-of-fact when she speaks of one of Bill's evil acts. She lived in a pocket of calmness, it seems, surrounded by chaos. I saw her tear up one time: when she heard Bill's testimony on tape for the first time.

This woman grew up in the arms of a dangerous man—knowing eventually that her husband was a murderer and a robber and an arsonist and a thief and a philanderer—and talking about it all might have been cathartic at times. Like Shane, she wanted to tell the truth about what Bill did, and now, thanks to someone who knew, she had solved another mystery.

"All these years, it's always bothered me who was shot that night," she said. "Now that I know, it hasn't crossed my mind again."

According Ruby's unidentified informant, it didn't cross Bill's mind either, until later. After killing Hester and stashing the body, Bill drove the car to a place near Jody's and sister Frances's homes and left it. He was in another state, maybe Tennessee—no one knows for sure—when he remembered leaving the body in the trunk. He drove home immediately and disposed of it.

In the fall of 1978—about seven years after Hester disappeared—his skeleton was found in a shallow grave about a mile from a dynamited well where the body of Charles Martin of Jackson County was discovered in 1976.

If opposites attract, then Ruby and Bill were perfect attractions for each other. She has found a consistency in her life, being decent, honest, spiritual, loyal, giving. Bill was a giving person at times, but most of the time, Ruby said, everything was all about him. But Ruby never spoke negatively about the father of her children, especially in front of them, and she didn't allow others to put him down when her children were listening. She wanted them to respect their daddy, to think he was there for them, even when he was not.

Just to say Ruby Birt is generous doesn't begin to describe her irresistible urge to give of herself, and to describe her as religious is grossly understated. Ruby appears to have an umbilical connection to God: through prayer, through her thoughts, through her living. And, unless she loses her cool with someone, she doesn't do anything she thinks might offend her Lord. When an item she was buying at a store totaled six dollars and sixty-six cents, 666—the symbol for the beast, or anti-Christ, in the Book of Revelation—Ruby refused to pay. "I'll pay six dollars and sixty-five cents, or I'll pay six, sixty-seven," she said, "but I won't pay six dollars and sixty-six cents." And she didn't.

When she cut her hand severely working at the restaurant one day, she went to Dr. Huff's office across the street to get the wound stitched up. Looks like it will take six stitches, Ruby, the doctor said. "No, it won't. I want seven stitches," she demanded, seven being the number of perfection and completion in the Bible. She got seven stitches.

That may seem like superstition to you, but to Ruby it is as real as the King James Bible that escaped damage when fire destroyed the Birt home on Picklesimon Road in Winder many years ago. The Bible and a Christian cross necklace were about the only items left following the nighttime fire. Their survival, she'll tell you, was not happenstance. Neither was the fire, Shane said. His father torched the home, or had it torched, for insurance money. Jody, who was living with the Birts, lost all of her basketball trophies in the fire. She was an outstanding left-handed basketball shooter in high school and won awards for her athleticism. "You'd think I'd know better than to bring my trophies in there," Shane quoted Jody.

Truth is, Ruby Birt breathes thankfulness as she melds practically everything that happens in her life with what she reads in her Bible. She is childlike in her faith, and she finds opportunities to pray all day long. As she said, she prays after hearing the siren of a fire truck or ambulance, asking the Lord to watch over whoever is at the end of the call. "Lord, bless them. Lord, take care of them," she will pray. Her favorite saying is, "Do your best, and the Lord will do the rest."

She has a small nursery of plants thriving around her house, which she owns. She leases the three acres of land that surrounds it. She set out thirteen dogwood trees and with each planting prayed: "In the name of the Lord and Savior Jesus Christ, please let this tree live and become a thing of beauty." They all lived. She also has growing on her property muscadine grapes, pomegranate and fig trees, roses, petunias, and yucca and pineapple plants. "The squirrels and chipmunks get some (of the small pineapples), but they all live," she said. No doubt, she prayed over each plant.

Her tiny back porch and her immaculate backyard are her daily altars. But she knows that God is everywhere, so she prays everywhere. Her chief prayer years ago was, "Lord, let me live long enough until the children can take care of themselves." She has lived well past that time—but is still praying, mainly for the safety and well-being of her children, grandchildren, and great-grandchildren. She also prays for another Christmas and Easter with her family all around her.

Along the way, she instilled in her children two things: Work for what you get, and do the right thing. It's wholly ironic, but Bill told his children the same thing: Do not steal. Do not cheat anyone. Do not claim for your own anything that does not belong to you. Treat people the way you would want to be treated. If you do wrong, you pay for it, seven-fold. His mother told him that many times.

Unfortunately, Bill was in prison at the time for doing the opposite of what he preached. And he was paying for it.

Despite Bill's past, Ruby considers herself a blessed woman. She said it many times. If she hadn't been married to Bill, she wouldn't have five children she loves dearly. So don't even suggest she'd be justified in feeling sorry for herself. Her philosophy is, bad things happen to people, and why should one person be spared? "I'm no better than anybody else," she said. Besides, she doesn't have time for self-pity.

You might conclude the Lord got her through hell on earth, but she wouldn't say it that way. He has just been there for her, she would say. She was blessed.

Many of us, me included, usually say that a person is blessed when he or she acquires good fortune. But Jesus called some people blessed when they appeared just the opposite. In the Beatitudes, for example, scholars believe Jesus was contrasting the secular notion of happiness with true blessedness, or spiritual prosperity. That comes from a right relationship with God. I would say Ruby has achieved a relationship with God that others might find hard to understand, especially when it comes to forgiveness.

God, she said, has led her to forgive everyone who wronged her. She is a walking testimony of Colossians 3:13: "Forbearing one another, and forgiving one another, if any man have a quarrel against any: even as Christ forgave you, so also do ye."

She forgave Bill's girlfriends, every one of them. She was even grateful to the one who moved close to Ware State Prison, Bill's last place of incarceration. The woman visited Bill often during his last years, relieving Ruby of the need to drive hundreds of miles merely to walk down that long, dark hall and visit briefly with a man who would never again breathe air as a free man.

She forgave Billy Wayne Davis, the used car dealer who came up with several of the banks to rob, people and places to hit, jobs that sometimes led to murder. "I don't blame him," Ruby said. "Bill was responsible for his own actions."

She forgave her children when they were disrespectful and detoured into drug use.

Most of all, she forgave Bill.

"My daddy was the mountain my mama had to climb," Shane said.

As if she needed reminders to be Christlike, two portraits of Jesus—the One who embodies forgiveness and forgives all sinners

CHAPTER THIRTY-TWO   BY PHIL HUDGINS

who ask, believing—are displayed prominently on her living room wall. One of them is 19 by 28 inches and even has her Savior's image embedded in the glass on the reverse side. Two depictions of the Lord's Last Supper overlook the dining room table, one of them a tapestry Bill brought home one day.

If Jesus ever visited Ruby Birt's home in the flesh, He might be overwhelmed, and even blush, humbled by this woman's devotion to Him. Scriptures from Psalms and Philippians adorn the walls of Ruby's bathroom.

"Ruby is one of those people you can depend on to pray and seek the Lord for every decision that she makes," said Tim Hammond, pastor of her church, New Life Apostolic Church in Watkinsville. "She has a lot of empathy for people because she knows what it's like to go through tough times. She rises to the occasion. Some people would shake hands with someone in trouble and then walk on by. But she always took the time to talk to them and to empathize with them. . . . She is a joy to be around. Pleasant and always uplifting. It would be nice to pastor thousands of people like her."

Her devotion to God has always been there, ever since she was a little girl attending the Nazarene church, but, as a married woman, she couldn't attend church regularly until Bill went to prison for good. "We did not dare try to sneak off and go to church," she said, reminding me that she was allowed only one way to drive to school or work. If she went a different way, Bill somehow knew it and wanted to know why.

Ruby longs to be the person God wants her to be, but she doesn't claim to have lived a spotless life. Throwing a tricycle through a rolled-up car window is not exactly child's play. And sneaking a hacksaw blade into a state prison is frowned upon, too.

But if God can forgive Bill Birt for all the evil and cruel acts he committed, he certainly can forgive Ruby, who believes that no matter how great the sinfulness of sin is, God's grace is greater.

Besides reading the Bible and praying, Ruby gets her joy from helping and giving.

"When I broke my ankle some time ago, Ruby Nell was the first one up here to help out," Ruby's best friend, Lynn Walls, said. She came in one day with two air fresheners for Lynn's dogs. "Are you saying my house stinks?" Lynn asked her. "No," Ruby said, "these are humidifiers. They will help your dogs." Who has ever thought of buying humidifiers for dogs? Ruby Birt has.

Ruby insisted on buying shoes for her best friend. Lynn said one day, "Ruby Nell, I'm not paying you to work here and then have you go out and buy shoes for me. I don't need any more shoes. And then she'll show up with another pair. I had to hurt her feelings to get her to stop buying me shoes."

When John Mobley was running for mayor of Winder, he asked Ruby if she'd help with his campaign. She did. And she was effective, he said.

"Ruby lived a different life, a hard life," he said. "But when it gets to the end, Ruby prevails."

At the projects in Winder, Ruby and her family, minus Bill, lived next door to Eloise Burton, an African American woman. "When she had something to cook, she cooked enough for me," Eloise said. "We ate together, we talked together, we rode together, we looked after our kids together. She was a good neighbor."

It was at the projects that the Birt children learned to accept people as people, regardless of culture and skin color.

Andrew Jackson was in his early teens when he got to know Ruby, hired to help his mother, Kathy Elaine Allen, who was burdened with serious illnesses. Ruby cleaned the Allen home between school bus routes twice a week.

"You wouldn't let your manners slip around her, for sure," said Andrew, now forty-six and a resident of Texas. "You just notice that in people. You know how some people can come into a room, and you don't have to say a word. They automatically demand a little bit of respect from you. That was the way Ruby was then and is now. Not in a harsh way. It's just 'yes, ma'am.'"

CHAPTER THIRTY-TWO   BY PHIL HUDGINS

Ann Power, who taught elementary school in Winder, said when PTA committees were being formed, she wanted to serve on one with Ruby. "She was a worker, I'm telling you," she said. "And if she was the leader of the committee, she wouldn't ask you to do anything she wouldn't do herself. She was quite industrious."

Ruby's children seemed to respect everybody, but especially adults. "They were expected to be respectful of other people, and they were," Ann Power said.

"Ruby has a heart of gold," she said. "I am proud to have had the chance to work with her."

Motherhood for Ruby eventually became a battle against hunger, peace of mind, and simple existence, and part of her therapy was work. Even now, though she has plenty to eat and her children are grown and gone, she works.

"She is the hardest-working person I know," daughter-in-law Jill Birt said.

During some holiday seasons, especially Thanksgiving and Christmas, Ruby and Lynn Walls often work seventy-two hours straight cooking for their customers. When they get so tired they can't stand up, they sit down, lean against each other, and take short naps.

One day when I visited Ruby at her home, I couldn't find a place to sit at the dining room table that didn't have a pile of clothing in front of me. She had sewn nine slips, ten shirts, turned nine long-sleeve shirts into short-sleeve, and produced eighteen pairs of skorts. She had to explain to me that skorts are shorts with a flap across the front, and sometimes the back, to give the appearance of a skirt.

"The doctors say stay busy," she had told me earlier. "If I stayed in bed, I wouldn't be able to move."

So she moves. From early morning to late evening, she moves, holding her head straight, her gray hair curled high, green eyes focused on the task ahead, whether it's baking a cake, tending her garden, sewing a pair of skorts, or peeling and boiling and frying at the Master's Table. One day, a doctor came by the restaurant and scolded her for cutting grass and trimming hedges in the hot sun. She told him she was fine.

She loves collecting pretty knickknacks. More than a hundred teapots, some of them from foreign countries, are displayed throughout the house. Figurines in all sizes, photos of family members, and paintings of calm scenes grace the walls and cabinets.

But don't let the frilliness of the home fool you. Ruby can be tough. Every year, about a week before she began bussing troubled kids to Rutland Psychoeducational School in Athens, she visited every student's home to introduce herself and explain her requirements. One of them was punctuality. "I would pull up, toot the horn, count to three, and leave," with or without the student, she said.

She was issued a metal detector to scan each student for weapons. If someone misbehaved on the bus, he was left behind. But if everybody—she transported about fifteen students—was well-behaved all week, she would stop at a store on Fridays and buy chips and drinks for the whole crowd.

"Some of the kids did not like weekends," she said, "because they didn't like spending all weekend long at home." For them, home was not a happy place.

One of her duties as the school's receptionist was to fill out various reports and then read the information aloud over an intercom. At the end of each report, she quoted a verse or two from the Bible.

"You know you can't do that," she was told repeatedly. But she did it, every time.

She received only one traffic ticket driving the bus. She stopped on a bypass in Athens as a funeral procession passed by, and a state trooper charged her with obstructing traffic.

"I'm going to stop for a funeral," she said. Besides, "there was another lane there; people could have gone around me."

Ruby threatened to call news media when officials at the Alto, Georgia, prison refused to allow her to visit Bill. They let her in.

And you read about the time a television newsman interviewed her on the front lawn of her rental house, a toilet from her rotting bathroom floor sitting by her side.

Ruby has been a good mother. As Norma Jean said, she had to be both mother *and* father to her offspring, especially after Bill went to prison for good. She encouraged her children to be honest in everything they do. You have done nothing wrong, she told them, so hold your heads high.

Shane certainly is honest about his father's past when he speaks at churches and prisons. He tells his listeners about the work of Gideons International, which hands out Bibles all over the world, and about how God gave him hope. He also praises Sheriff Earl Lee.

The sheriff said he never dreamed he would see Bill Birt in church. It took twenty years of knowing and befriending Bill, but that's where his inmate/friend ended up on September 6, 1992, a day before Labor Day: in church for his baptism.

"I never dreamed that I would see him in church either," Shane tells his listeners. "That man is my dad.

" . . . Against all odds, Jesus saw fit to step into what seemed like a hopeless case and allow me to be standing before you today. I know that it is only by the grace of God that I am serving Him today. This great Book," he would say, holding up his Bible, "is my only hope in this life. I am here to encourage you to allow His Word to continue to spread throughout our world."

Speaking at a men's group, Shane said, "A lot of people don't understand how I can say this, but I know what it's like to be loved by murderers, because all my life, I've been loved by murderers." To know Harold Chancey, he said, was to love Harold Chancey. To know Ruth Chancey, someone Shane called Nana, was to love Ruth Chancey. His father also could be a loving human being.

"He loved us," Shane said of his dad, "but he loved his untamed, uncontrollable life more." Bill, whom Sheriff Lee described as one of the smartest people he'd ever met, could have had it all. He had a faithful wife and five beautiful children and could have lived inside a house filled with love. He chose to live outside the law.

But everyone agreed that Billy Sunday Birt, once the deadliest man in Georgia, had regrets at the end of his life. "Daddy would have been the perfect husband," Shane said, "if he could have lived his life over again, he would have been a perfect husband." He would have stayed at home and out of trouble.

Theologian Karl Barth said, "It is always the case that when the Christian looks back, he is looking at the forgiveness of sin." Perhaps that describes Bill Birt in his later years.

Without trying to be a psychologist, a layman could argue that Bill was his own worst enemy. Ruby would argue that the second person—the bad person—inside her former husband's psyche was the real enemy. The first person really wanted to do the right thing. As a result, Shane said, Bill's love was totally unpredictable. He loved his youngest son, but he threatened to blow him up if he didn't leave Ruth Chancey's home. "It didn't matter that I was his son, his own blood," Shane said. "Daddy would've done what he said he would do if I hadn't left."

He threatened Ann, too, but she didn't believe he would hurt her.

Ruby's love for her children, on the other hand, was and is unmistakable: easy to embrace, mostly consistent, uncompromising. Even when she rebuffed Shane during his drug-using years, she did it out of love—tough love. She thought she was doing the right thing.

Ruby Nell Birt is a formidable woman. Probably the only person who could cow her was Bill Birt. She is a determined woman. With all her trouble, she has not felt sorry for herself. She is a faithful woman. She's not perfect—she'll be the first to say that—but in the end, she mainly wants the approval of her God of unconditional love. And she believes Bill Birt accepted that love, and His forgiveness, at the end and accepted Christ as his savior.

CHAPTER THIRTY-TWO BY PHIL HUDGINS

Most of all, Ruby is a survivor. She survived Billy Sunday Birt, she and her five children, all in one piece. And she has survived with a smile and a blessing for everyone she meets. "God bless you," she would always say as I left her home or ended a phone conversation. I would respond, "God bless you, too."

"He does constantly," she would answer.

Chronicling the life of Ruby Birt has been an adventure, believe me. Writing about all that she went through being married to a Dixie Mafia hit man was difficult at times. Remembering, for her, surely was even worse. Ruby grew up in a family of grace and disgrace. But through it all, as Shane said, "Mama was the hero of the family."

A *blessed* hero, his mama would say, even if she agreed to the word "hero," which is not likely. She would prefer just the word "blessed," blessed both in her relationship with God and in her good fortune as a human being who was afforded opportunities to serve.

If her close friends had to describe her in one word, they would say she has been a blessing, a blessing to nearly everyone she meets, and even to those she will never meet.

My prayer is that she will continue to be a blessing—and blessed, as she says—the rest of her earthly life. In her next life, this woman of faith knows she will be without any worry or turmoil at all.

A plaque hangs on the screened-in front porch of Ruby's house. It says, "Life is not about waiting for the storm to pass . . . It is about learning to dance in the rain."

Ruby Nell Birt learned to dance in a flood.

Ann Birt with Shane during her July 2021 visit.

EPILOGUE

It's midmorning of February 4, 2022, a Friday, a rainy Friday. People who own heavy equipment businesses usually can stop and talk on rainy days. And Shane Birt wants to talk.

It has been about five months since the manuscript of this book went to the publisher. I thought the writing was complete. But a lot has happened in five months, and an epilogue to this gripping story is desperately needed. So Shane is sitting at his mama's dining room table to talk about it all. I'm here to listen.

Not surprisingly, Ruby is at work at the restaurant. The house is quiet. The only sound besides our voices comes from the tall grandfather clock that chimes loudly and often and an occasional telephone ringing.

The first time I talked to Shane—it was about writing this book—was in May of 2018. Now, approaching four years later, we're meeting again to talk about the latest developments in his complicated life.

As we sit at the table, I remember that he telephoned me on a Wednesday in August of 2021. But I wasn't sure which Wednesday. It was August 25th, he says.

"I'm getting ready to go to jail," he told me on the phone that early evening, his voice breathless and shaking.

"Why?" I asked.

He wasn't sure why, but he was the one who wanted someone to call 911 to get the cops there to arrest him.

"What do you want me to do?" I said. "I don't have your bail money."

"Oh, I got the money," he said. "I need you to call Bob Ingram and tell him I'm going to jail. See if he can help me."

I did call Bob Ingram, the retired GBI agent, later that night, but what could he do? If Shane had done something that called for his arrest, he would be arrested.

Sitting there today, more than five months later, Shane says he's not sure what he did that evening. He had been drinking heavily. He had been clean of drugs for years, but he drank occasionally, and not just a little. On a rainy day when work slowed down or stopped, he could drink a fifth of Captain Morgan rum mixed with Diet Mountain Dew, and nobody but his family could tell he'd been drinking, according to him.

Jill, his wife, always knew. And she didn't like it. They had fussed before about his drinking, but Shane said a man ought to be able take a drink if he wants to.

But on this evening, August 25th, the arguing presumably turned into yelling, then screaming, and Shane wanted to be arrested, he guesses, to prevent him from doing something drastic, or stupid. Jill objected to calling the cops. But the deputies came anyway, and Shane was hauled off to the Barrow County Jail, where he would reside for the next three or four nights. He's not sure if it was three or four.

Shane vaguely remembers calling me, but, still, he's still not sure why he called.

It was Lynn Walls, his mama's best friend, who picked him up at the jail after he was released on bond, charged with simple assault. But he had not struck Jill. Never had, he says.

This wasn't the first time Lynn Walls came to Shane's rescue. It was she who took him in, fed him, cared for him when he was on meth, first separated, then divorced, from his wife.

Lynn drove Shane from the jail to a hospital in Monroe, next door to Barrow County, and while they were sitting on a bench outside, waiting to be summoned inside, they could hear a man parked nearby yelling and cursing at a woman, presumably his wife or girlfriend.

EPILOGUE

"Every other word out of his mouth was vulgar," Shane says.

Shane got up from the bench, walked over and said to the man, "Buddy, you let one more vulgar word come out of your mouth, and I'm going to show you what God put men on this Earth for."

The man was drinking beer. "He drank another can or two of courage," Shane says, "and got out of his car. When he got out of the car, I slipped my boot off, put my finger in the loop on the back. The man started toward me, and I said, 'Man, you got about two more steps and I'm going to lay you flat.' He went back to his car. That was the way I was raised. You didn't cuss in front of a woman."

Even his daddy, the hit man, taught him that.

At the hospital and later, Shane thought he was thinking with a clear mind. He wasn't under the influence of any substance, but bad things were running through his brain. Maybe some people "needed to disappear," he thought. Whatever that meant. It was unsure.

Doctors at the hospital told him he was suffering from complex PTSD, post traumatic stress disorder. "I never been to war," he said. Doesn't matter, they said. You don't have to be a war veteran to be a victim of PTSD.

After being released from the hospital—Shane thinks he was there three days—"everything rocked on and rocked on," he says, "so I went to Dr. (Gary) Huff." He's a Winder physician. "He agreed with the hospital that I had complex PTSD. He put me on Zoloft," a medication to calm his brain, to smooth out some of those rough thoughts.

And then a close friend—Shane decided not to use his name—told him something he needed to hear. "He was the first man I'd ever had any kind of admiration for that told me I needed help," he says. "I told him more than I told anybody. I realized that I can't handle this on my own anymore."

Shane trusts this friend, so when he recommended that Shane and his whole family see a counselor, that was it. He, especially he, needed to see a counselor.

Shane found a place to live—he couldn't go back home to Jill yet—so he was destined to live alone, except for several months with a daughter's dog, Haggard, named after Merle Haggard.

His friend found him a counselor. (Shane doesn't want to name him, either. He says he doesn't want the counselor or his friend to be bothered by curious people asking questions about his father's crimes.)

On their first meeting, Shane started telling the counselor everything that was in his head and asked if he could come twice a week. The counselor balked at the suggestion.

Counseling twice a week would be too much for both him and Shane, he told him. It's just too much bad stuff. Once a week is enough. There was a time, Shane says, when the counselor said: "Shane, don't tell me any more. My mind can't take it."

Like the others who evaluated Shane's emotional problems, the counselor says Shane has complex PTSD. Shane's response: "You tell me what PTSD is, and I'll tell you if I got it or not."

PTSD, the counselor said, causes its victim to react to every situation. If you're going to fight—"they say it's fight or flight or freeze," Shane says—the Birts have always fought. "Your brain would start pumping blood to every part of the body to take care of it. The last part of the body to get blood is the part of the brain for reasonable thought. That made a lot of sense."

In every situation, a male Birt was going to win, no matter what it cost. "It didn't matter," Shane says, "if it took our fists, took our brain, took our voice. We were going to win. And it could be against the one we loved the most or the one we hated the most."

The counselor says Shane also gets anxious being around people in certain situations. And he's narcissistic. "I knew my daddy was narcissistic," he says, "but I never dreamed that I was." The symptoms and layers of narcissism are many, but Ruby put it simply in explaining Bill Birt's personality: Everything was about him.

EPILOGUE

"Jill and the kids couldn't say no to me," Shane says, "because it was my decision, whatever it was." If he wanted to buy a car, he went out and bought a car, without asking anyone's opinion.

But things are changing. A few weeks after Shane began counseling, he asked Jill to join him and his customers for business meetings—to talk about the company, tax matters, bookkeeping. Shane wants his wife to be fifty percent owner of the business. She will now be consulted on certain matters. She's never been consulted before. She did some of the business's check-writing, but that was about it.

Jill Birt has not been her own person, Shane says. She said as much one day at Ruby's dining room table, talking about the time before she and Shane were divorced: "You sometimes lose your identity. Instead of being me, it was always Jill and Shane."

But she has an opinion, and she will be allowed to voice it, Shane says. And she has. He wanted to buy her a new Ford Bronco recently—payments would be nine hundred dollars a month, and we could do that, he told her—but Jill said no. We don't need to do that. And Shane, uncharacteristically, did not argue.

Jill sometimes wants to apologize for something—she apologizes for nothing, really, Shane says—but there's no need. "She has no reason to apologize for anything. 'You don't owe me or anybody an apology,'" he told her.

"I told Jill that for the first time in my life, I realize that my enemies are not anywhere outside of my head. It's all me."

As the writer of this book, I was concerned that recalling all the murders and arsons and robberies—all of the evil actions of his father—had added to Shane's emotional disorders, energizing the demons in his mind.

Recalling it all hasn't been easy, for sure, Shane says. At one time during our interviews, he told me he was suffering with sleep deprivation and mental anguish, mostly due, at that time, to the tension wrought by months of sordid recollections.

But today, February 4, 2022, he says it's not the book that's the problem. "Actually, it's been more helpful than hurtful," he says. His counselor even told him it will be good to get it all out, even if it's in book form. If someone asks about his father's criminal acts, he can say, "Just read the book."

What has been upsetting most recently, he says, is "all the lies" that the podcast *In the Red Clay* disseminated. Particularly distressful was the podcast's last episode, which bashed his mother, quoting his brother Stoney as saying she enjoyed the high life because of her husband's ill-gotten money. She was portrayed as one who did not object to her husband's criminal activities. Many of Ruby's friends were angry about that portrayal.

"The fact is," Shane says, "my mother is the reason we all survived my dad's horrible life as a murderer and criminal. She is the hero in my life."

Because of the podcast and because he's a Birt, Shane has become somewhat of a celebrity at times, and that makes him uncomfortable.

When someone heard his name called out at a Cracker Barrel restaurant recently, he wanted to pose with Shane for a photograph.

"If you wouldn't want to take a picture with Charles Manson, why would you want to take a picture with me?" He wanted to ask the man that question, but he didn't.

The podcast, Shane believes, "is just making a mockery of all the victims and the victims' families. If I could apologize to everybody, I would."

EPILOGUE

Phil Hudgins.

A few days after I interviewed Shane for this epilogue, we learned something confirming that at least one hoped-for result of this book has been partially fulfilled. The Watauga County Sheriff's Office issued a news release announcing the case-closing of the grisly triple murder that occurred during a heavy snowstorm on February 3, 1972, in Boone, North Carolina. The announcement came February 8, 2022, five days after the fiftieth anniversary of the slayings.

Once she learned the murders of her parents and brother had been solved, Ginny Sue Durham, Bryce and Virginia Durham's daughter and Bobby Joe's sister, said she wanted to "thank all of the people who worked for decades on my family's case." She said she appreciated their sacrifices, knowing some officers worked weekends on the case and continued to investigate even after retiring. "I just read what she said," Shane said, "and that's one of the reasons we did this book. It brought closure. I'd like to bring closure to more of these cases."

In a press conference February 11, Watauga County Sheriff Len Hagaman said the daughter and her uncle—Bill Durham, Bryce Durham's brother—were relieved the fifty-year-long nightmare had finally ended. Several local and national news media picked up the Boone story.

But let's remember that this case would not have been closed if Shane had not recalled what his father told him about almost being trapped by the fierce snowstorm that night in February 1972. After remembering that conversation, Shane and I met with Bob Ingram, who was instrumental in getting a confession from Billy Wayne Davis, now eighty-one, the last survivor of the four murderers. The other three were Billy Sunday Birt, Bobby Gene Gaddis, and Charles David Reed.

Who ordered the hit on the family? No one knows for sure. But Sheriff Hagaman said he wished he could have interviewed Troy Hall, the former son-in-law, now deceased. Bob Ingram said the same thing several times.

Chapter Twenty-three explains how the investigation progressed after Shane, Bob Ingram and North Carolina authorities got involved.

After getting together for business meetings, Jill and Shane met one day to do a little yard work at their home. Shane still wasn't living there, but being in the yard together was a good start toward reconciliation, he figured. Maybe he could move back in. One day.

Then he thought dating again might be a good idea. First, he asked Jill if she would like to see the play, *An Officer and a Gentleman*, a musical, at a theater in Athens. That was December 13th. A musical is not something Shane would enjoy normally. But he did enjoy it, he says. Jill was sitting next to him.

On December 18, they attended their church's Christmas party together.

A few days later, he asked if she'd like to see *The Nutcracker*, a Christmas ballet, at the Classic Center in Athens. She said yes.

The seating arrangement was not comfortable for a broad-shouldered man sandwiched between a strange woman and an estranged wife, somebody he didn't want to assume would welcome a stretched-out arm on the back of her seat.

EPILOGUE

Finally, sitting there with his shoulders severely retracted and his arms and hands reaching awkwardly below his lap, he couldn't stand it any longer.

He told Jill he wasn't trying to be fresh, but he needed some relief. Not a problem, she said. She was prepared to let him suffer, though, if he didn't ask. He put his arm around the woman he loved.

Jill didn't think Shane could sit through *The Nutcracker* because, as he put it, "they run around in tights and just burst into song." But he did enjoy it. Jill was sitting next to him.

Beginning that month, December, he would spend an occasional night back home. Then, on New Year's Day 2022, probably his best start ever to a new year, he moved back in permanently.

Nowadays, everybody in their family—Mom and Dad and the four children—has his or her own counselor. Shane and Jill also are seeing counselors, hers and his, together. They're learning a lot about each other.

On Sunday, January 30, 2022, they took part in what their church calls a "cardboard testimony." Couples who want to participate—and there were several of them—hold up pieces of cardboard or poster board. On one side, they write briefly what their problem or concern is. On the other side, the solution.

On one side, the Birts had written: "Marriage destroyed and all hope lost." On the other side: "But God healed and restored."

Shane says he will need more church than most people, and he talks to his pastor, Tim Hammond, practically every day.

Shane Birt says frankly that he's tired of being a Birt. He's proud of his mama for not leaving Barrow County, her home, to start a new name somewhere else. But some Birt kinfolks, especially the men, just need help, even if they won't admit it, Shane says. And he is one of them.

He can drive in any direction in Barrow County and not be far away from where one of Bill Birt's victims was killed—or buried.

Twenty-seven victims in this one Georgia county. "There were some within four or five miles from where we are sitting," he says from his mama's dining room table.

Despite all the bad stuff swirling around in his head, Shane is trying to get a handle on his life in general as a family man. His mother didn't have a life unless Bill gave her permission. Shane doesn't want that for his family.

He is working to always be considerate, especially with Jill. She said she thought he'd look good in a beard, so he grew one. Both of them knew he needed to lose weight, so he has lost about a hundred pounds. When he has time, he walks, sometimes five or six miles. It's not so much to lose weight, he says. "I realized that when my whole body is moving, my mind is standing still."

Jill, his barber, had cut his hair recently. He looks sharp.

I took several photographs of Shane later at a Mexican restaurant, where we had lunch. I wanted to show how much he has changed in appearance. But Shane, unlike his father, doesn't like being photographed. "That's enough of that," he told me, finally.

Shane doesn't drink alcohol anymore. In fact, he doesn't even drink his mixer, Diet Mountain Dew, by itself. He has switched to Diet Sprite. He's getting more work done these days, mainly because he's on the job more often. If a person wants to avoid something, he can find a reason to get away. Shane apparently was good at that.

Shane is still taking Zoloft, the calming medicine. He says he can't tell any difference when he takes it, but he can when he doesn't take it.

The charges against him at the sheriff's department have been dropped.

He's learning how to deal with what his counselor calls the three R's. In most situations, Shane would react, retreat, and reflect. But that's backward, he says. He should retreat, reflect, and react.

He had said a couple of years ago that all of the trouble he went

EPILOGUE

through—the drugs, the divorce, the homelessness at times—was worth it "to have what I have now." But he apparently didn't know what he had, or appreciate it. He led me to believe that theirs was a happily-ever-after story after he and Jill remarried. But I failed to get Jill's take on that happiness. They were happy at times, of course, but it was on Shane's terms.

No doubt he'll continue to see his counselor. It might be once a week, once a month, every other month. But he'll need more counseling, he says, and he's not ashamed, anymore, to admit it.

Billy Shenandoah "Shane" Birt—youngest of the Birt five—is working hard to change. For the first time in his life, he says, he doesn't see himself simply as Billy Sunday Birt's son. He's Shane.

His close friend, the one who told him he needed help, said one day: "We're breaking century-old curses, if not more."

Lord, Shane Birt prays that's so.

—Phil Hudgins

ACKNOWLEDGMENTS

When I talked to Shane Birt in the spring of 2018 about writing this book for him and his mother, I was a little apprehensive about taking it on. Jessica Phillips Henricks and I had finished writing *Travels with Foxfire*—a fun book to do—and I had thought about tackling another major writing project before aging out. But not this soon. And not one featuring the former wife of a hit man who had killed dozens of people. Perhaps something a little more inspiring.

Turned out, Ruby Nell Birt is as inspiring as just about anyone I've ever met. If you've read this book, I don't need to remind you of the conditions under which she lived—and emerged, she says, blessed. Always selfless, she takes no credit for herself. She gives her Lord all the credit and all the glory.

So at the top of the list of people to acknowledge and thank stands Ruby Birt, the matriarch of a family who rose above the notoriety wrought by a dangerous husband/father and refused to give up and give in.

Next on the list is Shane Birt, who asked me to take on this unbelievable but true story. It was Charlene Stamps, a great friend at Community Newspapers Inc., my former employer, who recommended me to Shane. So thanks, Charlene.

The inspiration behind anything I do, both for paid and unpaid projects, comes from my wife, Shirley, who has always encouraged me. Writers are often critical of themselves and their work—"This is not good enough," their inner voice tells them constantly—so it helps to have someone to say, "This is good." Shirley has been that someone for me.

Four friends read the manuscript before it was submitted and made suggestions. They are: Billy Chism, Emory Jones, Myles Godfrey, and Johnny Solesbee. Thanks, guys.

A number of people from law enforcement, most of them now retired, contributed considerably to this story. None was more helpful than Robert "Bob" Ingram, a former GBI agent who has been there from the beginning. I can't thank him enough. Ingram has retired, again, this time as chief deputy at the White County Sheriff's Office in Cleveland, Georgia, and is teaching criminology at nearby Truett McConnell College.

I also thank Ronnie Angel, Jimmy Terrell, Stanley Thompson, Sheriff Len "L.D." Hagaman, Captain Carolynn Johnson, Sheriff Tim Pounds, and Sheriff Gary Hutchins. I quoted extensively from a report prepared by the late Jim Earl West and Jack C. Berry of the ATF.

I gleaned information from several books, including Stoney's two memoirs, published in 2017 after his father's death. "You can use anything you want from this book," Stoney said after autographing his first book, *Rock Solid: The True Story of Georgia's Dixie Mafia*, an inscription that included his grandmother's oft-repeated warning to her son Billy: "You will reap what you sow." His second book, *Rock Solid: In His Own Words*, contained numerous letters from his father that provided insights for this book.

Other titles that offered useful information were: *Alone Among the Living*, by G. Richard Hoard; *A Conspiracy of Silence: The Murder of Solicitor General Floyd Hoard*, by Mike Buffington; *A Breed Apart: A True Story About U.S. Treasury Agents During the Moonshine Years*, by Charles H. Weems; *That's Rufus*, by Rufus Edmisten; and *Barrow County: Photographs from the Stell-Kilgore Collection*, by Myles Godfrey. Several newspapers filled in gaps in Bill Birt stories. They included *The Augusta Chronicle*, *The Winder News*, *The Jackson Herald*, *The Dahlonega Nugget*, *The Times* of Gainesville, *The New York Times*, *Athens Banner-Herald*, *Winston-Salem Journal*,

ACKNOWLEDGMENTS

The Atlanta Constitution, The Atlanta Journal, and *The Atlanta Journal-Constitution.*

Other individuals who were helpful, either in their encouragement, in providing information or story ideas, help with publication, or pointing us in the right direction for research, included Dr. C.B. Skelton, Lynn Walls, Ken Hudgins, my brother, who published *The Winder News* for many years; Ann Birt, Norma Jean Birt, Jill Birt, Myles Godfrey, J.C. Mathis, Dick Hoard, Jimmy Anderson, Ann Chenault, Shane Coley, Coroner Atha M. Lucas, John Mobley, Andrew Jackson, Eloise Burton, Ann Power, Pastor Tim Hammond, William "Bill" Blalock, Ann Hughes, Andrew Hughes, John Latty, Harold H. Smith, Norman Baggs, David Morrison, Millard Farmer, Sister Helen Prejean, Steve Cronic, Rebecca Hamby, and Michael DeLoach Sr.

Two useful podcasts featuring Stoney and his remembrances of his father were:

+ CSI Atlanta, interviewers Karyn Greer and Sheryl McCollum, episode one, "Strength and Love," January 2, 2020, and episode two, "The Deadliest Man in Georgia," January 9, 2020, produced by CBS46 Atlanta, https://www.cbs46.com/podcasts/csiatlanta/csi-atlanta-georgia-s-dixie-mafia/audio_8e84facc-3310-11ea-886b-dfa50341b20e.html.

+ "In the Red Clay," interviewer Sean Kipe, episode seven, "Billy and Billy," and episode nine, "A Letter from Death Row," October 6, 2020, produced by Imperative Entertainment, https://www.intheredclaypodcast.com.

Finally, I want to thank Chris Yavelow of Asheville, North Carolina, the award-winning composer, multimedia producer, and author who did the final edit and design of the book.

As noted earlier, writing this book was not always easy and carefree. Recalling past crimes of Bill Birt was even harder for Ruby Nell Birt and her offspring, especially Shane, the youngest. On top of it all, he was hospitalized with COVID-19 for four days.

But he wanted to get the story told—the true story, as best he could remember and document it. And, as the famous author Ernest Hemingway said, a writer can't tell the good and beautiful without telling the bad and ugly.

Ruby had her own health problems. On Sunday, February 21, 2021, she fell leaving her church and broke a hip. She underwent surgery and immediately looked forward to therapy so that she could return to her daily activities. Church, she said, is the best place to break a hip, "because people will pray for you."

Five months after her fall, Ruby worked at the Master's Table for twelve hours, from 5:30 a.m. to 5:30 p.m. She was back there at 6 a.m. the next day.

One of Shane's recollections eventually emerged from a conversation with his dad more than three decades ago. And it led to identifying the killers of three people inside their Boone, North Carolina, home on the snowy night of February 3, 1972, a murder case that had remained a mystery for forty-nine years.

"Closure" is an overused, over-appreciated word. It means "a feeling that an emotional or traumatic experience has been resolved." But closure doesn't change what happened.

Let's hope, however, that for the surviving relatives of the Boone victims, for their many friends and associates, for all the law enforcement officials, and even a former state attorney general who worked on this case for decades, knowing what happened is at least better than not knowing.

ABOUT PHIL HUDGINS

Phil Hudgins worked more than half a century in the newspaper business, retiring as news training officer for a couple dozen papers owned by Community Newspapers Inc. of Athens, Georgia. He is co-author of two other books: *Travels with Foxfire: Stories of People, Passions, and Practices from Southern Appalachia* (2018), and *I Took the Fork* (2008), a memoir of journalist and philanthropist Lessie Smithgall, who died at 110. Phil is a 1964 graduate of the University of Georgia and a 1974 Nieman Fellow of Harvard University. He and his wife, Shirley, have two daughters, four grandchildren, and one great-grandchild.